Textures of Struggle

Textures of Struggle

*The Emergence of Resistance among
Garment Workers in Thailand*

Piya Pangsapa

ILR Press
AN IMPRINT OF
Cornell University Press
Ithaca and London

First published 2007 by Cornell University Press
First printing, Cornell Paperbacks, 2007

Printed in the United States of America

Library of Congress Cataloging-in-Publication Data

Pangsapa, Piya.
    Textures of struggle : the emergence of resistance among garment workers in Thailand / Piya Pangsapa.
        p. cm.
    Includes bibliographical references and index.
    ISBN 978-0-8014-4591-0 (cloth : alk. paper)—
ISBN 978-0-8014-7376-0 (pbk. : alk. paper)
    1. Women clothing workers—Thailand—Case studies. 2. Women textile workers—Thailand—Case studies. 3. Women in the labor movement—Thailand—Case studies. 4. Industrial relations—Thailand—Case studies. I. Title.

    HD6073.C62T57 2007
    331.4′88709593—dc22

2007011166

Cornell University Press strives to use environmentally responsible suppliers and materials to the fullest extent possible in the publishing of its books. Such materials include vegetable-based, low-VOC inks and acid-free papers that are recycled, totally chlorine-free, or partly composed of nonwood fibers. For further information, visit our website at www.cornellpress.cornell.edu.

Cloth printing   10 9 8 7 6 5 4 3 2 1
Paperback printing   10 9 8 7 6 5 4 3 2 1

I dedicate this book to my mother, Jittima,
and to the loving memory of my father, Supreecha

Contents

Acknowledgments

On completing this research project, I express my deep gratitude to the many remarkable women who so openly and readily shared their lives with me. This book would not have been possible without their participation. I especially thank Sripai, Nay, Pik, Saneh, Soey, Taan, Mai, Pai, Dao, Patcharin, Thim, and Khun Chawkieng. I also thank the factory owners for graciously allowing me access to their factories, as well as Phil Robertson for his help and support in ensuring access to the women at YCW Rangsit. Without his help, I would not have had the opportunity to develop contacts during the initial stages of my fieldwork. I also thank P'Lek Junya Yimprasert of the Thai Labour Campaign for her incredible energy and impassioned commitment to workers' rights and social justice. For inspiring my work, I would also like to acknowledge Pasuk Phongpaichit and Chris Baker, and for guidance of the early stages of my project, I would especially like to thank Ji Ungpakorn.

An important guide in my journey was Jim Petras, who provided moral support and encouragement throughout my time as a graduate student in the Department of Sociology at Binghamton University (SUNY). His guidance and supervision helped me get this research off the ground, and Jim remains a great inspiration for me. I also thank Martin Murray and James Geschwender for carefully guiding my doctoral research and for providing constructive feedback on developing the book.

At the University at Buffalo, I thank the Department of Women's Studies, The UB College of Arts & Sciences, The Julian Park Fund, The Baldy

Center for Law & Social Policy, and The Gender Institute at the University at Buffalo. I especially thank Masani Alexis De Veaux for her wisdom and friendship as well as inspiration through her poetry. Lynn Mather and David Engel reviewed drafts of the project and provided valuable insights at a crucial stage in developing the research into a book (as well as moral support beyond the call of duty). I also thank the participants of the Baldy Manuscript Workshop, including Lynn, who organized the workshop, David and Jaruwan Engel, Frank Munger, Rebecca French, Jim Atleson, Roger des Forges, Ruth Meyerowitz, Kari Winter, Susan Cahn, and Rami Sreenivasan—all of whom provided me with helpful comments and suggestions. The Baldy Center invited two accomplished ethnographers with a burning concern for women's rights in the workplace—Susan Tiano and Ping-Chun Hsiung—to comment on my research. As a result, I benefited greatly from their expertise, and I thank them for their positive encouragement, valuable comments, and constructive criticism which were very helpful in the final revisions of this book.

I thank my commissioning editor, Fran Benson, for recognizing the original contribution of my research and for helping me bring this book to fruition. I couldn't have asked for a better editorial team at Cornell University Press, and I thank Teresa Jesionowski and Patricia Sterling for their sharp and perceptive editorial work. I also thank the incomparable Do Mi Stauber for her brilliant work on the index.

I could not have written this book without the love and support of my family. I thank a remarkable woman, Jittima, my mom, for her love and wisdom, and I dedicate this book to her and to the loving memory of my dad, whose kindness, generosity and down-to-earth sensibility taught me the meaning of compassion. A great inspiration for me was one of the most accomplished scientists of her generation, my grandmother, Nuanchan Bunnag. I thank my sister, Nim, whose wit and wicked sense of humor kept me going. This book is about feisty women who take control of their own lives against all odds, but a kind and extraordinary man has always been there when I needed him—Thank you, Ekk. I have been very lucky to have such a supportive family. My faith in this project has been sustained by my Buddhist spiritual mentor and guide, Khun Nussornpan. Last, I thank Tig for being there for me.

PIYA PANGSAPA

Buffalo, New York

Textures of Struggle

Introduction

The Condition of Women Garment Workers in Thailand

Imagine having to work twelve straight hours every day of the week, 360 days a year, in a rundown building, a converted car garage, or a makeshift warehouse with floors made of cardboard boxes and roofs of thin aluminum siding. Imagine working when it's hot and humid, 98 degrees outside and over 100 degrees inside, and there's only one old ceiling fan whirling above. Imagine not being allowed to drink any water when you work. Imagine that the only drinking water provided comes from a pipe attached to the sewer. Imagine having to tolerate your thirst until you get home at night because you simply refuse to drink water from that pipe. Imagine having to prop open an umbrella above your work station because the rain is trickling in through the cracks and holes in the ceiling, and then imagine the risk of being electrocuted because all the sewing machines are electric. Imagine working alongside 800 other women every day under these conditions and having to share six toilets with this many co-workers. Imagine voluntarily giving up bathroom and lunch breaks because you need to put together at least 1,000 pieces to make enough money that day. Imagine being paid less than 80 cents at the end of that day.

In outsourced manufacturing and export processing zones throughout the world, women continue to be subjected to the same conditions: meager wages, long hours, hazardous work environments, physical and verbal abuse, and job insecurity. Fewer and fewer manufactured goods today are made in the West but have been outsourced to countries and regions around the world where labor is very cheap and where labor regulations are weak or nonexistent. On a global scale, the situation of women workers in transnational factories has been well documented following the extensive relocation of manufacturing industries to low-wage countries: garments in Cambodia, Vietnam, and Thailand; shoes in Indonesia; electronics in China; leather goods and garments in India and Bangladesh.

Who makes the many products that you use or wear on a daily basis? Consumer goods are sometimes assembled and finished in Western countries, but for the most part the clothes, shoes, socks, handbags, toys, electronic gadgets, and all those objects in which we invest our identities and through which we reveal our personalities are made in sweatshop factories that lie out of our sight and out of our minds. The conditions of these factories are often harmful to the people who work in them, and many of the rules we expect factories to have in place to protect workers do not exist—or, if they do, are often not observed.

In the garment industry the global supply chain consists of a range of actors who are involved in the marketing and production of ready-made apparel. Typically, a large retailer or brand-name company sends its production to hundreds of thousands of workers in over a hundred countries because it is cost-effective for them to do so. Large retailers such as Wal-Mart and JC Penney and brand companies such as Tommy Hilfiger, Nike, and Gap outsource their production in this manner. Workers are hired by outsourced factories that are, in turn, contracted by manufacturers acting as the main suppliers for the brand-name companies or retail giants that sell and distribute finished garments to the consumer.[1]

You, the consumers, are at the top of this supply chain, and at the other end hundreds of thousands of people are sweating away fifteen hours a day, seven days a week, to get those goods out "just-in-time" for you.

In a nutshell, the outsourcing of textile and garment production depends very much upon the low cost of labor at the end of the global supply chain. The competitive nature of the retail business drives down wages and conditions for workers around the world, who essentially are competing with one another to make clothes for the global consumer. For the most part, this reserve of labor is readily available in developing countries of the Global South. It appears that nobody can do anything to stop it because we want the goods to be there when we need them, whether they are cell phones, PCs, shoes, clothing, or accessories. This book is designed to alert people in developed societies about where the things they buy (and use and throw away) come from, the conditions in which they are made, and who is making them.

Many of these trends have been identified by various local, student, and international pressure groups such as the Clean Clothes Campaign (CCC), Sweatshop Watch, Campaign for Labor Rights (CLR), Labour Behind the Label, Committee for Asian Women, Global Unions, Labour Start, Maquiladora Solidarity Network, and United Students Against Sweatshops, all of which seek to raise public awareness about the conditions of workers in manufacturing industries around the world. The Clean Clothes Campaign, for example, hopes to improve conditions in the global garment and sportswear industry by raising consumer awareness. One of its campaigns, by keeping track of current actions being directed against the company, mobilizes consumers to press companies for improved working conditions in subcontract factories that manufacture apparel for Nike. Similarly, Sweatshop Watch boldly declares, "Shop with a Conscience!" on its website as it aims to empower workers and inform consumers. Although Sweatshop Watch specifically targets garment factories in California, the consumer movement group seeks to raise general awareness about the exploitation of low-wage workers both in the United States and abroad. All these labor campaign groups believe that workers have the right to earn a living wage, to reasonable working hours with overtime limits, and safe and decent work environments, and they emphasize that those responsible for pay levels, hours, and conditions must be held accountable for their practices.[2]

To raise awareness among consumers in the West, these well-organized campaigns generate shock and horror stories about the work and living conditions of the women, men, and children who "labor behind the label" in developing countries. Yet very little is known about what it is really like for a woman to work in a factory, day after day, and even less is known about what happens to the women themselves: how they survive in these conditions, the sacrifices they make, the pain they endure physically and emotionally. My intention is not to paint a hopeless picture but to present evidence of what life is really like for women workers. More specifically, I want to show how women in factories actually respond to their situation, how they take their future into their own hands, how they challenge the conditions they face, and, even if they are not able to make significant changes, how they use more subtle ways to challenge and undermine how they are controlled in the work situation.

Although Thailand has long been a provider of low-cost female labor, producing goods for global consumption, there are few in-depth, ethnographic studies of the women who slave for export industries in developing countries and none of those in Thailand. Conditions in some places may be better than others, and my study illustrates how women respond to different work environments. Some employers are kind; some employers are mean. Furthermore, many of us probably assume that high-tech goods and gadgets are made by highly skilled and highly paid workers in pristine, state-of-the-art factories, but in fact, most of the things we prize in our personal lives are really "Made in China," "Made in Thailand," "Made in Cambodia," and so on in conditions that are anything but pristine. Apple's popular iPod is a good example. An investigative journalist, tracing the "incredible journey" of the portable digital audio players from conception to completion in the Chinese factories where they are made, found that in just one factory, 200,000 workers work an average 15 hours a day, earn less than US$60 a month, and live in crowded dormitories 100 to a room in highly secured sites surrounded by barbed wire and security guards on duty 24/7.[3]

At the same time, those factories that are aware of the codes of responsible conduct that Western brand-name companies have developed also face some difficult choices. If they apply such codes, they can make themselves uncompetitive in the marketplace and lose business to companies with fewer scruples. One of the biggest problems identified by the CCC is that even outsourced manufacturers who formally sign on to social responsibility feel forced to behave differently in order to meet production deadlines. In other words, they need to get the next batch of clothes or shoes out "just-in-time" to hit the shelves for the season.[4] All in all, outsourcing is characterized by speed and efficiency on the part of a supplier to deliver quality products to retailers according to the demands of the market. Hence there is enormous pressure on outsourcing companies that are expected to deliver so many goods within a particular time frame, and it is no surprise that workers end up bearing the costs of such a business environment with excessive hours and work-related accidents.[5]

Some of this is the responsibility of consumers in the West, and some of it is the responsibility of the corporations that outsource to the manufacturer. But we also need to consider the responsibility of those outsourced manufacturers, the governments that allow labor violations to happen (and even actively encourage them for the sake of economic development and modernization), and the factory workers themselves (many of them women). This book, contrary to the altruistic and humanitarian characterizations of those in the West, shows how factory women can and do take responsibility, can and do struggle to make a difference, and can and do improve their conditions. It shows how factory workers assert their own agency and autonomy and have power to act on their own behalf. It is very difficult for factory workers to do so. It is much easier for Western consumers to make ethical shopping decisions than for a factory worker in a special economic zone in Thailand, China, or Vietnam to look for less exploitive jobs or organize a union or protest against excessive overtime without pay, yet this is exactly what they are doing.

The international division of labor is nothing new. Global supply chains have existed previously, but what is different about global supply chains today is how they operate. It is no longer a colonized production process (where raw materials were exported to the West and manufactured products were sold back to the colonies) or transnational companies running subsidiaries in many different countries (where codes of conduct could be enforced more easily) but an outsourced one (where firms in developing countries sell finished products to brand-name companies in North America or Europe which have no obligation, responsibility, or liability to the workers hired by these firms).[6]

We tend to fixate too much on the manufacturing jobs lost in the West and not enough on the actual conditions of work for those people who have notionally "benefited" from outsourcing but at the same time experience the harsh realities of low-wage employment. When considering the conditions under which women labor, the following questions are central: *Why* are some women less tolerant of their working conditions than others? *How* is it that women who have similar levels of education, come from the same socioeconomic background (i.e., predominantly rural farming families), and enter the same occupation nevertheless emerge with different experiences and reactions to their wage employment?

So, why Thailand, and why this study now? Thailand has been and continues to be a major center of outsourcing production, which means that its workers live and labor at the end of the global supply chain especially in the apparel industry. Although Thailand is known as a tourist haven that welcomes 6–10 million tourists each year, export manufacturing contributes over half of its GDP.[7] Textile and garment production is the country's second leading export industry and, in 2004, represented approximately 4 percent of GDP.[8]

In the Western media, factory women are often infantilized or portrayed as victims who have no choice and dare not question or challenge their situation for fear of losing their jobs. Even the picture painted by campaign groups gives us this image of the fearful, browbeaten, and subservient worker. But factory workers do mobilize on their own sometimes and thus come to challenge our expectations as well as their employers. In many instances, women are not passive victims; they are not completely driven into the ground, despite the enormous hardships they face. They employ different strategies in different circumstances, and I have tried to provide some understanding of the conditions that can lead to outright militancy and other strategies that can and do make a difference. The workers I have studied take responsibility for their situation, and it is important to recognize that they do.

In the case of Thailand, following the 1997 financial crisis, some factory owners used economic instability as an excuse for becoming more "flexible," which allowed them to shut down production and relocate elsewhere (sweatshop production was "on the move"), to circumvent labor laws, and to demand increased productivity levels from workers while reducing wages. Consequently, workers became so exhausted or so fearful of losing their jobs that resistance was made virtually impossible. What I seek to do in this book is examine such economic restructuring from the point of view of women workers and labor activism.

The Story of Chawkieng

Hara Textiles was a modern manufacturing establishment that dispersed its base of production to many small factories in and around Bangkok. It had a workforce of about 1,000 in 1975.[9] The sweatshops that made up the factory were housed in rundown buildings, converted car garages, and makeshift warehouses constructed out of aluminum siding and cardboard boxes. The workers were mostly young women and girls between the ages of thirteen and thirty, who were paid daily wages of 9 to 20 baht (US$0.36–$0.80) without benefits. One day in October of that year, the employer announced that the factory was going to be shut down and relocated. For the women at this factory, this job was their only source of income, and upon hearing that announcement the women decided to retaliate by stopping production. Their struggle lasted four months.

During this time, the factory owner consistently refused to negotiate with the workers. Meanwhile, the workers were finding it very difficult to survive without an income. As their financial situation became more severe, the women decided to take matters into their own hands. A demonstration ensued, and a takeover of the factory by the workers followed. During the takeover, the women formed a collective, which they called *Rohng Ngarn Sahmakee Kamakorn* (Factory of Unity for Workers), and reopened production with a revolving credit fund. Using the company's machines, they assembled ready-to-wear garments and sold their items in the local market, equally dividing the proceeds their sales generated. During their demonstration, the women spoke up about the appalling work conditions in the factory sweatshops and made factory profit levels public, announcing that a shirt costing 60 to 70 baht to produce was sold by the factory in the market for 200 to 400 baht.

This famous demonstration at Hara Textiles was led by a young woman named Chawkieng. On a Sunday morning in October 1999, I met with Chawkieng at her factory building, which was also her home; she had been working and living there since 1992. She told me about her experience at Hara and of how she came to own and operate her own textile business after the Hara incident.

I was only twenty-one years old when I got the job at Hara. I applied there because the factory was near my house. I received some training on the very first day on the job, and being a very quick learner, I mastered the task in no time and did the job well and fast. All workers were paid by the piece.

Hara was a very successful factory back then. It had about a thousand employees. The place where I worked was fairly large, but the employer put no money into the factory. He just rented a large space and put up thin aluminum roofing to cover and surround it. The floors were made of cardboard boxes, and they were always wet when we lay down to sleep or rest. The factory even provided rice, but the rice was not edible, full of rice moths and maggots. These kinds of conditions were suitable for animals, maybe, but not for human beings.

The factory wouldn't allow water or food on the premises because they were afraid it might dirty or stain the garments. They didn't even provide drinking water and expected us to consume water that came from a pipe attached to the sewer. So we had to sneak in water to drink; otherwise, how could we work?

I used to work every day from 7:00 a.m. to 6:00 p.m. Because we were paid by the piece, there was a race to get to the factory every morning to see who would be the first to choose the largest batch of work. Work came on a "first come, first served" basis. In the morning, you would see women lined up at the gates like at a race track, and when the bell went off, we would all run like crazy to beat each other to the finish line! We would work without looking up once from our stations, going twelve hours straight so we could make enough money for the day. It got to the point where we refused to take lunch and bathroom breaks. My mind and body fully adjusted to working like that, and to this day, I can't have breakfast or lunch. The work environment then was such that taking time out to eat meant a lot of money out of my pocket, and during that time, I also had three children to feed.

There was never any kind of unity or friendly relations among the women. We came together only when our jobs were threatened. My friends and I couldn't find any work after the Hara strike because no one would hire us, especially me, given my reputation as the one who led the strike.

The public exposure of the incident forced Chawkieng to go into hiding for several years (she not only was blacklisted but feared for her life). Then, with only one sewing machine, she started to take in subcontracting piecework in her home. The contractor who hired her was so struck by the excellent quality of the work and the quantity she could produce that he wanted her to produce more, but she had only one sewing machine. As the work orders kept coming in, though, eventually she acquired five additional sewing machines. Soon enough, she had ten people working in her house. The work orders kept piling up, forcing Chawkieng and her crew to eat while they were working at the machines.

I worked so much then. I counted the hours. I worked twenty-two hours every day for one full year, and I am living to tell it. I slept only two hours a day, but I could never do that anymore. Where we are sitting right now, this factory literally came from my blood, my sweat, and my tears. During those long days when I was working nonstop, tears would constantly be flowing from my eyes because I never slept.

In time, needing more space for the growing number of workers and sewing machines, Chawkieng moved her crew into a *tukh taew saarm chun* (three-story building). But the work orders kept increasing and because of the way she treated her employees, so did her workforce. She moved again into a *tukh taew see chun* (four-story building) to accommodate the expansion, and by that time, she had purchased thirty more sewing machines. In 1992 she finally moved with her family into this factory building where we met.

Ironically, my standard of living has improved because of Hara: had the employer not threatened to shut down the factory, I would have just kept on working. But when we stood up against him, we realized how low the wages he was paying us were. We deserved to be making a lot more for what we were doing, and we didn't want to be stuck working like this. I believe this was a lesson that the employer gave the employee.

Today, wherever there is a strike, that is where you have smarter workers. But to protest or to strike doesn't mean much nowadays, because nothing seems to come of it. Employers all have some excuse to shut down factories and lay off workers. Nevertheless, whenever there *is* a strike or protest happening somewhere, I tell my workers to stop what they're doing and to go and see that strike, and I would urge them to support the demonstrating workers. But my workers refuse to go because they feel that it doesn't concern them.

Chawkieng's account highlights the many effective forms of coercion and control over labor that continue to persist in factories today. More significantly, her account of factory work at Hara very well describes the kinds of conditions that women workers in labor-intensive factories continue to be subjected to. In fact, accounts of deplorable factory conditions go back to the early nineteenth century, such as the case of the Lowell Mill Girls, employed in Lowell, Massachusetts.[10] Nearly two centuries later, we continue to hear countless stories of women factory workers around the world who are struggling to live on their low wages and who labor under increasingly oppressive conditions. But every so often, we hear stories of women who are trying to do something about their situation through collective mobilization at their workplace. I chose to begin with the Hara incident because it represents an extreme case of worker rebellion: rather than object to the harrowing conditions under which they labored for so long, the women rose up only to protest against a direct threat to their livelihood, the shutting down of the factory (a practice widely referred to today as "cut and run"). Chawkieng's story offers insight into the complexities embedded in notions of worker consciousness, which in her case can be observed as a curious and abrupt transformation from accommodation to resistance and rebellion. At the same time, Chawkieng provides an insightful reflection of her own life, the hardship she endured in building her own business, her views on worker protest, and her rationalization of who she has become.

The story of exploited female workers has been repeated time and again, regardless of their location. Why then continue to write about them if their situation has not changed? One must continue to write about them precisely *because* their situation has not changed. In a global economy where women workers are compelled to sell their labor for the lowest possible price, one can even expect their situation to get worse.

During Thailand's export boom (1985–1995), textile factories were thriving, and rural women gravitated to where factory jobs were available because they simply had no other choice. As a result, they put up with a lot of hardship to improve their lives and provide subsistence and opportunities for their families and their children. These women were mothers, wives, daughters—women who were living up to their duties toward their families and communities but were also willing to fight for what was due to them, to demand a fair day's pay for a fair day's labor. I chose to do this study because women workers are often taken for granted and because there are so few accounts of women who work in these places. And I believe that conditions in sweatshops around the world continually need to be exposed.

I also wanted to look at consciousness because I had always assumed that militancy had a masculine connotation, and I wanted to find out if that was true. Most of the literature on the labor movement in Thailand is highly gendered, focusing primarily on male workers and male-dominated unions, and thus reinforcing the gender stereotype of the male worker as more assertive: that is, willing and able to become more engaged in militant action. By contrast, my ethnographic study focused exclusively on women workers at the end of the global supply chain and sought to establish whether these stereotypes were accurate. Doing so is especially pertinent, since Thai factory women are marketed by the state as compliant, disciplined, nimble, patient—in short, exploitable. But, born and raised in Thailand, I have always been aware that Thai women are not like that. Although Asian women are often projected in the media as being submissive, this was never the case in my experience with Thai women of all social backgrounds (it could be accurate for younger women sold into the sex tourist industry, but even there it is a blanket generalization based on preconceptions). Naturally, then, being skeptical about these characterizations, I went into the factories to find out whether they were true. Although Thai men and women are generally polite with Westerners (whom they call *farang*), they are not genuinely passive in everyday life. I have to say that many women I encountered in working on this book were quite cheeky, spunky, feisty, often domineering, witty, and confident. In fact, there is a Thai word that captures these attributes—*dhet*, which also means "bold," "daring," "fearless." The women workers I studied were clever, resourceful, courageous, and innovative in ways that gender stereotypes do not capture.

Seeking out what was genuine and authentic was what I wanted to do, and the only way was through in-depth qualitative research. Therefore, I used ethnographic research techniques to reveal women's experiences for what they were and to provide a picture of their daily lives. I used their voices to assess the accuracy of these widely held characterizations.

Ethnographic research uniquely offers insights into these kinds of questions because it presents a picture based on the first-order social constructs of everyday life rather than on the researcher's own assumptions. In other words, ethnographic studies carried out over a long period of time, where a researcher immerses herself in the lives of her research subjects, can reveal what life is really like for them. Ethnography seemed appropriate in this context, and qualitative research can sometimes reveal things other methods cannot. In-depth interviewing and spending time with the women really allowed me to get into the *chiwit jing jing* (what Westerners refer to as the "nitty gritty") of what it was really like for women factory workers.

In this book, then, I explore the very diverse experiences of Thai female textile factory workers in the context of production and the different structural conditions under which they labor. More specifically, I examine how the all-encompassing nature of wage work speaks to issues of worker accommodation and/or resistance within various factory settings. Questions informing this research included these: What are the circumstances surrounding women's lives that contribute to their accommodation, acquiescence, or resistance? What inhibits a female worker from speaking out against her wages and working conditions? What triggers a female worker to rise up and speak out against her employer?

I address what happens to women once they have settled into wage employment and focus specifically on how wage employment differentially shapes women's collective and personal consciousness. Because the sweatshops of Thailand involve almost complete immersion of one's life and identity in the processes of work, factory employment influences and defines women's entire perceptions and outlook on life as well as their ways of living. It seems that even their limited social and personal lives outside the factory cannot escape completely the binding economic ties women have to their factory employment.

Studies of worker consciousness inevitably draw one to consider (neo-)Marxist conceptions of productive processes and relations. For this reason, I started my analysis by considering the general tenet that the dynamics of the capitalist accumulation process shape and transform social relations in production, which, in turn, influence and shape worker consciousness. Marx had indicated that consciousness is a social product and "is at first, of course, merely consciousness concerning the immediate sensuous environment and consciousness of the limited connection with other persons and things outside the individual who is growing self-conscious."[11] Indeed, workers who are not politicized also form strong personal bonds through the adversities faced on the factory floor, working cooperatively to ensure that production goes smoothly and efficiently; thus, they develop a social consciousness associated with accommodating behavior. Worker consciousness is therefore not necessarily synonymous with collective action against the employer.

For politicized workers, growing self-awareness about their poor working situation can become a collective concern and can lead a handful of workers to mobilize other workers—the conditions for labor solidarity. It is possible to trace the development of worker consciousness by looking at women factory workers in different settings and their varied experiences at work. As Michael Burawoy writes, "Any work context involves an economic dimension (production of things), a political dimension (production of social relations), and an ideological dimension (production of an experience of those relations). These three dimensions are inseparable. Moreover, they are all 'objective' inasmuch as they are independent of the particular people who come to work, of the particular agents of production."[12] So, despite the formal institutional separation of the economy, the polity, and ideology or culture in the capitalist mode of production, Marxist approaches highlight the existence of crucial connections between these dimensions (which other Marxists describe as regions) of the social formation.

The sense of objectivity implied by Burawoy refers to the mystification of capitalist relations of production as a natural and voluntary product of the operation of the economy. Burawoy develops critical ethnography in order to help explain why people accept exploitation as inevitable. For these reasons, the privileging of the economic dimension (in this case, women's experiences at work) enables a more nearly adequate explanation of how the political and ideological dimensions evolve and change along with transformations in production, both at the factory level and at the level of the global market.

The factories I investigated demonstrate the vital linkages between local elite capital and multinational capital, although the size and scale of their operations reflect the marked disparities in managerial policies and treatment toward their employees. One factory, for instance, started out as a small family business that produced men's undergarments for the domestic market. The success of this local enterprise allowed the company to grow, and it soon started producing ready-made apparel for export. The company's benevolent managerial practices resulted in a highly skilled, experienced, and devoted workforce, which was good for business in the long run. Another factory, with strong commercial ties to major multinational clothing companies, ran on a business model more common to labor-intensive factories, one where antagonistic relations between workers and management prevailed. Nonetheless, this second factory also continued to thrive, even as management had to combat a disruptive workforce.

I hope to demonstrate the importance of looking at the objective conditions surrounding women's productive lives along with the ways their subjective experiences are shaped by their engagement. At the same time, it is important to recognize that these conditions of production are constantly changing. It is not sufficient simply to state that women do or do not realize they are being exploited. Rather, it is necessary to look at the individual and collective experience of work in different locations and how this experience plays a large part in determining the potential for active resistance among women workers. As John French and Daniel James write in their introduction to a collection of studies on women workers in Latin America, "This emphasis on material or structural constraints does not take analytical priority over the investigation of the specific forms of subjectivity and consciousness through which women negotiate their material and affective relations. Indeed, this integration of what has sometimes been called the 'objective' and the 'subjective' is linked to a redefinition of the subject of labor history, the concept of agency, and the role of language and discourse."[13] Perhaps the stories I present here will shed some light on the specific issue of women's engagement with social transformation.

The body of texts in the research literature on women and work has mainly focused on the effect of the state and of capitalist and patriarchal ideologies and their effects on the gendered division of labor. The state and the capitalist employer often have economic interests that coincide and both exercise similar mechanisms of direct and indirect control over female labor. Capitalist owners are interested in the immediate profit from this labor; the state is interested in expanding the national economy (via foreign exchange earnings, foreign direct investment, and so on); and these interests are often realized through the recruitment of cheap, primarily female labor. Correspondingly, feminist scholars have been able to identify and specify how forms of control over labor are acquired, maintained, and reproduced. In Hong Kong, for example, subcontracting agents relied on parental pressures at home to make young girls work for long hours and low wages. In short, sociologists, cultural anthropologists, feminist ethnographers, and historians have made significant contributions to the field of women and work.[14] But only a few studies have looked specifically at worker consciousness as it pertains to women in labor-intensive industries at the factory level in developing countries.[15]

Often, empirical case studies of women workers do not sufficiently highlight the all-encompassing aspect of wage work as a daily routine that becomes a permanent fixture in women's lives. My examination of women in different factories and work settings highlights this aspect and contrasts "militant" and "nonmilitant" behavior in the contexts in which they arise, enabling me to consider how consciousness evolves and transforms during periods of economic growth and economic crisis along with changes in production. My findings reveal how one factory "produces" a nonmilitant and compliant workforce and how another "produces" the exact opposite. Women's stories portray individual and collective efforts to overcome adversity at two different levels: accommodation to factory work on the one hand, and full engagement in a struggle against the employer on the other. I contend that the structure of the work environment, women's particular experiences within the workplace, and their personal and social relations both inside and outside the factory must be looked at contextually for an understanding of the varied and complex factors behind *why* and *how* mobilization among workers takes place in today's globalized world. In essence, this book captures diverse forms of worker consciousness before and after the Asian financial crisis in 1997 and traces how consciousness evolves and changes in the context of Thai industrial development. Such an analysis may offer important implications for the situation of low-wage workers in labor-intensive industries in other developing countries.

The Centrality of Women's Experiences

All Marxists inherently believe that factory work is exploitative because workers do not profit from the fruits of their labor. Women are integrated into the labor market and exploited as a reserve army of low-wage laborers for accumulating capital at minimal cost. Consequently, financial independence, liberation from patriarchal structures, and social mobility are often severely constrained within the economic limits of wage work, since women spend a large portion of their time at work. I wanted to start from women's own experiences by using a micro-level approach to the social construction of work relations specific to a particular industry, occupation, and locality. This kind of approach from below is necessary to an explanation of what is going on at the larger macro- (or global) level and offers a more comprehensive and sensible approach to the study of women in different working situations. Women's experiences cannot be deemed as essentially micro and ahistorical, because everyday life and interactions can inform us about the larger picture. As Burawoy points out, the technique of participant observation suffers from the problem of significance. In other words, case studies may supply very interesting results but provide no measure of their generalizability precisely because "the study of face-to-face interaction, of the social situation, is said to be inherently micro and ahistorical."In his discussion of the extended case method, however, Burawoy argues that the significance of a case study lies in its ability to tell us about the world in which it is embedded. In so doing, the extended case method "seeks to uncover the macro foundations of a micro sociology," and this gives us a more in-depth context within which to look at social transformations.[16]

So therefore, I looked on my fieldwork as a way of learning about and as a forum attempting to present what these women have to say about their living and working conditions. As French and James state, "The objective is to achieve a fullness of representation and understanding that is adequate to the multidimensional, integrated nature of how people actually experience their lives."[17] I hope this research contributes to the growing body of literature that incorporates women's voices and narratives and adds to the array of existing studies on female factory workers in the countries of East Asia that have been central to the global apparel industry.[18] A case study on one of the region's largest textile manufacturers, Thailand, and their female laborers is greatly needed.

A Note on Terminology

I use several terms (e.g., adaptation, accommodation, acquiescence, passivity, powerlessness, exploitation, oppression, subordination, coercion, resistance) to describe, define, and qualify women's experiences at work and their responses to factory employment. "Subordination," "exploitation," and "oppression" are the common terms employed in the theoretical and empirical literature on women. "Subordination" and "oppression," according to Maria Mies, are "widely used to specify women's position in a hierarchically structured system."[19] Both oppression and exploitation are the result of women's subordination to patriarchal authority either at work or within the home, and subordination adds another dimension, for it involves the social and cultural mechanisms that are exercised over women and that shape their roles in society, thereby oppressing them, and that can lead them into situations where they can be exploited. As Edna Acosta-Belén and Christine Bose note, "The understanding of the subordination of women…requires the recognition of these various layers of oppression."[20]

Women in third world countries are seen as simultaneously subordinated, oppressed, and exploited under the two mutually reinforcing systems of capitalism and patriarchy.[21] In this context, capitalism refers to the material basis of women's oppression in the market economy; patriarchy refers to a social system that subordinates women to men on the basis of gender. The forms and bases of women's subordination are thereby embedded within the labor market, the household, and the workplace. Case studies of family firms in Taiwan, for example, found that most businesses were owned by men and that preexisting social norms of the Chinese family system allowed men to exploit women's labor.[22] My book, however, draws explicit attention to the oppression of women in the context of the capitalist organization and system of production.

Marilyn Frye also considers oppression in relation to exploitation. She characterizes oppression as a "systematic network of forces and barriers which tend to the reduction, immobilization and molding of the oppressed." The factory system can be seen as inherently oppressive for women (and men) because it physically confines workers and restricts their mobility—leading to the issue of coercion, which, according to Frye, involves the act of forcing someone to do something by the manipulation of circumstances and limiting options. The paradigm of coercion is very significant in an examination of women and factory work: the factory owner employs various mechanisms of control within the factory system in order to ensure efficiency and productivity. The employer uses women's low wages to put into place an effective system of overtime work and pay. The same applies to the subcontracting piece-rate system of production, where workers are coerced into a situation in which they can to some extent determine their own wages (such as deciding whether or not to produce 3,000 items that day). The structures of production thereby alter the situation of the worker who is presented with options in such a way that she can make her own judgments and set her own priorities. But the circumstance surrounding her decision (necessity to earn the extra wages) places great limitations on her options and the choices she makes. In this regard, "the force involved in coercion is applied at some distance," so that workers seem to be engaged in controlling and determining their own movements and making their own decisions at work.[23]

In Frye's definition, coercion does not involve direct physical force but is a situation in which "choice and action do take place." In the case of one factory, for example, all the workers chose to work overtime hours because the opportunity to make extra wages was presented to them. In this situation, coercion is applied at some distance by the factory owner with the setting-up of an overtime system that coerces workers to make their own choice about whether or not to work the extra hours. This manipulation lies at the root of coercion and in this regard, "coercion is extended, ramified and laminated as systems of oppression and exploitation."[24] By the same token, James Scott uses the term "passivity" to refer to an exploited group that "actually accepts its situation as a normal, even justifiable part of the social order"; it "assumes at least a fatalistic acceptance of that social order and perhaps even an active complicity."[25] In my research, I found that women were actively complying with a production system that required them to work over ninety hours a week for many consecutive years of employment. Women commonly uttered the phrase *yoo dai pai wan wan* (getting by day to day), but rather than suggesting a sense of resignation, a fatalistic outlook, or the unfortunate fate of being "born poor," their expression carries a hint of cynicism toward a system that is openly oppressive and unresponsive to their situation while leaving them powerless to do anything about it.

Susan Tiano applies the terms "acquiescence," "alienation," "accommodation," and "resistance" to measure consciousness in her study of women assembly workers in Mexico. She defines the four terms as follows:

> "Acquiescence" represents women who unquestionably support the system of productive and reproductive relations that structures their lives and who have little personal empowerment. "Accommodation" refers to women who believe in the system and feel empowered to act within its strictures to improve their circumstances. "Alienation" indicates women who are mistrustful of or reject the system but feel powerless to change their lives. "Resistance" denotes women who reject the system as unjust and believe that they are capable of effecting positive changes in their conditions.[26]

According to Tiano, accommodators can be described as "individualists," workers who have a strong work ethic and are interested in improving their lives through hard work and dedication. Alienated women blame an unjust system for their problems and harbor a sense of hopelessness because they do not know what to do or who to turn to for help, and they feel that any effort at making change would be futile. Resistant women also blame the system but feel so angry and frustrated about their situation that they believe they must do something about it and decide to take matters into their own hands.

Borrowing Tiano's terminology, this book explores the experiences of an accommodating group of women at one factory and a resistant group of women at another. Accommodators are characterized by the longevity of their employment and their devotion to work and to the factory, and by the absence of any form of collective protest. Resistant or rebellious women may have started out as accommodators but felt unhappy about their situation and wanted to take action. Either way, it would be inappropriate to place women into such heuristic categories when women themselves, personally or collectively, often experience shifts from one mode of consciousness to another. Not all women in unionized factories, for instance, can be described as "militant" women, since the term "militant" in the context of my research applies to those women who have been actively involved in organizing labor struggles at their factory. Moreover, the factory women in my study are not acquiescent per se, because they do question the gender-biased nature of the system and have a strong sense of control over their lives and their wages.

The majority of women in the factories studied were poor rural migrants who readily adapted to the factory's rules and regulations. Once they settled into the factory system, women were accommodating because they felt empowered by the wages they were making and their ability to support themselves and their families financially. But poor work conditions and low wages eventually alienated one group, and as conditions worsened, a handful of women became agitated and rebelled. Although women were generally critical of their work conditions and regarded their situations as exploitive, only one group of women was willing to take risks by engaging in collective action. At the nonmilitant factory, women generally appeared to accept a system they regarded as unfair but felt powerless to change.

Moreover, following the 1997 Asian financial crisis, another story of worker consciousness emerged: the resistant group of women became accommodators once again because the shift in the system of production diminished their ability to organize. Another explanation for the decline in labor union strength in the militant zone at the factory-firm level had much to do with the significant decline in textile production, which meant a significant decrease in workers' wages. In 1999, Thailand had a per capita annual income of US$1,690, down from US$2,740 during 1990–95.[27] The workers I interviewed at both factories reported considerable reduction in their biweekly and monthly wages because of a sustained slump in work orders and consequent reductions in overtime work and pay. Subsequently, accommodating women, becoming resistant to a system that drastically slashed their wages, collectively banded together in order to slow down production.

By examining workers' responses to the changing socioeconomic situation and its consequences, one can see how consciousness evolves and transforms in diverse ways, even within a relatively short period of economic change and restructuring. In other words, worker consciousness shifts from accommodation to alienation to resistance as a result of new structural conditions of work at one place, while at the other, worker consciousness shifts from resistance to alienation to accommodation. In this instance, workers at the nonmilitant factory felt compelled to exert control over a production system that was affecting their wages, while workers at the militant factory felt more and more disempowered as their union leaders were fired, as their union became co-opted by management, and as the piece-rate system took over the former assembly-line system of production.

Like Susan Tiano's work, this case study "challenges the conception of women workers as uniformly passive" and thereby calls into question the idea of collective identity and a collective consciousness. But if consciousness does not develop in a uniform way, then how does it manifest itself for working women in this particular segment of the working class? Tiano contends that a more complex schema is required in order to look at "alternative subjective orientations that may underlie women's seemingly quiescent behavior."[28] I suggest that subjective orientations can be observed through an in-depth look at women's work histories, women's perceptions about themselves and about their work situations, women's views of management, and their relationships with one another, inside and outside the factory setting.

Research Methodology and the Composition of the Sample

At the time that this study was carried out in 1998, Thailand had a population of about 60 million, the urban population constituted 21 percent of the total. The country is divided into five regions (see map of Thailand, opposite the title page)—Central, Eastern, Northern, Northeastern, and Southern—comprising seventy-six *jungwat* (provinces).[29] The women I interviewed came from major cities in various provinces of the Central, Northeastern, and Northern Regions. The majority of manufacturing establishments were located in Bangkok and the surrounding five provinces of the Central Region. Of a total working population of around 29 million, women made up 50 percent of the labor force. Fifteen percent of the total workforce was employed in the manufacturing sector. Women outnumbered men in all the leading export industries—which included electronics, textiles and ready-made garments, food processing, precious stones and gems, and footwear and leather products—and constituted about 80 to 95 percent of the total workers employed.

The economic crisis in Thailand that began in the summer of 1997 came just a year before I embarked on my fieldwork. My interviews focus both on women's retrospective accounts of their work experiences up to 1997 and on those following the crisis through to 2005. They told me stories of both joy and hardship, about what it was like working at a time when Thailand became a world-leading exporter of ready-made apparel and during the post-crisis transition in the system of production.

The Factories

Factory One (F1) was founded in 1957 by a Thai Chinese businessman whose son still oversees and manages all operations. The factory successfully established itself as a leading manufacturer of men's underwear in the domestic market and later expanded its production by specializing in infant and children's clothing for export to European niche markets. The factory is one of the few remaining in the Bangkok metropolitan area. At the time of my interviews, F1 was a non-unionized factory and employed about 800 workers, mostly women. It provided no dormitory facilities for its workers. In addition, the business had expanded its operations and had set up a larger, more modern facility outside of Bangkok which employed more than 3,000 workers and produced brand-name adult clothing for export. My interviews, however, took place at the factory's original location, which occupies about four and a half acres of land in the city district of Prakanong, Bangkok.

Factory Two (F2) was established in 1987 by a Chinese-Thai businessman whose family owned one of Thailand's largest textile conglomerates, operating several large-scale factories in the Rangsit industrial zone.[30] During the export boom of the late 1980s, F2 had a workforce of about 800 women and became unionized in 1994. It specialized in brand-name clothing and sportswear and exported ready-made apparel for several large multinational companies, including Nike, Gap, Adidas, Timberland, Old Navy, Champion, and Gymboree.

I thought about a way of summing up what one might describe as "responsible" and "irresponsible" factories and considered giving F1 the name *Thai-Jai-Dee* and F2 the name *Thai-Jai-Rai*—as taken from the women's own descriptions (*jai dee* meaning "kind or nice" and *jai rai* meaning "mean and heartless"). But I decided to label the factories simply "F1" and "F2" in order to capture the experiences of women workers in textile factories everywhere around the world and also to maintain some degree of neutrality and anonymity, given the close ties and interfamilial associations of members of the Thai business community. Abbreviated pseudonyms are therefore used for all the factories (except Hara), labeled numerically from 1 to 4, plus two subcontract factories, SF1 and SF2.

Factory Three (F3) was established in 1978 and is located in the Samut Sakorn industrial zone, about one hour out of the capital city, in the district of Krathumbaen. It manufactures pressed fabrics for export and specializes in the dyeing and inspecting of cloth. The factory had a non-unionized workforce of about 1,800 during the time of my visit in 1999. At F3, there were ten production departments with up to 200 women working in each department. Regular working hours were Monday through Friday from 8:00 a.m. to 5:00 p.m., but the plant was operating three eight-hour shifts for a 24/7 operation. Workers were required to wear pink uniforms, were issued a card to be punched three times a day, and were routinely frisked by male or female guards at the entrance gate. F3 provided dormitory facilities that accommodated up to 300 workers. My interviews with women who lived in the dormitories took place in their lobby and canteen areas.

Factory Four (F4) produced brand-name apparel for export and had a unionized workforce of about 1,300, mostly women. F4 also provided some dormitory facilities, although many of the women lived in rented rooms near the factory. F2 and F4 were both located in the industrial zone of Rangsit, in the outlying district of Pratumthani, and belonged to the same parent company (PF).

In 1992, F2 opened two subcontract factories (SF1 and SF2) in the northeastern provinces of Korat and Ubon Ratchatani. After the financial crisis, F2 became heavily reliant upon outsourced production at these two factories, which employed about 400 and 600 workers, respectively. SF1, which had an ordering relationship with Nike, subcontracted parts of its large orders to SF2.

Of the first four factories, F1 was the only factory located in the Bangkok metropolitan area; F2, F3, and F4 were all located in major industrial zones on the outskirts of Bangkok, where a majority of textile industries were concentrated and where unionized textile factories were strongest.

The Women

I constructed two ideal types of women workers, "militant" and "nonmilitant," in order to compare what actual empirical experiences would lead to such differing and contradictory responses to factory employment.[31] Interviewing these very divergent groups of women allowed me to better understand the two extreme poles of workers' consciousness. Thenceforth, significantly, my sample allowed me to compare a large group of non-unionized factory workers against several of the most militant women in the recent history of the Thai labor movement. This sample included both women who had never been involved in any form of protest or demonstration and women who took on a central role in the formation of a labor union at their factory. Women I interviewed from the latter group included those who had been dismissed for their union activities.

My data were collected during fieldwork that took place from September 1998 through January 1999, and from September 1999 through January 2000. Follow-up interviews were conducted with some respondents in 2002, 2003, and 2005. The qualitative data come from in-depth interviews with women who had been employed for extended periods of time in medium and large textile factories located in and around the Bangkok metropolitan area (see Table 1 on page 33).[32] I focused primarily on women who had been employed for ten, twenty, and thirty consecutive years or more, a characteristic in stark contrast to the general profile of female assemblers elsewhere. The typical or "ideal" female factory worker in the eyes of employers is young and single, and willing to work long hours for low pay for a short period of time. The temporary nature of her employment is correlated with societal expectations for marriage and childbearing. In her study of female *maquila* workers, Tiano found that employers tended to favor young, single, childless women rather than older, married women with children on the assumption that younger, unmarried women would be more committed to their jobs, since they lived at home and had no domestic or child-care responsibilities. Young women are also perceived to be more docile and submissive because they often live under the patriarchal authority of their fathers and brothers. Women thus occupy a disadvantageous position in the labor market: because of prevailing cultural stereotypes and preconceived notions of gendered biological traits, they are deemed suitable for low-skilled, low-paying jobs—recruitment standards that deepen existing gender inequalities.

Maintaining a young, temporary workforce also frees employers from having to pay older workers seniority benefits. Yet I found just the opposite to be the case at one factory: there, the workforce was made up of many older, married women who had families and who were receiving seniority pay. These women had long employment records, and some were the primary breadwinners in their families. This unusual situation says just as much about the owner of the factory, though, as about the women who worked there.

An intensive study of specific groups of women therefore has many methodological advantages. First, one can learn what wage work *means* to these women, most of whom come from rural farming families. Second, one can get a glimpse of these women through the eyes of those engaged with them on a daily basis as workers or as members of a workers' union. Finally, one can closely examine women in times of crisis by assessing their responses and reactions when their daily lives and, in many cases, their livelihoods, are disrupted. For me, being a young Thai woman in the field was a bonus, for three main reasons: my fluency in the Thai language enabled me to capture the many nuances and meanings in the women's speech and conversation; coming from a similar cultural background made the women more comfortable around me and more willing to talk freely and openly; and, because there were no language and cultural barriers, women readily invited me into their homes, enabling me to spend time with them outside of the workplace. Women became subjects rather than objects in my research, as they were also in Lourdes Benería and Martha Roldán's landmark study of subcontract homeworkers in Mexico City.[33] Those authors examined the lives of female homeworkers by visiting and talking to the women in their neighborhoods, which enabled them to better understand the effects of this kind of work on women and their families. Women's life histories helped them capture the important socioeconomic links between the household and industrial homework at the local level and between subcontracting production and the global market.

I interviewed women on factory premises during working hours and outside the factory in their homes and in various social milieus (e.g., in temples, at soccer games, at union meetings, and in labor court), sometimes in the presence of co-workers and friends. Informal conversations took place during workers' lunch and dinner breaks. By talking to women inside and outside their work settings, I was able to see how work shapes social relations and how women build their own worlds around work. During my interviews, women revealed things that they had never really thought about before and were often caught by surprise by the profundity and eloquence of their own illuminating comments. Similarly, spending this time with the women led me to think about questions I would otherwise never have thought to ask. Many women did not want the interviews to end because they were so delighted that someone was actually interested in hearing about their lives and what they had to say about their experiences. Questions that elicited their views and opinions especially about work triggered in some women a strong sense of empowerment and entitlement as they reflected upon their many years of factory employment and what that work had meant to them.

There were some practical limitations to the research, such as the number of factory women a manager would allow me to interview; because these interviews were conducted during the work week, those workers had to take an hour or more out of their production time during the workday. The proprietors of three factories (F1, F3 and F4) were kind enough to allow their workers to take off a few hours from their shift. The women themselves expressed initial reluctance about coming into contact with an outsider and were quite cautious about my presence. Outsiders were easily detected because most factory employees were in uniform, and only factory employees were allowed on the premises during working hours. But once I sat down with the women individually, and immediately reassured them that I was there only to ask a few general questions about their lives, they quickly came to accept my presence.

Outline of the Book

The first of the following chapters tells the story of "nonmilitant" women who had been working for many consecutive years in the same factory, performing the same tasks seven days a week, fourteen hours a day, 353 days a year (all but Thailand's traditional holidays). Their stories unravel the factors that contribute to maintaining a long-standing and compliant workforce. Wage work became an integral part of almost every facet of their lives, not just a means to an end. Women's lives inside and outside the factory were embedded within the structure of their employment and deeply intertwined with the pace and nature of factory work. My findings suggest that notions of powerlessness, passivity, and accommodation can be attributed to less oppressive forms of control over labor at this factory than at others. One highly effective mechanism of control over labor is the institutionalization of overtime work and pay, which creates a rigid dependency on factory work, though providing few or no benefits. At the same time, an assembly-line production system forces women to work side by side every day, which inevitably causes them to develop intimate personal affiliations and attachments. The tightly knit group of friends created within this constricted scope of social relations leads to the development of an intimate work setting, which, in turn, strengthens employees' dependency on and attachment to the factory. A distinct social consciousness is thereby rooted in a common need to ensure the stability of their employment without any interruption to production. Meanwhile, low wages and long working hours have entrapped these women in an unending cycle of struggle for daily survival, which both fails to improve their living conditions and inhibits possibilities for mobilization.

Chapter 2 tells the stories of a handful of women also with continual years of factory employment, but highly oppressive forms of control over labor led to their resistance and rebellion at the factory. Retrospective accounts of their experiences help to uncover the many factors behind their struggle and help to explain how certain controlling mechanisms over labor managed to provoke worker rebellion. In spite of the deplorable work conditions and ongoing labor violations at the factory during the first few years of their employment, these women stayed on because they too became accustomed to the routine and derived a sense of satisfaction and self-worth from doing quality work—and for the most part they found comfort in knowing that everyone around them shared the same plight. The factory indeed became the setting where women bonded, even as they became increasingly unhappy with their work conditions and began to question their situation. The lives of the women who led the protest against it no longer revolved around work but instead revolved around union organizing efforts. Women's collective experiences of struggle against the employer and their own experiences of militancy and activism thereby came to shape and define every facet of their lives.

Chapter 3 situates workers within the context of a changing production environment following a period of economic crisis and discusses the implications for women in both factory settings. I examine the disruptions and continuities in the lives of the women in an atmosphere of recession and a weakened economy and look at new mechanisms of control over labor as they became manifest in the system of subcontract piecerate work. Workers were no longer selling just their labor power but were now selling their bodies, their health, and their well-being to produce maximally and meet a quota that provided less than a minimum wage. I draw once again upon the actual experiences of workers from both F1 and F2 in order to examine how these "new" forms of control, along with worsened structural conditions of work, could produce highly reactive responses while, at the same time, invoking a fearful and accommodating workforce. Moreover, the piece-rate system fostered tension and animosity among workers as individual women competed for piecework, thereby inhibiting their socialization and solidarity. Such a production system not only forced women to work longer hours but acted as an essential tool to circumvent labor law, rupture the unity and cohesion of organized labor, and shut out latent forms of mobilization for women at non-unionized factories in Bangkok and the surrounding industrial provinces.

The conclusion reviews the arguments presented in this book, examines their implications for future research, and emphasizes why it is important for researchers to recount and analyze women's stories. What happened to women in Thailand in the 1990s is now happening to more vulnerable groups, so even though the women I studied made progress through their own efforts, the forms of exploitation that blighted their lives are still at work among "new victims." Of course, the women featured here would not see themselves as victims; nevertheless, their economic position and their duties toward their families and siblings, combined with their need to survive, placed them in a situation where employers could take advantage. It is the dynamics of these relationships that this book seeks to explore and illuminate. I hope to have cast light not only on the specific experiences of women in Southeast Asia but more generally on the economic processes that take advantage of the most vulnerable workers.

Economic Development and the Thai Apparel Industry

During the 1960s, multinational corporations began to penetrate Thailand and other East Asian nations by setting up production plants in export-processing zones and by taking advantage of the abundant supplies of cheap female labor.[34] In Thailand, the massive influx of young female migrants flowed into the urban informal sector and into labor-intensive manufacturing enterprises. The Thai economy continued to grow rapidly during the 1970s and 1980s. Temporary and short-term migration into the city began in the 1970s and increased steadily as labor opportunities in the countryside fell along with the drastic decline in agriculture. Internal migration resulted in a mass movement of 1.5 million people from the rural provinces into the city to look for work in the early 1980s. Many remained for a year or two before returning to their villages; some stayed for short periods of time between harvest seasons; and others relocated permanently. Pasuk Phongpaichit and Chris Baker indicate that "Bangkok continued to dominate urban growth, and expanded from a city of 2.6 million in 1960 to 4.6 million in 1970, and 5.9 million in 1975," in tandem with the acceleration of employment in manufacturing.[35] During this period, Bangkok experienced one of the highest rates of population growth in its history, with almost half of the urban population consisting of people from the countryside.[36] Development policies since the 1960s, however, resulted in an unequal distribution of resources, widening the gap between the urban and rural areas and between the rich and poor in Thailand.

Meanwhile, there was a marked rise in the percentage of female workers in manufacturing, given the proliferation of labor-intensive industrial establishments that preferred to hire women. At the same time, organized labor in Bangkok and the surrounding industrial provinces gained prominence, along with the rapid expansion of export-led industries. In the garment and apparel industry, women were the "preferred" workers because of the preconceived notion that the task of sewing was naturally suited to women, and the paternalistic attitude that women were easier to control. Such patriarchal views have had an important impact on managerial policies and have resulted in the generally poor treatment of women in labor-intensive factories. Textile factories in particular were among the few channels of employment for women from rural areas. Women were therefore drawn from the agricultural sector into the industrial sector on a large scale, and their employment became more permanent than seasonal. In addition to the apparel industry, the employment of women expanded into sales and retail businesses (supermarkets, department stores, and shopping malls), including real estate sectors (construction and related occupations), during the export-oriented phase.

In 1981 there were 38,476 manufacturing establishments throughout the country, 17,319 of them in Bangkok. By 1991 there were 57,033 manufacturing establishments with 20,248 in Bangkok.[37] In 1999, Bangkok registered more than 1,645,000 establishments—26,000 located in the five surrounding provinces—and employed a combined workforce of over 5 million workers. Most establishments were small firms employing no more than nine persons.[38] These small-scale factories made up about 60 percent of the total number of manufacturing establishments in Thailand; medium-size factories made up 30 percent, and large factories only 10 percent. Of a total of more than 8 million establishments throughout the country, however, large-scale firms employing 1,000 or more workers hired the most women.[39]

The free-market phase of the late 1980s and early 1990s was characterized by a high degree of liberalization, deregulation, and privatization, and a decline in state intervention. While the agricultural sector had dropped to about a 17 percent share of Thailand's GDP by 1989, the manufacturing sector increased to 35 percent and the service sector to 48 percent.[40] Foreign corporations were seen as a source of capital that could replace state investments and provide technical skills and training for workers. Meanwhile, domestic capital, especially banks, profited greatly from larger businesses and joint ventures. More important, the local capital market developed new ways to mobilize new sources of investment capital, and it was this period that saw the growth of finance and securities companies.[41] Foreign direct investment, mainly from within the region, started to flow into Thailand in massive quantities after 1985 and accelerated dramatically with heavy capital investment from Japan.[42] From 1985, finance firms were able to offer high interest rates to mobilize savings, which they then lent to the expanding manufacturing sector. Initially, much of the incoming portfolio investment came from Hong Kong and Taiwan and later from the United States and Europe.[43] Major international stock brokerage firms and merchant banks established offices in Thailand between 1989 and 1992. In 1991 the government made the local currency, the baht, freely convertible to allow for easier capital inflow. This led to a heavy inflow of foreign portfolio investments and loan funds into the Thai market in 1992–93.[44]

In the 1990s, Thailand became one of the most popular destinations for foreign investment in Southeast Asia, attracting over US$50 billion. Much of this "hot" capital went into the stock market, real estate, credit cards, auto loans, and currency speculation. Lured by the prospect of quick and easy profit, owners of large manufacturing establishments themselves became major investors in the stock market and in real estate, thus investing their earnings from profitable export businesses.

Thailand's "bubble" economy eventually burst in July 1997, resulting in massive layoffs of workers from many export manufacturing establishments and the downsizing or closing of many firms. External debt had accumulated to $94 billion baht by 1999. The social impact of the crisis was severe as working women and men, already struggling to survive on their paltry wages, now had to face rising inflation and an increasingly unstable job market. The impact was heaviest on the working poor, and by the end of 1998, thousands of men and women were returning to their home provinces, having lost their jobs in factories and on construction sites.[45] Unemployment at the end of 1997 reached 1.4 million and rose to over 2 million in mid-1998. In August 1997, Thailand received a US$16.7 billion bailout package from the International Monetary Fund (IMF). The situation contrasted markedly with that which had prevailed during the 1970s, when the state provided a certain degree of protection from the instability and volatility of the free market. Toward the end of my fieldwork, the repercussions of the economic crisis had set in along with stagnation, recession, and inflation.

Much of the literature on Thailand's economic development reflects a neoliberal approach to the Thai experience, which considers industrialization, accompanied by foreign trade and investment, as a mechanism to raise the country's living standards and reduce income inequalities over time.[46] Many articles discuss in great detail the industrialization policies responsible for Thailand's rapid growth and the various internal and external factors behind the country's miraculous economic success.[47] But what they often overlook is the significance of female labor to this "economic miracle" and the consequences to women workers within this context of dramatic economic change.

As Richard Doner and Ansil Ramsey indicate, Thailand's garment industry did not begin to develop until the late 1960s. Domestically and internationally, ready-made garments became increasingly popular in the early 1970s as rising per capita income helped to create demand. When the garment industry first developed, it was divided into two parts: one aimed at the domestic market and the other at the international market.[48] In 1967, the National Economic and Social Board of Development questioned the future of import protection, and in 1969 the Bank of Thailand set forth its case for export promotion.[49] This occurred within the context of World Bank involvement and the Western model of export-oriented growth. Nonetheless, the government continued to sustain the growth of import substitution, arguing that Thailand should still protect its primary industries. Local merchants and entrepreneurs who were protected under Import Substitution Industrialization (ISI) from international competition were thereby opposed to the transition.

Although initially, most apparel production was for the domestic market, from 1970 on, there had been a considerable increase in export production for the global market. Consequently, the value of exports rose from US$1.3 million in 1975 to nearly US$2.6 million in 1990.[50] In 1989, more garments were exported than were sold domestically, according to Doner and Ramsey. By 1994, there were approximately 18,000 textile manufacturers in Thailand but rough estimates from the late 1980s suggest that only 1,000 to 1,400 companies produced for export and of these, about 50 companies accounted for 60–70 percent of total exports (including the factories on which this book focuses).

Doner and Ramsay contend that the textile industry's rapid growth depended on ties between the state and society, or what they term state-societal linkages. They point out that the relative autonomy of central economic agencies, such as the Bank of Thailand and the Ministry of Finance, played a central role in Thai economic growth because it enabled the state to pursue macroeconomic policies. In this regard, Thai businesses operated in a setting of economic stability that was lacking in many developing countries. Moreover, "the relatively fragmented nature of the Thai state has allowed many competing firms to emerge in the garment industry and in other sectors of business."[51] Overall, state-society relations, the changing world market, and exchange rates facilitated the rapid growth of the Thai textile industry.

In the late 1970s, the government tried to extend the import substitution policy into capital and intermediate goods, but Thailand had already begun to face a major decline in global demand for primary produce. Moreover, stagnation of agricultural export revenues led to declining demand in the domestic market.[52] This slowdown in growth prompted bankers and businessmen to press for immediate economic restructuring, arguing that the current strategy had saturated the domestic market and that Thai business had become mature enough to compete in the world market. During this time, the textile industry was Thailand's largest manufacturing industry, with a very high export potential, which prompted its leaders to pressure the government to improve export production.[53]

Through the 1970s, U.S. and European Union (EU) restrictions on garment imports from Hong Kong, South Korea, and Taiwan gave Thailand's garment producers an opportunity to expand their exports to these markets. Further growth for the Thai garment industry came with a major devaluation of the baht in 1984.[54] Currency shifts made Thai garments more competitive in the world market, and consequently, there was big jump in garment exports in 1986 and 1987. Nevertheless, despite increased foreign investment, the garment industry remained largely in the hands of local Thai-Chinese businessmen who were among the most powerful and influential figures in the Bangkok business community, as they were the ones who had expressed initial interest in exporting garments overseas.[55] The World Bank also insisted on a change of strategy in return for loans to relieve the country's growing foreign debt.

The realignment of the economy in the mid-1980s therefore had dramatic results, and by 1988, Thailand had become the region's highest performer in economic growth. In 1989, it attained the status of NIC (newly industrializing country) and became known as "Asia's Fifth Tiger" (after South Korea, Taiwan, Singapore, and Hong Kong). Real GDP growth reached 13.2 percent in 1988, and total exports quadrupled in value between 1985 and 1991.Thailand enjoyed one of the most rapid economic growth rates in the world during the 1980s and 1990s and ranked among the world's top fifteen garment-exporting countries in 1990.[56] Between 1986 and 1990 the textile industry became Thailand's largest export earner. The mid-1980s to mid-1990s were the years that some of the women I interviewed recalled with nostalgia as "the golden days"—times when work orders were high, enabling many women to earn overtime wages.

According to the Thai Garment Manufacturers Association (TGMA), as of 2005 about 800,000 people were working in the local textile and garment industry in around 4,000 medium and large factories, of which only 2,300 are registered with the government. Seventy percent of these 2,300 are small manufacturing establishments (SMEs). And in spite of the effects of the 1997 financial crisis on the Thai textile industry, Thailand is the world's thirteenth biggest clothing exporter today, and garment exports are continuing to expand.[57]

Overall, Thai capitalist development has gone through roughly five phases: first, a pre–import-substitution phase (1950s–1960s) characterized by the central role of a traditional agricultural sector and a rural-based peasantry; second, an import-substitution phase (1960s–1970s) characterized by heavy state involvement in industrialization, the gradual shift from agriculture to industry, and the subsequent transformation of peasants into commercial farmers and wage laborers; third, an export-oriented industrialization (EOI) phase (1970s–1980s) characterized by the penetration and expansion of multinational corporations and their manufacturing bases, a rapid increase in foreign trade, high export growth, and the considerable absorption of women into the workforce; fourth, a "free market" phase (1980s–1990s) characterized by the massive influx of Japanese capital and "hot" capital in the form of portfolio investments, speculative capital (currency attacks), and the deregulation and liberalization of global capital and finance; and fifth, a bubble economy (late 1990s and into the new millennium) resulting in an economic crisis and recession accompanied by a decline in state protection, as well as by financial bailouts, structural adjustment policies, and massive layoffs of workers.

My analysis of female textile factory workers and worker consciousness is situated within the latter three phases of Thai economic development. The EOI phase captures the initial entry of young, inexperienced rural female migrants into labor-intensive factories and illuminates a "golden" period in the lives of women who settled into their factory jobs and benefited financially from the surge in textile production. The free-market phase saw the textile industry at its height but was also a period of much labor unrest. Organized labor took to the streets and staged sit-in demonstrations against what they viewed to be "ruthless" factory owners who were gambling their profits in the property market. And last, the post-crisis period signaled a difficult time for women, as their factories shut down production, restructured their work processes, cut back on working hours and pay, and laid off workers en masse. All these factors further debilitated possibilities for worker mobilization, though they triggered other forms of struggle and resistance.

From the mid-1970s until the mid-1990s, the Thai textile industry enjoyed much growth and expansion, thanks to a marked increase in global demand for ready-made apparel, especially from the West. During this period of economic prosperity, two extreme poles of worker consciousness could be observed. At one factory, women were enthusiastically working to earn the extra wages from overtime hours, providing the factory with a highly efficient and productive workforce. At another, the employer also relied upon highly skilled and experienced laborers but refused to compensate workers adequately for their efforts and used illegal means to maintain productivity. Consequently, a handful of workers, increasingly frustrated with management, took action and successfully won their very first victory against the factory. Given the rapid proliferation of manufacturing establishments throughout the country during this time, skilled workers were in short supply; this situation imbued in some workers a sense of agency and led to antagonistic relations between labor and management, especially in the outlying urban industrial zones. Occurrences and nonoccurrences of union activity can therefore be examined within the context of industrial production at the local firm level and within a broader picture of socioeconomic change. According to Doner and Ramsey, the availability of a large, poorly organized and a politically weak workforce, owed primarily to tight state control, was a major contributor to the expansion of the Thai apparel industry. Although the textile industry has the highest density of labor unions in the country's private sector, only about 2.5 percent of textile firms in 1990 were unionized.[58] Nevertheless, organized labor in Bangkok and the surrounding industrial provinces gained prominence along with the rapid growth of the apparel industry.

Walden Bello specifies that 1973–76 saw the height of organized labor in Thailand: "Key strikes during this period included a five-day strike by 50,000 textile workers, most of them women, at Sanam Luang, in October 1973, and a massive street protest of over 80,000 workers at the Rama V Monument outside the Government House.... Over a thousand strikes were registered in Thailand in that period, and by late 1976, some

TABLE 1. Composition of sample

Factory	Union status and no. of workers	Location and services	Type of women	Informants	N
F1	non-unionized (800), low turnover	Bangkok, no dormitory	nonmilitant	34 women employees, 3 male employees, 3 supervisors (2 female, 1 male), 1 manager (male)	36 women 5 men
F2	unionized (800), low turnover	Rangsit (industrial zone, outskirt of Bangkok), no dormitory, vans for transportation	militant, leaders of workers' union	6 women (5 dismissed), 1 woman employee	7 women
F3	non-unionized (1,800), low turnover	Samut Sakorn (industrial zone, outskirt of Bangkok), dormitory	nonmilitant	18 women employees, 1 manager (male)	18 women 1 man
F4	unionized, affiliated with F2 (1,300), low turnover	Rangsit (industrial zone, outskirt of Bangkok), dormitory	nonmilitant	4 women employees, 1 manager (male)	4 women 1 man
PF	unionized (5,000; parent factory of F2 and F4), low turnover	Rangsit (industrial zone, outskirt of Bangkok), no dormitory	nonmilitant	2 laidoff women workers	2 women
Other	2 small-scale factories (non-unionized); 1 ceramics factory (unionized); 1 food processing factory (unionized)	Omnoi-Omyai industrial zone of Samut Prakarn and Nakorn Prathom provinces, Prapadaeng industrial zone in Suksawat Rathburana district, and Bang Na Traad industrial zone of the Central Region	militant	1 former textile worker now factory owner, 3 women employees	4 women
SF1	non-unionized (400)	Korat province, no dormitory	militant	1 woman employee	1 woman
SF2	non-unionized (600)	Ubon Ratchathani province, no dormitory		none	
Non-factory				3 labor academics/ researchers	1 woman 2 men

185 unions had been formed."[59] Bello believes that the Thai labor union movement will never again reach the prominence that it achieved then. When the military returned to power in October 1976, organized labor was forced underground by the disappearance of several union leaders. Nor did organizing efforts become any easier during Thailand's "boom" years; rather, they brought continued suppression of independent unions and the fragmentation and dispersal of workers throughout the manufacturing sector.[60] Nonetheless, many militant workers' unions, such as the one I discuss, reemerged in the early to mid-1990s. The early to mid-1990s were the years that saw the rise of militant labor activism led primarily by women workers in the export processing zones on the outskirts of Bangkok.[61]

Successful union drives and labor campaigns have often been illuminated by well-publicized demonstrations occurring at certain factories that manufacture brand names or at factories where unions receive strong external support. Citing a report on cross-border organizing in the apparel industry in Guatemala, for example, Dan Clawson indicates that by 1993 only 6 out of 300 *maquila* factories had managed to form a union and only one had managed to negotiate a contract.[62] These figures are likely to be representative of the ratio of unionized to non-unionized factories in free-trade zones, suggesting that labor militancy is the exception rather than the norm, since unionizing is often prohibited in free-trade zones, and workers are fearful of losing their jobs. Workers employed in low-paying, labor-intensive industries typically have low educational levels, little work experience, and few skills, making them vulnerable in a job market where companies can easily hire and fire workers or move elsewhere.

Adaptation and Accommodation

The "Nonmilitant" Women

The factory represents the predominant physical space where women build close personal relationships and an attachment to the stability that work offers. This chapter tells the story of a group of women workers who have never been involved in any form of direct action against their employer. These are women who have been working for ten, twenty, and in some cases thirty or more consecutive years in the same factory, performing the same task often seven days a week, fourteen hours a day, 353 days a year. Why were these women, young and old, working for such extended periods of time in an industry recognized for its high turnover of labor?

Thailand enjoyed one of the most rapid economic growth rates in the world during the 1980s and 1990s and ranked among the world's top fifteen garment-exporting countries in 1990. Between 1986 and 1990 the textile industry became Thailand's largest export earner. This was a period that the women referred to as "the golden days": with work orders high, many were able to earn higher wages. My analysis of worker consciousness among the nonmilitant factory women, based upon their own retrospective accounts of work and living, is situated within this export-led industrialization phase of Thai economic development.[1] Their personal stories also highlight the limitations of social life among working-class women. This is not to say that the women themselves perceived their lives as having poor quality or to suggest that they did not have social lives but to underline the time constraints imposed upon women as a direct consequence of their employment.

In-depth interviews with thirty-four factory women at a non-unionized textile factory in Bangkok, F1 (Factory One), along with additional interviews with several women from F3 and F4, help to unravel the many factors that contribute to a long-standing and compliant workforce.[2] What emerges is a distinct social consciousness embedded in a group of women who had been working together over a long period of time and whose nonconfrontational attitudes are shaped by their particular work experiences at the factory. As such, worker consciousness did not culminate in collective action against the employer, even though the workers were aware of their exploitive situations. Instead, relatively harmonious work relations fostered a committed and nondisruptive workforce. At F1, women who were voluntarily adjusting and accommodating to a system that was their only means of survival were driven by family obligations (such as caring for their children or supporting their parents, younger siblings, or other family members) and thus needed to maintain the stability that factory work offered them. At the same time, their experiences of work delineate the highly adaptable mechanisms of control and subordination over labor within the factory. Their accounts help to identify the reasons why women at this factory did not engage in any form of collective protest at a time when the Thai textile industry was booming and urban labor unrest was widespread.

My findings suggest that powerlessness, passivity and accommodation can be assessed, in part, by women's responses to factory work as they are shaped by the structure of wages, working conditions, working hours, the production process, and the behavior of the *nai jarng* (factory boss) and the *hua na* (supervisors) toward them.[3] The case of F1 reveals how certain controlling mechanisms over labor manage to shut out active resistance among women who have come to fully accommodate themselves to the pace and nature of work and their work environment.

The Women at Factory One

In-depth interviews that I conducted with the thirty-four women during September to December 1998 and September to December 1999 showed that—contrary to the stereotype of the young, single, female assembly worker—the women in my sample had an unusually high median age of 31.2 years; they had been employed for a mean average of fifteen years; and more than half of them were married. Of the thirty-four women, only eleven had been working for less than ten years, and seven for ten to fifteen years; the remaining sixteen had had sixteen to thirty-two years of consecutive employment at the factory.

The majority of these women came from large farming families in rural provinces of the Central, Northeastern, and Northern Regions, and most had had some experience with agricultural tasks such as farming, gardening, harvesting, or raising livestock. Most of the women started off-farm work at eighteen, the age at which Thai citizens are officially issued their *batr pra cha chon* (citizenship identification cards) and can legally apply for employment.[4] For most, this factory job was their very first paid occupation. They cited economic necessity caused by the drastic decline of subsistence agriculture as the main reason for leaving their homes.[5] Because crops can be harvested and sold for only a few months out of the year, many farmers have found it very difficult to support their families, given the seasonal nature of farming, the high costs of fertilizer and insecticides, and the lack of income during the off-season. Furthermore, small farmers have been increasingly squeezed out by larger, commercial farmers who have the capital to invest in technology and machinery. Women's out-migration, then, was primarily motivated by rural impoverishment during farming's off-season and by low yielding crops.

In her study of young rural Thai migrants, Mary Beth Mills describes women's experiences as mediated by their aspirations to attain material progress and their sense of responsibility to their families. My findings indicate that the migration of these young women into the city was primarily motivated by their economic need and their longing for the sense of personal freedom that they anticipated would derive from financial independence. Another common reason women gave for leaving home was boredom: "We had nothing else to do during the off-season and we felt bored and unproductive." Daughters under eighteen often leave school after the fourth grade to help their parents on the farm, and when girls enter their teens, many decide to migrate into Bangkok.[6] Typically, an older sibling, a relative, or a friend already working in the city informs a younger woman about job openings and encourages her to apply. Realizing the benefits of wage employment, women's parents typically have little objection to their daughters' decision to leave as long as they know of a friend or relative living in the city.

Although a desire to be "free from parental authority" was not mentioned by my interviewees as a motivating factor, many women did stress the need for some personal autonomy, which they believed they could attain only by becoming economically self-sufficient. The harsh reality of low factory wages, however, immediately diminished their high expectations.

F1: Objective Realities

Factory One (F1) was founded in 1957 by a Thai-Chinese businessman whose son oversees and manages all operations. The factory became a leading local manufacturer of men's undergarments and later expanded its business by specializing in infants' and children's clothing for export mainly to Europe. F1 is a non-unionized factory employing about eight hundred workers, all women except for ten males who worked in the shipping and packing departments and as maintenance technicians. My interviews took place at the factory's original location, which occupies about four and a half acres of land in Bangkok.

The Production Process

The very first stage in the production process involves the processing of raw cotton fiber, which is spun into reels by large machines supervised by two or three men. Another machine weaves the reels of spun raw fiber into huge spools of cotton fabric and into large sheets of cotton, which are then sent out to be dyed. Brought back to the factory, the dyed cloth undergoes an inspection process with a steam folding machine that is monitored by two or more women who look for marks or flaws. Cloth to be printed is sent to a subcontractor and then returned to the factory. The rest of the production process involves five departments that make up the core of the factory: Cutting and Sewing; Overlocking and Buttoning; Ironing and Folding; Retouching and Inspecting; and Packing and Shipping.

In my interviews, I discovered that the women perceived the "Cutting and Sewing" and "Ironing and Folding" to be the most physically demanding. Curiously, older women who had been with the factory for twenty years or more belonged to these departments, suggesting perhaps that older women were not as frail as one might expect—indeed, were physically stronger and more tolerant than women half their age. Their presence could also be attributed to the very fact that few women from these departments had retired, eliminating the need for the factory to hire new workers. Samlarn, a former worker and sewing department supervisor at age fifty-four, was proud to say that she had not taken a day off in the previous three years; she boasted, "The young women in my department are constantly amazed that I can work so much at my age!" In "Ironing and Folding," women are not only required to stand while lifting a heavy metal iron to flatten and fold the clothes but must also be able to tolerate the oppressive heat and steam coming from the iron with only one ceiling fan to provide ventilation. Puan believed that the women in this department held the longest record for years of employment, noting that "young girls are not as patient." Noy, a twenty-year-old from the packing department, expressed her amazement of older peers: "My job is to put labels onto the clothing and it's a pretty easy task even though it requires a lot of concentration, but it's not like I'm working in the ironing department where you have to stand all day long lifting that heavy iron. And to know that the people there have been working for twenty, thirty years!" None of the women hesitated to point out that the ironing section had been unsuccessful in retaining young newcomers. The incredible persistence of the older women is worth noting, as I found women in their forties working seven days a week, including all the overtime hours, and taking the fewest days off in a year.

Remarkably enough, most women did not report any major health problems, even though they were aware of such hazards in the working environment as the dust in their lungs and the damage to their eyes and ears. The recently issued health and safety protection law required workers to wear protective face masks covering the nose and mouth at all times, but many of the women found the face guards uncomfortable and refused to put them on except when instructed to do so, such as during safety and health inspection visits. Thus, the women knowingly risked compromising their health just to get through the work day "feeling comfortable." They told me that they would rather not know if their health was in danger but would go on working until "their bodies gave out." Khae recalled the first time the factory gave out the protective cloths: "When we first got them, nobody bothered to put one on because we were never used to wearing anything over our faces. But they forced us to put them on because the factory was up for inspection, and when the inspectors left, we took off the masks and we were shocked to discover how much dust we had been breathing all this time! We were all thinking how much dust must already be in our lungs. I've refused to get a medical checkup because I'd rather not know. I'm just going to continue working until I drop."

Khae estimated that only about half the women at the factory wore protective masks on a regular basis. Yet few women reported having experienced major health problems, which, according to the women, meant an operation or surgery. A handful of women, however, did suffer from chronic health problems. Only three had had operations: Nisa for a bladder problem, Malee for a stomach tumor, and Ouan for a mastectomy. Malee still suffers from chronic stomach pain, and Khae's sister, who was also employed at the factory, had to quit because of serious menstrual cramping. Other women whom I would categorize as having serious problems included Lek, who suffered from stomach flu; Maam, who experienced chronic migraines; and Laek, who was treated for an irregular menstrual cycle. Interestingly, none of these women explicitly attributed their health problems to their work conditions except for Noy, who had been treated for pneumonia and blamed dust particles for making her cough up blood. All of the women, though, had suffered from occasional headaches, colds, fevers, stomach pains, and such work-related health problems as allergies, strained hand and leg muscles, varicose veins, and weakened eyesight.

Working Hours and Wages

Working hours set by the factory were Monday through Saturday from 8:00 a.m. to 5:00 p.m., overtime (OT) hours on any day of the week from 5 p.m. to 8 p.m. (and sometimes up to midnight, depending upon the volume of work available) and on Sunday from 8 a.m. to 4:30 p.m.[7] According to the factory owner, working hours should not exceed 56 hours per week, although under the labor protection act, working hours are not to exceed 8 hours per day and 48 hours per week. Thai labor law also stipulates that an employer must allow an employee one day off per week, but there is no clause prohibiting overtime hours on Sunday. In reality, the women at F1 work an average 80–96 hours per week, seven days a week.

One explanation for employers' ability to circumvent labor regulations is weak enforcement and implementation of labor laws in general. Another reason has to do with the small fines that are imposed on employers who violate or fail to comply with legal stipulations: under the Labour Protection Act of 1998, fines are not to exceed 5,000 baht (US$125). And even though there may be criminal penalties as well, an employer must be convicted in order to receive punishment. If convicted, an employer may receive a term of imprisonment of up to one year and/or be fined an amount not to exceed 200,000 baht (US$5,000). Grievances against the employer are rarely brought to court, however, because employees are often unaware of the illegality of these practices. Furthermore, within the Bangkok metropolitan area, cases are immediately dropped so long as the offender pays the imposed fine within thirty days.

At F1, workers were paid a daily minimum wage of 157 baht per day on a biweekly basis.[8] This rate rose with length of employment, however: the longer an employee worked at the factory, the higher her daily wage, which meant that F1 workers were essentially rewarded for their perseverance.[9] Because the majority of the women I interviewed had worked there for over ten years, their wages stood at around 167–175 baht (US$4.51–US$4.72

in 1998) per day. Overtime pay was 30 baht ($0.82) extra for each hour.[10] There were no yearly or other bonuses given to workers; overtime work and pay was considered the only *bonus* opportunity for workers to earn extra money. Workers themselves claimed that they could sometimes earn more income than workers elsewhere who did receive annual bonus pay.

Permission for leave of absence at F1 had to be obtained directly from the factory owner, whom many found to be "fair and reasonable." But very few women took leaves of absence except in the case of an emergency or a death in the family.[11] Because there was little job mobility within the factory, a woman remained in the same department, performing the same task, regardless of her length of employment; this may explain why many older women remained in the more physically demanding departments. Newly hired women received some form of training from the floor supervisor or from experienced co-workers and were given a two-month probation period. Training usually took place right away but lasted for only a few days, since the tasks were relatively low-skilled and fairly easy to learn.

For many of the older women, F1 had been their first place of employment upon arrival in the city. Others, however, had left a previous place of employment out of practical necessity. For Maam and Saiyon, the factories for which they had been working were located too far from where they were living. Waew had worked in a food-processing plant that shut down her production unit, and Moey in a factory that exported golf gloves until it went out of business. Still, other women who had prior working experience had been employed in smaller-scale factories or in lower-pay occupations: Laeyd at a small-scale textile factory for ten years before she came to F1; Win as a janitor in a department store; Maam in a shoe factory; Saiyon in a sweatshop that made T-shirts, Anne in a company that printed name cards; Thong as a security guard; and Ouan as a domestic servant. Ouan felt she was "better off" as a factory worker because she didn't have to "be on call 24/7."

Interestingly, Khae, who had had no previous work experience, was the only woman who openly compared the working conditions and the wages at F1 with those of other factories she knew of and eagerly pointed out that "women at F1 are better off. We don't need permission to use the restroom, and our wages are always paid on time," she said, "and there has never been a late payment. We are even given advance pay on Friday if a payday falls on a Saturday!" Khae's observations not only point to her general awareness of conditions elsewhere but indicate the rather unusual behavior of management toward workers at F1. This was something that the workers themselves openly and frequently acknowledged.

Overall, the women said that their factory imposed few restrictions and regulations, especially with regard to bathroom use, talking during work, and getting a drink of water. But more important, the women felt that the factory provided them with more work and high overtime pay, even though none of them explicitly compared their experiences at F1 to those at their previous places of employment. For the women it seems, then, that work was just work and the factory was simply another place of employment. Though they were happy about the stability and security it provided, the fact that many of them had had long working histories at previous jobs, probably in poorer work conditions and at lower pay, suggests that migrant women often try to accommodate to any working situation as long as they can generate an income.

Aside from dust and noise pollution on some production floors, such as in the "Cutting and Sewing" and "Overlocking and Buttoning" departments, the factory itself was clean and provided convenient facilities for its workers. Work areas were well lit, and ceiling fans provided ventilation in addition to standard ventilation systems on each work floor. There were restrooms on every floor, tanks of purified drinking water, a large canteen dining area with new ceiling fans, a shower and wash area behind the canteen, and individual lockers for each worker.

Because there were no dormitory facilities or transportation services for the workers, most employees lived within walking distance to the factory. Those who lived a distance away spent anywhere from one to three hours to commute to work by public transportation. Workers were allowed a one-hour lunch break from noon to 1:00 p.m.; those staying on for overtime had a half-hour dinner break from 5:00 to 5:30 p.m. and on Sundays, a half-hour lunch break at noon.

Workers received medical treatment and compensation under a government-mandated Social Security system that automatically deducted 30 baht per month of a worker's salary into a compensation fund that could be used by the worker for any type of medical illness (though not for complete physical checkups). The factory had a contract with a public hospital whose services and facilities were considered by workers to be substandard, however, so many women opted to pay out of their own pockets for better medical care at a private clinic.

Income Remittance

Much of what women earned was often remitted to their parents back home, to support younger siblings or their own children, most of whom were cared for by grandparents or other relatives. Women kept enough money for themselves to pay for rent and utilities, transportation, food, and other living expenses. The wages of women with young children were almost entirely devoted to supporting their children. Unmarried daughters were expected to care for their aging parents. Because Noy had to support her young son, her sister would send money to their widowed father, who lived with grandchildren and other relatives in the province of Tangsalakram. Nisa, who came from a large family of eleven children, had worked at F1 for thirty-two years. Forty-six years old and still single, Nisa lived with her father and remitted all of her income to her parents. Puan continued to send money to her mother, who lived alone.

Thai women are expected to financially support their younger sisters and brothers. It is common in Thai culture, as it is in many Asian and Latin American countries, for the oldest female child to make sacrifices for her younger siblings (though we should bear in mind that self-sacrifice is seen by Thais as "making merit").[12] Unmarried daughters in my study were working to put their younger siblings though school. Manee, who has no children, financially helped her younger sister, a full-time student.

Other women, many young and single, preferred to spend their earnings on themselves but sent money home whenever necessary. Dee, a fair-skinned Thai Chinese woman from a large farming family of ten children, came to Bangkok with her aunt when she was eighteen. Twenty-eight years old and single, she had been working at F1 for five years but said that she did not remit income to her parents because she liked to spend money on herself. This flexibility is a reflection of the fairly open and liberal attitude of parents who are not in urgent need of financial assistance and who leave income remittance to the discretion of their children. Similarly, Sunee admitted: "I spend most of my money on food because I eat out a lot, and on personal stuff. I earn just enough to get by in Bangkok." Like Sunee and Dee, Porn stated that she made enough to get by and that she lived "somewhat comfortably because my parents seldom ask me for money." Overall, women who did not remit their incomes either came from well-to-do farming families or had families of their own to support and were saving up for future investments in a house, a motorbike, or a small business.

I discovered some remarkable things about older factory women. Despite having families, older women devoted themselves more to their jobs than younger, single, childless women and worked more hours during the week. In addition, they were less likely to take sick leave or leaves of absence, and they remained employed for longer periods of time and had the lowest job turnover. These characterizations contradict the common rationale on the part of managers elsewhere who believe that "single, childless women can more easily devote themselves to their jobs than can partnered women and mothers." The majority at F1 were young and single when they were hired initially, but some who later married and had children continued to work at the factory for twenty to thirty consecutive years. In her discussion of Mexican recruitment practices, Tiano found that *maquila* managers had begun to change their preferences in favor of recruiting older women with children, because children were considered "an asset to women's successful job performance": their child-care responsibilities supposedly made women "more reliable in all aspects of their lives." Employers wanted a stable and productive workforce and felt that workers who were mothers were also mature women who were less likely than younger women to miss work or quit their jobs. Tiano reported that managers believed that "marriage often leads a woman to 'settle down' to her work because she need no longer be concerned about finding a husband."[13] At F1, the owner may have started out by hiring many young, unmarried women but ended up with an experienced and loyal group of workers, many of whom had later married and had families.

Emotional and Physical Sacrifices

One theme that pervades the literature on women and work stresses the high emotional and physical sacrifices women make in their integration into the paid workforce. Likewise, the women I studied had been forced to give up their provincial lives, sever ties to their children and families, compromise their own health and physical well-being, and sometimes give up on their hopes of having a better life beyond the factory. Of the thirty-four women interviewed at F1, twenty-three were married (one separated and one widowed), sixteen of whom were mothers. Only two of the sixteen had young children living with them in Bangkok, to be left in the care of neighbors or relatives when their mothers went to work; the other fourteen had left their young children behind with their parents or in-laws back in their home provinces.

In Thailand it is common for working parents to leave their children in the care of grandparents, other family members, or hired care workers during the day. But for many working-class women, leaving one's children behind is a matter of practical and economic necessity. Consequently, married women with children are the ones who make the largest emotional sacrifice for factory employment, because many endure a total physical separation from their young children.[14] In her study of Filipina domestic migrant workers, Rhacel Parreñas discusses the emotional difficulties of mothers whose children are cared for by extended kin. She describes the women as being "trapped in the painful contradiction of feeling 'the gap caused by physical separation' and having to give in to the family's dependence on the material rewards granted by this separation."[15]

Employers directly benefit from the strong kinship ties of rural migrant women who have no choice but to fall back on the support of immediate family members in the absence of social welfare services in the city. The likelihood that a working mother will be physically separated from her children has not only caused disintegration of the nuclear family unit while adding the burden of child rearing to extended kin members (such as a woman's parents and siblings) but also drastically reduced family size: given the heavier financial responsibility that comes with raising a family, married women have often had to limit the number of children they had. Many women who grew up in large households of seven or more siblings could not afford to raise more than one or two children of their own. For women of rural backgrounds, the decision to have fewer children is a contrast to past practices where children were seen as potential agricultural laborers.

Working mothers were able to see their children only a few days out of the year because transportation is costly, and they are given very little time off.[16] Women stayed in touch with their children by mail, exchanging letters as soon as their children were old enough to read and write. Communicating by phone was not only expensive but "incredibly inconvenient," given the lack of telephone facilities in many of the rural provinces.[17]

Da, who had been working at F1 for over twenty years, spoke of the estrangement from her own daughter, who was raised by her grandmother: "I had to send my daughter home when she was still a baby. My mother took care of her while I stayed here to work and send money home. My daughter has grown so close to her, she's *tid khun yai* [attached to her grandmother], and she treats me like a stranger when I visit and she sees me again for the first time in a long time. She's just shy at first, and then she gets used to me, but still, it can be heartbreaking. I've become used to it though."

Sumalee, a thirty-five-year-old woman who had worked at F1 for eighteen years, had a five-year-old girl being cared for by her parents back in their home province and got to see her daughter only three or four times a year. She and her husband rent a small place in the city, and both work to send money home.

As soon as Noy's son was born, she sent him off to live with her mother-in-law. She is able to visit him only once or twice a year and complains about not being able to see her son as often as she would like to. Taa and Songh's two young girls are cared for by Songh's mother in Udon Thani province; they speak to their girls once in a while by phone. Thim's two children live with her family back in Ayutthya; Mai's daughter is cared for by the grandparents; Win's newborn is in the care of her mother. Nid has a one-year-old boy who is being raised by her father and mother-in-law. She visits him once every three or four months because she cannot afford to travel to Korat any oftener. One woman (at F3) broke down and cried as she spoke of her five-year-old son, whom she gets to see only a few times a year.

Although the women enjoyed talking about their children and were always eager to show me family photos, doing so was a painful reminder of how long it would be before they could visit them again. "If I had a child, I would like to take care of him or her myself," said Manee. None of the factories I visited provided any kind of day-care facility for its employees; there were no affordable facilities in Bangkok; and few women had close relatives living in the city. Therefore, those who chose to be with their children had to rely on extended kinship networks or their neighbors during working hours. The women mentioned that private day-care centers in Bangkok were too costly, and only one woman had once paid for child-care services.

It is not uncommon, however, for children to be reunited with their parents as soon as they are old enough to take care of themselves, typically when they reach the age of twelve. Some parents may have saved enough money by that time to build a house of their own (as in the case of Patcharin and Damrong) and send their children to *rohng reyn ratr* (city public schools) or *rohng reyn wat* (temple schools). At F4, for example, Oy, a thirty-nine-year-old mother of two who had been working at the factory for eighteen years, initially sent her kids to their grandparents (her son to her mother and her daughter to her mother-in-law) until the children were old enough to move back in with her. She and her husband were living in proximity to the factory, and their children attended a public school nearby. Oy, who made 213 baht (US$8.52) a day, was still working to pay back the debt her family owed to the bank for money they had borrowed to build their house. Noy, who had a two-year-old son, wanted her son to start attending kindergarten, but public schools do not admit children before the first grade.

Parreñas brilliantly captures the experiences of Filipina migrant domestic workers who leave their own families behind in order to perform the work of mothering and caring for other families, and the emotional pain they endure as a consequence. Because of complete physical separation from their own families, working mothers placed their ability to provide materially for their children over their family's emotional needs: "Time with children is less important than giving money to children."[18] As rural migrants living in the city, however, Thai women factory workers were able to maintain regular and sustained contact with their children and made deliberate efforts to provide both material and emotional support for their families.

Mechanisms of Control and Subordination: Women's Lives in the Factory

Although management seeks, in Michael Burawoy's words, "not merely to coordinate...but also to control" labor, there is a process of coordination and control wielded by the workers themselves in ensuring that their work for the day has been successfully accomplished. According to Burawoy's definition of the *relations in production*, workers enter into relationships on the shop floor "both with one another and with management." In turn, these relations shape the form and development of the labor process.[19] The supervisors, the foremen, and the workers all relate in what Braverman calls the *social features* of the production process. These social features are introduced by the capitalist and dominate the labor process. But other factors that affected the work process and shape the distinct social consciousness of the women at F1. Workers' living arrangements, the daily rhythm of work, the overtime system, and the meaning women attached to work were important variables integral to production and relations in production.

Living Arrangements at Factory One

Because F1 offered no dormitory facilities for its workers, the majority of women lived in small rented rooms in "shop houses" scattered throughout Bangkok. The average room measures about 8 by 5 feet, and rent is mainly determined by room size. Tenants share a common bathroom facility. Since shop houses are not usually equipped with a kitchen area, cooking is done either outdoors or on a small portable stove in the room. Women sleep on mattresses, which they put up against the wall or in a corner when not in use in order to make space. Living with other co-workers in the same neighborhood or next door is not uncommon. Two single women or a married couple without children may share a room. Many women whose rooms are within walking distance to the factory live near one another, some in the same building, and commute to work together. Others sometimes spend the night at a friend's place on days when they leave late from work or live too far away.

It is common for married couples with children to live in the same neighborhood, either in rented rooms near the factory or in self-built houses in urban housing settlements. Some women find room in extended family households with their siblings or relatives. Another typical living arrangement is for a group of women to share a large room in an apartment building. Some older women choose to move into a place of their own and take out a monthly mortgage on a small house or flat. Lek, who had been employed for sixteen years, bought a small condo after she separated from her husband. She lived in the same complex as Boonyuun and several other women from the factory who traveled to and from work together every day by public transportation.

Rent per person ranges from 1,100 to 1,500 baht per month (US$26–36) or roughly one fourth of a woman's monthly earnings.[20] This rate varies according to the size and type of living arrangement.

Where a woman lives determines what time she needs to get up in the morning; those living near the factory can afford to get up later, around 6:30 or 7:00 a.m. Nuam, a single twenty-six-year-old, had been living for ten years in the same small room situated in a large *choom chon* (urban slum community). She shared the room with a friend. Kaek, a thirty-three-year-old who had been working at F1 for thirteen years, walked to work and found that living nearby allowed her to take her time in the morning. Kaek shared a room with her older sister, who also worked at the factory. Noy, twenty, would get up at 7:00 a.m. and walk to work from a small room she rented with her husband. Women who lived at some distance might need to be up by 5:00 a.m. to get to work on time, usually by public transportation. Ouan, who had been at F1 for twenty-three years (since the age of seventeen), got up at 5:00 a.m. and left the house by 5:45 a.m. in order to get to work on time, and she did not get home until 9:30 or 10 p.m.

Wake-up time could also depend upon a woman's marital status. Married women whose children lived with them needed to prepare breakfast and take their kids to school before coming to work, so a typical day consisted of getting up around 5:00 or 5:30 a.m., getting household chores done, and having a big meal before going to work. Dao, though she lives near the factory, got up at 5:00 a.m. to do laundry or housework and have breakfast with her mother, who cooked for the family. Moey, whose husband worked in an outlying province, lived so far from the city that she had to leave her house by 4:30 a.m. in order to get to work by 8:00 a.m. For her, commuting involved a one-hour train ride, a half-hour transfer by speedboat to the city's port, a one-hour bus ride in Bangkok, and finally, a short hop on a motorcycle taxi to get to the factory, where she had been employed for eighteen years. When asked why she had tolerated such a taxing journey for so many years, she simply responded, "I got used to it" and never bothered to look for a job that was closer to her home. This same rationale was commonly expressed by women whose commuting time involved two or more hours each way. I never thought to ask Moey *how* she was able to keep it up every day, but had I asked, I believe she would inquire what I meant by "how" and then simply tell me what her typical day was like and reiterate that she somehow "got used to it."

Living in Factory Dormitories

In her study of the lives of women and girls in the silk- and cotton-thread factories in Meiji Japan (1868–1912), Patricia Tsurumi looks at how the labor of young women and girls produced so much of the profit that built the "Meiji miracle" and Japan's modern military and industrial establishments.[21] She notes that low wages were maintained through long working hours and worker accommodations close to the factory.[22]

Factories that provide dormitories for their workers facilitate both a physical and an emotional connection between the worker and the factory. Women who choose to stay in dormitories find the accommodation to be "very convenient and comfortable," even with six to eight women to a room and one bathroom for each suite. The other main reason for staying in dorms is economic. In lieu of rent and utilities, some factories require women to perform additional tasks such as sweeping and cleaning the factory grounds, and women who live in the dormitories are paid only the minimum wage rate for overtime work on Sundays instead of the regular overtime rate.

At F3, women who chose to stay in the dormitories did so because it saved them money and was suitable for working various shifts. F3, a modern facility located in the Samut Sakorn industrial zone about one hour from Bangkok, manufactures processed fabrics for export and specializes in the dyeing and inspecting of cloth. In 1998 it had a total workforce of about 1,800, with ten production departments and almost 200 women working in each department. The factory provided dormitory facilities that could accommodate up to 300 workers. Regular working hours are Monday through Friday from 8:00 a.m. to 5:00 p.m., but in fact, there were three eight-hour shifts for a 24/7 operation.

My interviews with women who lived in dormitories took place in the lobby and canteen area of F3's dormitory building. I also interviewed a few women who lived in the dormitory at F4, which had a workforce of some 1,300 and provided on-site room and board to about a third of its workers.

Malee, a thirty-six-year-old woman, had been living in F4's dormitory ever since she started working there when she was eighteen. She shared a room with twelve other women and stated matter-of-factly, "I can't even sleep anywhere else but in my room here at the dorm." Malee is single and seldom goes out except to the nearby shopping mall with her friends: "I don't like going out because I'm not used to being outside." The only major change in her institutionalized life at the factory was moving from the old dorm building, where she shared a room with twenty other women, into a newly built one. For her, the safe and easy convenience of dormitory living in such a big city was very practical, reassuring, and such a large part of her daily life that she was unable to picture what it would be like to live out on her own, believing that she would find such an existence "very lonely." Like Malee, Sri, a thirty-three-year-old single woman, had been living in the factory dormitory since she started working there sixteen years ago. She chose to stay in the dorm because it saved her money and because she "never [got] lonely" in the company of roommates who were also co-workers. Mugh, twenty-four years old, particularly liked living in the dorms because of their feeling of *kwarm ob oohn* (warmth and comfort). Laong, forty-six, shared a dorm room with seven women and found it "enjoyable."

The rationalization and preference for dormitory living in F3 and F4 stand in contrast to the attitudes of women at F1, who had become used to living on their own and preferred the physical distance from the factory because it gave them a sense of freedom and autonomy from the workplace.

Kun, a twenty-five-year-old single woman from the knitting department, shared a room with five other single women. She had a small TV in her cubicle and could listen to music or watch television before going to bed at 8:00 p.m. Because the women worked in shifts, they slept in shifts: three women would go to bed at the same time and get up for the next shift and three women returning from their shift would take their place. Like some of the women at F1 who endured an arduous commute to and from the factory, women at F3 had to adjust their sleeping hours to shift work. Kun stated that they "got used to it very quickly," adding that it was the married women who moved out to live on their own. Yet, surprisingly, some married women continued to live in the dormitories. Paan, a twenty-eight-year-old mother of two, decided to leave her husband and children back home to find work in Bangkok and would visit her family every Sunday. For Paan, dormitory living saved her money and was just a place to sleep during the week because "I'm so exhausted by the time I'm done with my shift, that I just want to rest and not do anything."

Similarly, Nice, a thirty-eight-year-old mother of three who had been working at F3 for ten years, left her children in Suphan province with her parents. Nice took a leave of absence from the factory twice during her employment, to be with her kids, but came back in order to support them financially. She found it convenient to stay in the dorm because her home was too far away to commute to the city. Like Nice, Jita was fulfilling her dutiful role as a single mother. At forty, with a seventeen-year-old daughter, she had lived in the dormitory since she started working at F3 nineteen years earlier. Jita said that she planned to quit as soon as her daughter could support herself, but in the meantime she wanted to send her daughter to school, and staying in the dorm would enable her to do so. In the new dormitory building she shared a room with seven other women. Women like Jita often made sacrifices for their children, demonstrating that self-sacrifice is one of the major causes of sustaining arduous work in the factories.

The prevalence of older married women living in dormitories at F3 was startling. After all, these were women who had husbands and children, but they chose to live apart from their immediate families in order to maximize their factory earnings. In my interviews with them, they commonly uttered the phrase *tham ngarn pua luke* (I work for my kids) and were determined to put their children through school. These women embraced their roles as mothers and as caregivers to the point of keeping very little income for themselves. Dorm living helped them defray such costs as rent and utilities.

The convenient accommodation of dormitory living evidently acts as a very effective controlling mechanism over female labor at F3. While providing workers with a safe niche in the city, it draws women into an intimate physical bond with the factory such that they willingly surrender their lives to the factory system. What better way to control the movements and whereabouts of a workforce than to have the workers live, eat, and sleep as well as work within the employer's bounds? Thus, in a practical sense, management is able to wield control over a compliant and accommodating workforce.

At F3, I discovered that some of the younger women who live in the dormitories were taking continuing education classes on the weekends to finish *maw saam* (equivalent to the ninth grade). Kun, who finished *por hok* (the sixth grade), decided to continue her schooling because she felt that education was a long-term investment: "Women need more than a sixth-grade education if they want a better job, and if I can get a *maw saam* degree, my chances of getting a better paying job might be higher." The classes were affordable, and she attended with a few friends from work, though most of them later dropped out: "Some got lazy and left because they had a boyfriend, or they just quit. Only my friend and I finished the course." But after receiving her ninth-grade diploma, Kun no longer thought of leaving: "I would have to deal with making new friends again and adapting to a new job. I prefer to stay here." Kun's reasoning resonates with that of the older women at F1 who refused to leave the factory to look for other employment and thus represents another stark indication of the binding emotional ties to the factory that can hinder a woman's personal ambitions. Many young girls who took weekend classes decided to stay on after graduating primarily because they were unwilling to break away from the stability and support network the factory provided.

At F1, even though there were no such housing facilities, women still felt a deep attachment to the factory, many referring to it as "my second home," "a second family" for Moey, or "my only family" for Kuh. "I would get so depressed if I didn't come to work, because I would miss the factory. I would get so bored staying at home," said Kuh. In her eighteen years at F1, she was proud to state that she had never been absent from work. Moey and Kuh had become so attached to the factory that even on lunch breaks they would eat in the cafeteria instead of venturing out to the numerous food vendors in the *soi* (street). They found it "very comfortable" to be on the factory grounds and enjoyed taking a quick nap on their work benches before the lunch hour was over. Their relaxed attitudes toward factory work was characteristic of the general sentiment of women at F1, many of whom spoke of the dead-end, monotonous nature of their occupation yet at the same time attributed meaning and significance to the only place they had come to know well.

At F1, living in proximity to the factory had a similar binding effect to living in a factory dormitory, because it allowed women to settle into their work and living situations while finding a stable and comfortable niche in the city. Having established a safe and convenient residence close to the factory, and having built close personal connections with other workers, a woman was increasingly reluctant to leave and, consequently, more likely to move her place of residence than her place of work, since familiarity with her place of employment had become the center around which her life revolved. The married couples I interviewed believed that their employment at the same factory increased stability, a steady flow of income, and, in turn, a "happy marriage." In her study of factory workers in São Paulo during labor shortages in the early twentieth century, Theresa Veccia found that some employers provided basic, subsidized worker housing for employees and their families.[23] Indeed, housing and factory dormitories have become institutionalized in some larger factory operations today, especially as larger, more modern facilities relocate to remote industrial zones.

Routine Work and Daily Life at Factory One

Daily life at the factory was described as being "fast-paced when work is heavy" and "very slow when the workload is small." A woman's concept of time is indicative of the low wages she makes and the hand-to-mouth existence of factory life. As forty-one-year-old Malee put it: "These twenty-one years have gone by so fast because I haven't been able to save any money. I'm as poor now as when I came in." A typical response from women who had been employed there for over ten years was that "the day just goes by so fast because we've become so used to the *kwarm kuey chin* (routine) and the pace of work." Two forty-year-old women, Puan and Booyuun, both employed for over fifteen years, felt that "the workday goes by very fast especially when there is a deadline to meet." Samlarn, a supervisor, described the days as "going very fast especially when the work volume is high." She added that she had become used to the pace of work because "I've been doing it for so long." For these women, coming to work was like "a hard habit to break." Tuy, who had been working at the factory for twenty-two years, admitted: "I got so used to working and was always so very busy that I never had time to think about leaving or moving to another job." Once again, the notions of accommodation and adaptation were implicit in these women's general attitude toward work: that is, toward a routine they had become "so used to."

Samlarn, after twenty years at F1, admitted that she still looked forward to coming to work every day: "As soon as I enter the factory I forget the outside world." This kind of committed devotion to work was expressed not only by the supervisors but also by longtime workers who found the factory to be a sanctuary and refuge from the hectic and dangerous trappings of the city. As such, the factory was regarded as a safe haven and shelter for the women who already had enough *pa-ra* (burden) and stress in their lives. Empirical case studies on factory workers do not highlight enough this all-encompassing aspect of wage work: that is, a daily routine becoming a permanent fixture in women's lives, governing them from the time they wake up to the time they retire. According to the women, stress and tension on the job depended on the difficulty of the tasks involved. Noy's job, for instance, was to attach labels to the assembled clothes, a task which she describes as "requiring some concentration because you have to put the correct labels on the right clothes." But, compared with F2, work was less stressful at F1, because the women were not subjected to deplorable working conditions or harsh treatment by floor supervisors and management. Furthermore, F1 did not impose strict fines and penalties for flaws or defects, a system common in large textile factories such as F3 and F4.

For Porn, life was free of stress: "I'm not a stressful person because I don't want to *khid maak* [think too much] or *mai mee kang wohn* [have many worries], so it's better not to worry." Ouan thought of herself as a "happy, joyful person" who tried "not to worry." She was quick to point out that many other women, especially married women, were more stressed out than she was. Thong, like Porn, saw herself as a "good and even-tempered person" who liked to "take it easy." And Puan, who was thirty-nine and had been working at F1 for sixteen years, described herself as "quite a cool and even-tempered" person: "I just get by day-to-day without worrying about too much. Work is not that stressful for me. And I don't owe any debts," she added.

It may be important to note that many of the women *were* in debt and were working overtime to pay off money borrowed from family, friends, or local loan sharks, yet they did not cite their low wages as a factor that caused them stress outside of work. And although the few women who owed no money took much pride in the financial freedom they managed to maintain and made it a point to tell me that they had paid off their debts or had never had to borrow money, the women's generally laid-back attitude toward work and their insistence on leading a "stress-free life" could, nonetheless, be indications of accommodating behavior in a situation of *efficient exploitation*. According to Frye, efficient exploitation requires that the "exploited be relatively mobile, self-animating, and self-maintaining" but not determined enough to resist the exploitation.[24] At F1, workers were allowed to move freely about in the factory, felt fairly satisfied with the conditions under which they labored, and hence were not agitated enough to speak out in protest.

When considering the organization of production and treatment of workers in assembly line work, Harry Braverman illuminates the intricacies of the challenges that the capitalist employer faces with his employees: "In purchasing labor power,...he is at the same time purchasing an undefined quality and quantity. What he buys is infinite in *potential*, but in its *realization* it is limited by the subjective state of the workers, by their previous history, by the general social conditions under which they work as well as the particular conditions of the enterprise, and by the technical setting of their labor. The work actually performed will be affected by these and many other factors, including the organization of the process and the forms of supervision over it, if any."[25] In the same way, in Thai factories, the nature and efficiency of the production process itself is dependent upon the particular conditions within the factory system, which include how work is organized and the ways in which workers are controlled and supervised. At F1, workers and management appeared to have maintained rather cordial work relations, and the women themselves expressed concern over the quality of the product, because they had developed a sense of pride and satisfaction in their work.

Subordination and Control through Overtime

A seven-day workweek inevitably forces workers to adjust their minds and bodies to the pace and volume of work. Annual pay raises are incentives that incline women to stay committed to working in the factory. At F1, annual wage increments were awarded to women after several years of employment; in effect, seniority determined individual wage levels, which prevented many older women from quitting or going elsewhere. When women who had been working for fifteen years or more were asked whether they had ever thought about leaving for another job, the overwhelming response was that they did not want to risk "having to start all over again." That would have meant adapting to a new job and a new work environment, making new friends, and, more important, starting at the bottom of the wage ladder. Further they felt they were *kae kurn pai* (too old), pointing out that most factories preferred to hire younger women and believed that it would be "very difficult, if not impossible, to find a new job" with their low levels of education. Having worked at F1 for more than half her life, Ouan had made close personal friends who were still working at the factory: "Everyone in the factory knows me, and I like the warm atmosphere. I feel like I belong here, and I wouldn't want to make new friends."

The women at F1 were speaking on behalf of all the workers when they pointed out that "no one here would be able to live off the daily minimum wage" as it currently stood, because their living expenses exceeded that amount. As one woman said, "Not being able to work overtime means life or death for some of us"—particularly married women, who carried the heavier financial burden of supporting their children and sometimes other family members as well. One poignant example of the dependency on overtime pay was the effect it had on pregnant women. Under the New Labour Protection Act, pregnant women were not allowed to work overtime, and this remains the case.[26] One young pregnant woman, twenty-one-year-old Noy, was very unhappy with this stipulation because it restricted her from making the money she needed for such basic necessities as food and rent. Married women and single mothers said that they were always strapped for cash and found it "very, very difficult to live without overtime." (Of the women interviewed at F1, only two were single mothers; one was widowed and the other separated from her husband.) Single women without children, on the other hand, said that they could live without overtime pay but would have to be very careful with spending. Many young single women, though less pressured financially, said that they worked overtime "out of boredom." As Porn observed, "It's better than being at home and not doing anything." Such a remark may be indicative of women's collective frustration over wages too low to afford them enough material benefits to enjoy life outside the factory. Although one can be critical of the fact that married women did not have the option of staying at home when overtime work was available, with implications for parenting, one must bear in mind that most single women had significant financial burdens of their own (in particular, those supporting their parents and siblings) and therefore experienced much the same pressure to work as married women.

F1 women also spoke nostalgically of "the golden days," the boom of the late 1980s and early 1990s when work orders were at their peak. That abundance had enabled them to work until midnight and sometimes daybreak to catch up on orders, making "a lot of extra money" in the process. Their overtime pay during that period had amounted to more than twice what they typically earned in a month. According to Nid, "Back in those days, we used to go out in groups to restaurants, especially on birthdays, but we can't do that anymore except on rare occasions." Kuh, a thirty-six-year-old woman who had worked in the factory for eighteen years, did not hesitate to point out that overtime hours were not what they used to be. She commented on the "great team work and commitment" among the women during a time when they had to keep up with the heavy work orders: "We would help each other like crazy just to finish the job. On some days, we had to stay up all night without food, but the company would buy us dinner" as a reward. Her remark is indicative of how the women saw themselves as an integral part of the factory's prosperity.

After the financial crisis of 1997, as work orders declined and overtime work was virtually eliminated, many women experienced financial hardship. Overtime, a bittersweet reminder of more prosperous times, was now a rare opportunity that the women welcomed with enthusiasm. Pai called me one day to report that the factory had received a huge work order that week (December 2002) and said excitedly, "We had to work overtime every day this week until 8:00 p.m. because they were really rushing production for this order. Mai and I had to cancel our cooking class on Sunday because we had a chance to make 400 baht!" She informed me also that Win had requested a transfer to another department where more overtime work was available.

Not surprisingly, overtime pay was cited as the most important work benefit at F1 and functioned as a powerful binding mechanism of control, because the women were dependent upon this supplement to their daily wages to provide for housing, food, transportation, or basic medical care.[27] Women's lives were thereby structured by a system in which overtime pay was necessary to meet basic needs. Since regular wages were insufficient for survival, rather than being commanded to work overtime by factory owners, the women willingly did so out of necessity. Yet none of the women interviewed expressed a desire to leave their jobs or go into another line of work. They said they would stop working only when their bodies gave out or when laid off. When asked what they would do if they were laid off, some women responded that they would go back home to their families and find something to do there, such as "sell food," or "open a tailor shop." Among the older women, the most common response was "We're too old to change jobs." These women had become "so used to the work and routine and the relatively high wages" that they "didn't want to give them up." Ouan intended to work as long as she could because she had to support her children as well as pay off her debts.

Most women at F1 found that their *khunna parb chiwit* (quality of living) remained the same or had not improved while they continued to live and labor within the factory system, but they expressed general satisfaction with their jobs because of the steady income and comparatively fair and decent working conditions. Some offered interesting justifications for their longtime employment, such as that working in F1 has made them "stronger and healthier" than before. Kaek, who had initially been reluctant to work in a factory and suffered from dust allergies, discovered that as soon as she started making friends, she forgot about the heat and dust. "More friends, less dust!" she laughed. Moey, a "longtimer" of seventeen years at F1, had to leave the farm and come into Bangkok with her aunt because she was allergic to grass and pollen at home. "I'm not allergic to the dust here, but I'm allergic to the pollen at home," she remarked. These reactions suggest that women at F1 preferred to "play by the rules" rather than risk causing a problem that would disrupt the flow of income. The inability to shape or affect their own circumstances of work and living, itself a consequence of the high volume and fast-paced nature of factory work, meant that the women experienced a situation of powerlessness and that gender subordination was an unquestioned everyday reality.

Subordination through Loyalty and Paternalism

There are various other ways in which subordination is manifested within the sweatshop factories of East Asia. Christena Turner found that Japanese corporations (known for their use of parties, drinking outings, sporting events, and other recreational activities) have an interest in building a community for their workers to foster a sense of loyalty toward the company and a feeling of belonging to various levels of the corporate organization.[28] In Malaysia, the government designated free-trade zones as places where women are free to work but only under male authority. Subsequently, industrial ideology promoted a patrilineal family welfare model, which reflected a cultural emphasis on mutual obligations and loyalty, sometimes verging on "duty" and occasionally "bondage." In Aihwa Ong's study of Malaysian factory women, the male supervisors played a "fatherly" or "brotherly" role to secure workers' compliance.[29] At F1, however, women worked under the supervision of other women, with the exception of one male. (It is fairly common for factories to have female supervisors.) Supervisors received a monthly salary rather than a daily wage, plus added benefits such as health care and life insurance. One supervisor was assigned to each floor with the task of monitoring every stage of production for that particular department or unit or group of departments.[30] The supervisors were longtime employees who made up an integral part of the social fabric of the management hierarchy. Most were former assembly-line workers who had been promoted. The relationship between the workers and the one male and two female supervisors at F1 was equally cordial because all three had formed long-term emotional bonds with the women on the factory floor.

Maow, forty-six years old, working in the factory since he was twenty, and the only male supervisor at F1, oversaw work in the Cutting and Sewing Department. He believed that workers stayed on for so long because the factory owner was "good to them" and "there are not too many rules and regulations." He went on to remark on the many workers who had been there much longer than he had. Explaining his own commitment to the factory, he stated, "The boss takes good care of me and I've become so accustomed to the work and I like the stability. Besides, I have nowhere else to go." Jae Ngau, a fifty-five-year-old supervisor, had been working at F1 for forty-two years and oversaw the Ironing, Folding, and Packing Departments. Like Maow, she had spent more than half her life at F1 because she believed that the owner had always been very good to her and treated her like a family member. She commented, "This is a good factory because there are very few restrictions on workers unlike at other places—you can go and wash your face to freshen up if you want to but you can't do that somewhere else. And ever since I've been here, there has never been one late payment." Being a supervisor, she claimed, required a great deal of patience and understanding: "You can't scold your workers all the time because it would cause problems. You have to find a balance between being strict and being nice." Having been promoted to the position when she was twenty-four, Jae Ngau claimed she understood what workers needed and used her seniority to help the women when she could. An older worker mentioned that since the slowdown of production, Jae had intentionally figured out how to *toong ngarn wai* (delay the workload) so as to have it spill over into overtime for the workers. This gesture reflects the mutual understanding that had been developed between supervisor and worker (fostered by their long working histories) and illustrates the strong emotional bond between workers and management forged at F1.

Samlarn, fifty-three years old and never married, oversaw the Cutting and Sewing Department along with Maow and had been working at F1 for twenty-four years. Like Jae Ngau, she attributed job longevity to and emphasized the importance of "good wages that are always paid on time and the lack of restrictions here, which gives workers a lot of autonomy," and she added, "No one forces you to do anything. You just have to be responsible and get the work done." As a supervisor, Samlarn was very close to her co-workers, especially those whom she had known for twenty years, and felt that they treated each other as "equals." She admitted that her only friends were the women who had worked alongside her in Cutting and Sewing. Supervisors are trusted by managers (in some cases, they are relied upon to deliver results), and, likewise, experienced shop floor managers (at least in the case of such factories as F1) treat workers fairly and reasonably, compared with other places of employment in the apparel sector.

F1 workers referred to their boss as *seya* rather than *nai jarng*. Although these two terms are sometimes used interchangeably by workers, *seya* is commonly known to be a respectful term or positive expression for "factory boss" or "factory owner," whereas *nai jarng* carries a more negative connotation. By referring to their boss as *seya* instead of *nai jarng*, workers expressed their trust in and respect for the factory owner and, at the same time, the feeling that they were an integral part of the factory. At F1, women developed a deep sense of loyalty to both *seya lek* (younger generation or junior factory employer/owner) and *seya yai* (older generation or senior factory owner). Their loyalty was perhaps not always justified. For example, in periods of hardship such as in the post-1997 crisis, the women workers actually empathized with the plight of the family who own the factory and accepted the necessary hardships to ensure the long-term survival of the company in the hope that their employment could become more secure. "We have to sacrifice for the factory too, since we are getting paid by the factory," they would say when asked about their wages and the long hours they put in during the week. "They, too, have to cope in this economy. We're all just trying to get by," said Puan. "If you want the factory's money, you have to do their work," Ouan stated bluntly.

Realizing that the factory could easily hire younger workers for much lower wages, older women expressed their admiration for *seya lek,* who had remained loyal to them by refusing to fire long-term employees. Seniority instilled in them a keen sense of belonging and devotion to the factory. Many had started working there when the younger *seya* was still in school. At least five young women at F1 told me about a sixty-year-old woman who had been coming to work every day for over forty years and was "still going strong." Here, job longevity served as an affirmation of a factory that took good care of its workers. As Dao observed, "When younger women look around and see that they are surrounded by women who have been working here for twenty, thirty, or forty years, they take it to be a very good sign!" Even if the founder of the company was no longer involved, the emphasis on obligation within Thai business culture meant that long service on behalf of the family company should be recognized. *Seya lek* was well aware of the importance of sustaining the core workforce that had been with the family business for many years.

By and large, the women found *seya lek* to be "an understanding and reasonable person." Taa, for instance, saw him as "a good person because he would allow workers to take days off when it was necessary." Whereas matters such as authorizing a leave of absence would be left in other factories to the supervisor or the personnel officer, there was less bureaucracy at F1. As Maam noted, "There are too many channels to go through at other factories for a simple request. Here, you just go directly to *seya lek*." Rather than viewing workers' requests for leave suspiciously, "*seya* only wants to know the reasons for taking leave and would usually grant a request," said Moey, who suggests that this kind of assurance and fair treatment from the owner made the women feel comfortable with the factory and respectful of their boss. Such indications of deference but also mutual respect were nonexistent at F2, where women workers angrily referred to their boss as *nai jarng* and harbored only feelings of resentment and hostility toward the factory.

The relationship between the factory boss and his workers in F1 was very much like the dependent relation that Nancy Scheper-Hughes describes between master and servant, whereby the servant is "locked into an intimate and personal relationship with a *patrao*."[31] At the most practical level, a factory boss is always dependent on the compliance of workers, and vice versa, but unlike F2's, F1's factory boss seemed to appreciate hard work and commitment on the part of his workers and showed some kindness and understanding in return. A boss's behavior and attitude toward employees is thus a good indicator of the kind of working atmosphere one would expect to find in a factory setting. The workers, although dependent on their wages, develop a feeling of loyalty and trust toward "a kind factory and factory boss." Trust and loyalty are also qualities imparted by the factory supervisors toward both the boss and the workers.

All in all, women at F1 had internalized such feelings, and within these paternalistic arrangements, acquiescence and accommodation were expressed most profoundly in the women's willing devotion to the factory.

Subordination through Personal Ties and Self-Discipline

At F1, the women's familial connections within the factory further enhanced the family-like atmosphere at work, at the same time reinforcing loyalty and continuity among generations of working families. Many women had come into the factory through personal ties to family members (siblings or other relatives) already working there who urged them to apply for a job.[32] Ouan, who had been working at F1 for twenty-three years, was referred by her mother, herself a longtime cleaning lady at the factory. A friend of Maam's husband was working at F1 and referred her to the employer. Noy, a twenty-year-old tomboyish girl who had been working in the packing department for just over a year at the time of our interview, had come to Bangkok when she was fourteen to join her older sister, who had been working at the factory for six years; her sister and her sister's boyfriend both worked in the Machinery Department. Saiyon and Sunee both had relatives who were employed at the factory, and Khae, a long-time employee of fifteen years, was hired through her family's network F1. Her mother had worked at F1 for twenty years in the Dyeing Department (which no longer exists); her younger brother was promoted to the factory's personnel office; and her younger sister had been employed in the Sewing Department. Laeyd's mother, like Khae's, had also been working at the factory for twenty years, in the Machinery Department.

Even though F1 never deliberately set out to hire workers through family connections, the factory had inadvertently begun to rely on referrals from their own workers. These acted as a kind of screening process for the company, and the dependence of families on the factory at the same time conveyed a certain reassurance to the owner that the workers were likely to be loyal to their employer.

At F1, it was not uncommon for women to wind up dating and in some cases marrying men who worked at the factory. Kaek's older sister had met her boyfriend in the Machinery Department. Three of the women interviewed were married to men employed at the factory. Damrong and Patcharin had a nine-year-old daughter who lived with them and was cared for by Patcharin's sister while she and her husband were at work. The couple commute together to and from the factory. Anne, twenty-three, who had been working at F1 for seven years, met her husband, Catoon, in the Packing Department. "It's so convenient this way, and we see each other every day," she said. Taa, a pretty, personable, and talkative twenty-eight-year-old from a large farming family, who had been at F1 for ten years, met her husband shortly after she started working. Their two young girls were being cared for by Taa's mother-in-law in Udon Thani province. The presence of husband-and-wife teams means that family life is intimately tied to the workplace, especially when their livelihood is very much dependent upon a prospering factory business.[33]

When considering job satisfaction among apparel workers in the Mexican *maquila* industry, Tiano found that most workers reported liking *everything* about their jobs and derived satisfaction from their specific tasks and working conditions. Women there were often specific about the ways their wage work had improved their lives: it had helped them "understand people," "become more independent," "understand the value of money," and "value myself." Furthermore, apparel workers "took pleasure in performing specific tasks such as sewing in zippers and overstitching waistbands. Several others stated that they enjoyed sewing and would rather spend their time in this activity than in anything else. Others liked their work because they were good at it.... Attitudes such as these suggest that some apparel assemblers may have been engaging in personally rewarding games that led to 'relative satisfactions.'"[34] Similarly, Veccia notes that some women derived satisfaction from their factory jobs, such as the weavers who "expressed particular pride in their ability to master the skills their job demanded."[35] Likewise, women at F1 were proud of their skills and assigned value to their work. As Boonyuun declared, "I think my best comes out at work." Old-timers even expressed feelings about tasks that they collectively disliked, such as sewing the *chood meeh* (teddy bear outfits), an order that the factory received during the holiday season. "Those teddy bear suits for the Christmas season were the worst! They were the most cumbersome and difficult items to iron and fold," Patcharin recalled. "They were small and made of thicker material which made it impossible to place them on the ironing board," added Thim. "And how ridiculous I think it would look on those kids anyway!" exclaimed another woman.

The women at F1 not only derived a sense of satisfaction and self-worth from performing their work duties, however difficult, but attributed their overall feeling of contentment to the close social relations they had developed with their co-workers. The women took such pride in their work that during my return visit in 1999, I found out that they had asked the management to start providing factory uniforms. Interestingly, the main reason they cited was that they thought the factory needed to *mee rabeyb* (project a more orderly and "official" image). Several women said that they liked how uniforms looked on women they knew who wore them (such as roommates or friends who worked in other factories). The fact that none of the women, however, mentioned that wearing uniforms would be more convenient, or would save them the money otherwise needed for clothes, only confirms F1 women's unusual dedication to their factory.

In fact, work discipline at F1 was enforced primarily by the women themselves, owing partly to the amicable relations between the floor supervisors and the workers. Women not only wanted to keep up with the daily work quota but felt a personal responsibility in *kwarm rab pid chorb* (fulfilling their work duties). According to two longtime employees—Da, who was forty-six and had been working at F1 for over twenty years, and Boonyuun, forty and entering her sixteenth year at F1—"The work here allows us to *phen tua rau eng* [be ourselves], and we can do what we want to as long as we get the work done. It's stressful but it depends on the workload and the difficulty of the tasks. We help to train newcomers because we want to help make sure that the finished product is of the best quality. We're responsible for whether or not a product is good, and in this way we get to better our skills and show that we can do our best. Plus, we're doing something good for our families."

Docility or Contentment?

In sum, many factors contributed to job longevity and the creation of a long-standing and compliant workforce. The most common justification for staying was "not wanting to start all over again with new friends and a new work environment." The women felt that they led lives with very little stress and found the stability of their jobs reassuring. They did not want to risk losing their friends and their only reliable source of livelihood. Moreover, they had simply become so accustomed to the monotony and daily routine of factory work that they had gradually developed a sense of satisfaction and commitment to their job and defined their identities in terms of their role at F1. Women were not questioning the owner's control of the means of production because they themselves felt in control of their tasks.

The kind of collective solidarity exhibited by F1 workers may be perceived as "accommodating" because workers were primarily concerned with "getting through the workday with as little stress as possible." As indicated earlier, accommodators are characterized by the longevity of their employment and their devotion to work and the factory. Unlike acquiescent women, accommodating women have a strong sense of control over their lives and their incomes. As such, F1 women were interested in improving their lives through hard work and dedication. Once settled in to the factory and used to its rhythm of work, they gradually came to feel empowered by the incomes they were earning and their ability to financially support their families, a source of pride.

Although the nonmilitant women generally appeared to accept the system, they were not necessarily *powerless* in their ability to change the factory (see chapter 3). Overall, the mechanisms for exerting control over labor that fostered a nonmilitant workforce at F1 can be explained by the following factors: high overtime work and high overtime pay, a fair and reasonable *seya*, few physical restrictions during work, the apparent absence of penalties or fines, wages paid on time, acceptable workplace conditions (including the provision of drinking water and bathroom access), reasonable supervisory treatment, and a close-knit working environment made up of women's personal ties to their co-workers or family members. A situation of actual powerlessness may thus be mitigated by benign or covert mechanisms of control over labor which may not even be recognized by management or workers. Control is thereby maintained by providing workers with fairly acceptable conditions of work and by imparting a mutual feeling of confidence and trust (for example, workers are not routinely strip-searched, and the gates are not locked). At the same time, the factory is able to profit from the high productivity of its workers without having to provide bonuses and benefits based on performance.

The situation at F1 consequently works very well for the employer: an easygoing work environment leads to a highly committed workforce with a low rate of labor turnover, ensuring high returns with minimal investment in skills and training. Given a total absence of social protest at the factory, F1 women may be labeled as "passive" and "docile" from an outsider's point of view. But here, the "passivity" is really a reflection of workers' dependency on factory jobs and their satisfaction with the stability of work, and "docility" reflects their real sense of commitment and attachment to the jobs to which they have devoted so many years of their lives.

Insularity, Cliques, and Solitary Pastimes

How do women's self-perceptions and social consciousness become *products* of their social realities? And how do women's binding ties to their work shape their lives outside the factory? I first thought that the F1 women never had any time for a life outside the factory because they spent so much time at work. But during the course of my fieldwork, I discovered that they actually led dynamic and intensive social lives, usually among themselves, and made the most out of the little free time they had.

The F1 women usually spent their time off doing household chores, running errands, and resting. Their long working hours did constrain their social and personal lives and limit their opportunities to meet people outside of the work environment. Many single women, for instance, said that they did not have the chance to meet men, and so, in some cases, they developed personal relationships with the men working at the factory.

Several women admitted that they had no friends aside from their own small circle at work, especially those who worked directly next to them on the assembly line. Thong and Waew both said that they rarely socialized outside the factory and hung out only with their co-workers. "Once in a while, we would meet some newcomers during our lunch and dinner breaks," said Waew. "Even though there are hundreds of women working here, I don't have many friends outside the Packing Department," said Noy. Similarly, Anne, who worked in the Packing and Shipping Department, pointed out that there were only two men and three women in her unit: "I'm not really close to the women in other departments because we don't work together, and we only see each other during lunch." "I have no real friends on the outside, because all of my close friends are people I've been working with all these years," confessed Malee, who was forty-nine, yet despite here thirty-one years at F1, she said that she "never gets lonely." Likewise, Nuam admitted to not knowing anyone other than "the women I work with." Porn, who preferred to stay at home when she was not working, said, "My *puan sanid* (closest friends) are my colleagues at work. Our social environment is confined and limited to the workplace because we spend most of our time here at work, and after work there's no time left to meet other people."[36] Same-sex relationships were not uncommon. Dao and Nong, for instance, had been working at F1 and living together for ten years and likened their relationship to that of "a happily married couple."

Forty-year-old Boonyuun felt that factory work and its social networks allowed her some personal freedom when she could "be herself" (*phen tua rau eng*). On Sundays, after work ended at 4:00 p.m., some women would go shopping together, watch movies, go to the park, or visit temples, but Sunday was usually a day of rest. On rare occasions such as during a long weekend, some women would take a trip to the beach together. Others might gather at someone's place for lunch or supper. Mai and Pai had enrolled in free cooking classes at the Lumpinee Public Park, where they were learning how to make desserts. Mai and Pai were also avid soccer fans; they would stay up late at night to watch the games on television and regularly attended soccer matches with co-workers.

Other women preferred solitary pastimes. "I don't go to the movies or to the mall because they're not important to me," said Thong, who liked to stay home and watch television. Sunee, twenty-five, enjoyed being in the company of other single women friends, but when she got off work, she loved to watch television and listen to music. Waew also liked to "stay at home and watch television" but admitted that she enjoyed working much more than being "at home with nothing to do." Maam, on the other hand, enjoyed staying home on her day off: "I do some housework and I like to knit. There's always something for me to do at home, and I never get lonely."

I noticed that women tended to hang out in groups and they would always occupy the same spot during lunch. The formation of social cliques (*klum puan*) consisted mostly of workers of the same age group or from the same department, or just friends who shared similar interests and hobbies or lived in the same neighborhood or had the same employment histories. Some social circles did not get along with others, and women would readily point out to me the group or groups of women they liked (*chorb*) or disliked (*mai chorb*) and those they "just could not stand" (*thon mai dai*). Animosity was visible in group behavior especially among the younger women, where cliques generated social rivalries. One afternoon, I accompanied six women—including Mai, Pai, and Win—to a local soccer match, and at the entrance to the stadium another group of women from F1 walked past them, waving only to me. The group I was with described the other group of women as being "loud," "obnoxious," and "show-offs." Pai and Mai saw themselves as the "good girls," as opposed to the "bad girls," whose facial expressions had conveyed a *mai sohn jai* attitude (we don't care). These clique rivalries sometimes manifested themselves in snubbing—women using body language to convey their dislike of other women—but the cliques also seemed to provide an important context for social bonding and space for self-expression, in contrast to the constraints that factory work placed on their behavior.

After the soccer match, Mai and Pai invited me to hang out with them at Mai's place—a small but cozy one-room, self-built "shack" located in an urban *choom chon* (slum community) within walking distance of the factory. Mai wanted to show me pictures of her five-year-old daughter, her stamp collection, her pet turtle and fish, and the many posters of her two favorite soccer stars, Michael Owen and David Beckham, which she and Pai had recently bought together and which adorned what little wall space there was. When I asked Mai what her husband thought about their walls being covered with the faces of the English team, she laughed and said that he just had to live with it. Mai also enjoyed collecting old coins and telephone calling cards, recounting to me the time she went into a 7-Eleven to buy her first 50-baht calling card; she had been collecting calling cards ever since.

The following weekend, I visited Maam and Na, from the "rival" clique, at a townhouse belonging to one of Maam's relatives. Maam and Na, both single, had been friends for years, and they spent the afternoon showing me pictures from their many photo albums of family and friends. They particularly enjoyed sharing with me photos in which they and a few co-workers, ready for a party, were dressed up in flashy clothes and shoes and wore fancy hairdos.

Once I had spent time with both these groups of women, it seemed to me that cliques were composed of women who, though they had different personalities, seemed to be doing the same things as a group; in other words, their bonding relationships were very similar.

I also visited the home of Patcharin and Damrong, located in a small Muslim community on a riverbank not far from the factory. Patcharin and Damrong had a close, extended kin network living in their neighborhood. Patcharin's young nephew was the same age as her own daughter, and her older sister, who worked from home making dried flowers, took care of the two children while Patcharin and her husband were at work. Patcharin invited me, along with Thim and a few other women from F1, for lunch. She and Damrong had built their own home; spacious and comfortable, their house had a separate kitchen and dining area that looked out onto a small garden in the back. As the women prepared lunch, they gossiped and teased one another, talking about the men in their lives and about work. Two neighbors stopped by for help with baking a birthday cake for a party they were throwing for one of their daughters, and for about an hour the women amused themselves trying to figure out how to follow the instructions on the box of cake mix they bought as an "experiment."

During lunch, I learned that Patcharin loved to play the lottery and could talk incessantly about numbers. She often purchased lottery booklets that gave players tips about numbers and probabilities. She and her friends also particularly enjoyed telling ghost stories, and two said that they had seen apparitions and knew of people who communicated with dead spirits. The women also talked about their supervisor, Jae Ngau, and her "annoying" behavior: "She has an inferiority complex of sorts; that's why she's very nosy, which can be very irritating at times, but that's the way she is." In informal situations like this, women were openly critical about the factory but tended to personalize their discussion.

Conversations among F1 women often revolved around domestic and family interests: their children, their husbands, their relatives, and their friends. But they always came back to work-related issues: not making enough money, personal debts, the workload, and the factory. The women expressed their dislike of Bangkok's traffic, pollution, and congestion, and they voiced concern about the prevalence of drugs and violence in the city and the dangers that these posed to children, but they mostly enjoyed talking about their own children, the money they sent home, and what they would like for their children's future. Many expressed concerns about making enough money to pay for school fees.[37] They joked about how they worked so much and so rarely got to see their children that "our kids don't even call us *mae* [mother]." None of the women wanted their daughters "to end up in a factory." As Manee said, "We rural folk gave up school so we could work," and having made this sacrifice, the women were determined to see their children get through school, hoping that better work opportunities lay ahead for them while fearing the worst: "We don't want them to suffer like us." At the same time, the women were quite liberal in the upbringing of their kids and had a naturally laid-back attitude toward education. They considered it "okay" if a son or daughter decided to quit school, even though all the mothers I spoke to hoped to see their children finish high school and enroll in technical or vocational training. Ouan, a single mother of a twelve-year-old, wanted her daughter to finish school but was uncertain as to whether she would be able to support her financially.

Women's Self-Perceptions

The women generally perceived themselves to be easygoing, friendly, even-tempered, good-natured, and sociable. Many stated that they "try not to stress themselves whether at work or at home" and "to take things as they come." "Bold," "brave," "daring," "confident," "independent," "skillful" and "more open" were some of the words women used to describe both themselves and Thai women in general. These remarks came mostly from the married women who worked longer hours, some of whom made more money than their husbands. Unmarried women who had established their own financial stability and independence from their families likewise tended to have positive views of women but negative views of married men. Noy, for instance, regarded Thai women as "more *kau nah* [advanced] and *thansamay* [modern] because women are now holding important positions that only men used to occupy. Women are better because they can do more, and I think women are more independent and work like men. Thai men haven't changed all that much, but you really can't generalize."

Women's views about men were usually negative when they emphasized their primary role as caretakers and providers; thus the notion of the
family wage and a wife's wage as supplemental to the husband's hardly
justified paying women less than men. Perhaps more significantly, women
whose husbands were not contributing financially or doing their share of
housework had developed a strong sense of their own purpose and agency
as providers and thus identified themselves first and foremost through
wage employment—perhaps another explanation for accommodation and
acquiescence among women who needed to maintain a sense of certainty
and stability in their lives. Most of these women had worked for more than
half their adult lives and believed that "we work in order to survive"; more
important, "We can no longer depend solely on our husband's income." As
Laura Lee Downs observes in her study of women metalworkers: "Women
had some perfectly understandable reasons for choosing factory over
home.... [T]he woman metalworker enjoyed 'a relatively easy existence,
one that [was] less resigned' than that of the woman at home.... 'They want
no children or just a few.'... But it was the desire for money, above all, that
lured working women from the quiet path of housewifely self-sacrifice."[38]
For the F1 worker, there was no such compromise: a working mother always needed to provide for her family, and a single woman needed to
support her parents or siblings—which explains why prominent generalizations about working women often revolve around working mothers
and wives, or women living with large extended families.

In many cases, gender inequities within the Thai home were resolved
by way of economic necessity: both husband and wife worked outside the
home and so shared domestic responsibilities. A handful of women held
steadier employment and made higher wages than their husbands, which
enabled some women to assert their importance in the family. Noy, who
handled the finances in her family, however, felt that her role was exag-
gerated: "It's not a big deal because we only pay for rent and utilities. We
only have a fan, a television, and a few lights in our small room." Taa was
making more money than her husband, who also worked at F1, because
she had been at the factory longer. Kai, a thirty-five-year-old mother of
two, who had been working at F3 for nine years, earned more than her
husband, because he held only temporary jobs. It is important to bear in
mind that, regardless of family status, it was fairly typical for husbands to
share equally in household chores. As Manee and Dee put it, "Since men
and women both work outside the home, they must equally help each
other with the *pa-ra* [burden] of housework." Among the few couples who
had children living with them, however, household chores were carried

out by the daughters: "My husband used to help with all the housework, but now he wouldn't lift a finger because our daughter does everything."

Women's perceptions about gender equality indicated a marked shift from the traditional roles and expectations among working-class Thai families. Some women had reservations about the capacity of men to shed traditional values and treat women with respect and as equals; nevertheless, cultural norms and societal attitudes are typically more relaxed and *sabai-sabai* (easygoing) in Thailand than elsewhere, allowing men and women to adapt readily to their particular situations, especially to such practical day-to-day matters as cooking and cleaning. Interestingly, many women mentioned that their own parents had shared equally in household chores, a few women even commenting very casually that their fathers did the cooking and cleaning in the family.

Factory work has contributed to the breakdown of residual traditional boundaries in the division of labor in Thai households. In most instances, the issue of survival itself overrides gender inequities within the home, thereby breaking down the remaining conventional demarcations of the gendered division of labor. In the case of F1, some women enjoyed greater earning power than their husbands, but both husband and wife usually worked outside the home and contributed their wages toward the household. The burden of child rearing was often taken out of the equation, with children being sent away to be raised by relatives when husband and wife were both engaged in full-time wage employment; this situation inclined them to share equally in household chores. For the most part, F1 women had very strong opinions about women in general and were assertive, readily offering their views on men on the basis of their own experiences, but they were careful to avoid sweeping generalizations about men in Thai society. All but one of the interviewees believed in gender equality, and did not see themselves as inferior or subordinate to men, and prided themselves on not being dependent upon men.

In case studies of working women in East Asia, women have been often reported as regarding employment as a temporary transition phase to their ultimate roles as good wives and mothers. Seung-Kyung Kim, who examined the lives of young women workers in the export zones in South Korea, found that factory workers were typically working on a temporary basis until they married. Women felt that marriage and child rearing would free them from the burden of factory work; this meant that the industrial wages paid to a male worker in South Korea had to be sufficient to support a family, enabling women to become full-time housewives.[39] In Thailand, however, the minimum wage is not sufficient to meet the basic needs of even one person, which explains why both men and women are expected to work. Moreover, there is less expectation of full-time domesticity. As a result, Thai women constitute half the labor force.[40] For the women in my study, becoming a housewife was simply not an option, and many single women expressed the view that marriage and family responsibilities would be a burden and interrupt their full-time employment.

The increase in Thai women's participation in the workforce has been attributed not only to the high level of rural to urban migration and increased employment opportunities but also to delayed marriages and decreasing fertility rates. Busakorn Suriyasarn reports that between 1969 and 1979 the fertility rate of Thai women declined by about 40 percent, which resulted in a marked drop in population growth rates (from 3.2 to 1.6 percent) between 1960 and 1988. She also points out that there has been a marked attitude change, with women wanting to have fewer children. And even though rural women continue to marry earlier than urban women, the average age at marriage has increased for both groups. Suriyasarn reports that in 1970 the mean age of marriage was 21.4 for rural and 24.7 for urban women, but by 1980 it had increased to 22.0 and 25.5 years of age respectively.[41]

"Not marrying makes life so much easier and *mai puad hua* [without headaches]," married women would say to me. Realizing the negative effects of having to support a family, single women at F1 said they preferred to remain single, and married women, admitting they had a lot less *isra* (freedom), expressed envy of their unmarried friends. Porn, who hadn't married, was very happy to be single and considered herself "better off": "I can do whatever I want to but I mostly love to spend time alone at home. I think it feels like heaven." Kuh, a married woman, agreed with Porn about the positive aspects of being single: "You can go anywhere when you want to, and you don't have so many responsibilities." Significantly, however, she also pointed out that many women at F1 were probably single because "they work so much all the time!" As a single woman, Boonyuun made "just enough to get by in a big city like Bangkok" but said there was little money left after she paid for rent, food, and utilities. Nuam, also single, pointed out that "women are marrying much later nowadays because we realize it's better to be alone and independent than being tied down and burdened with all the worries and responsibilities that come with a family." Interestingly, factory women in F1 often combined the attitudes of "don't want" and "can't have" family responsibilities: economic independence was important to them, but they also displayed hardheaded (*hua khaeng*) realism about their situation.

Moreover, there was generally little parental pressure on unmarried daughters to "settle down" and become wives and mothers. "My parents had no influence in my decision to marry, and I could live alone or with someone anywhere I wanted," said Nuam. Twenty-five-year-old Sunee was indifferent to marriage, maintaining that there was no pressure from her family because "my parents leave my decisions up to me." The same was true for Porn, who claimed that she had never even dated; she did, though, mention that her parents were afraid she would end up without children to care for her. These women's very practical outlook toward marriage and motherhood was a consequence of the low wages they received from factory employment. Recognizing that their options are limited, many single women place financial independence and taking care of themselves (*doo rae tua eng*) and their relatives over having a family of their own, even at the risk of growing old and not having anyone to care for them later in life.[42] Some of their married friends expressed the view that they wished they could be free from the *pa-ra* [burden] of being married. Factory work had become the central focus of many young women's lives, shaping their expectations, prioritizing their needs, and defining their perceptions about work, men, and themselves. Marriage was not even a goal, nor was it an expectation, on the part either of the women themselves or their families. For many factory women, full-time employment was the primary objective, and factory work not only satisfied this priority but constituted the foundation for their entire support system.

Women's Perceptions of Factory Work

Kaek said that she had always looked down on factory work and found the label *sao rohng ngarn* (factory girl) condescending and degrading: "I thought, god, you must have to be so desperate to have to work in a factory! Even my brother felt the same way." Her uncle, a supervisor at F1, encouraged Kaek to apply and told her that if she did not want the position, he would have to give it to someone else. Kaek decided to give it a try and found that "it wasn't so bad after all." Having worked at F1 for thirteen years, her perception of factory women had changed: "The label *sao rohng ngarn* doesn't necessarily mean that you have a bad status. I actually think it's a respectable occupation." Similarly, Kun felt that *sao rohng ngarn* carried "more prestige and *tha na* [class]" than "construction worker," whose "job is heavy and dirty." The women's generally favorable attitudes toward factory work reflect a certain positive validation of an occupation some had initially regarded as low-skilled, low-status, and demeaning. Women at F1 saw themselves as more fortunate than women who worked as street vendors, beggars, or prostitutes. One of the older factory women captured their pride in the work they do in stating that they were "hardworking women in a respectable occupation, earning money by wholesome means without harming anyone."

On the one hand, then, the women were assertive, independent, occasionally domineering, but at all times they displayed a confidence in themselves that contradicted the stereotypes of Asian females. On the other hand, they could display some surprising insecurities in their sense of self.

In Thailand, women workers are traditionally known for desiring *pew kao phong* (a whiter, fairer facial complexion) because it reflects "more class" and is believed to be attractive to the opposite sex. Skin color is therefore a visible indicator of one's social class standing, particularly for women. *Pew kao neyn* (fair, smooth skin) is associated with upper-class women whereas *pew klaam pew dum* (darker complexion), a result of heavy manual labor in the field, is associated with women from a lower-class background, such as farmers' daughters. A woman's taking a factory job (spending so much time in a shaded environment) thus signifies upward social mobility, an act of entering into an occupation that shelters the women from backbreaking work under the scorching sun. Since this transition is accompanied by a desire to change the color of the skin, *tham hai pew kao* (to whiten the skin), skin-whitening products and creams are widely used by factory women who aspire to be more like "office women" or women of the upper class. The women believe that using these products can change their identities without their having to change their occupation, that by simply applying a skin cream they can embody the classy, higher-status, confident urbanite (*khon krungthep*).

One popular Thai television commercial advertised a cosmetic product specifically targeting "factory girls." Titled "Vampire," it punned on the word *rohng* (meaning "place or shelter") as in *rohng sob* meaning "coffin" and *rohng ngarn* meaning "factory." The ad translates as follows:

> FOUR GUYS: "Those evil bats are hiding in here! Go get them!"
> "Why are the coffins empty? Where did they go?"
> "Look! What kind of creatures are they? Why is that one not afraid of the sunlight?"
> The one lady vampire turns to the camera smiling, showing off two sharp long fangs, and says: "Because I use *Misteen Double Powder* before getting out of the coffin everyday."

MALE VOICEOVER: "New *Misteen Double Powder* has SPF 16, which helps
to protect facial skin from the sun's UV rays and contains a whitening
substance that helps to make your complexion whiter."
CAPTION: *Misteen Double Powder*, Double qualities in one!
SIGN OFF: *Misteen* is here!

This advertisement used the "vampire" to represent "the factory girl"
who needs to protect her face from the sun, since young working women
did not want their faces to become darker.

Most of the factory women had migrated from the rural provinces to
work in the factories, and such commercials capitalized on their desire to
reinvent themselves. According to Mary Beth Mills, rural migrants see the
move to Bangkok as an opportunity to be at the center of metropolitan Thai
society, to earn the cash necessary "to purchase the commodity emblems of
a modern identity." The city presents opportunities for a young woman to
be both a "modern woman" (*poo ying thansamay*) and a "good daughter."
The realities of low wages, minimal benefits, and harsh living and working
conditions, however, bring the two aspirations into conflict. Mills writes:
"In contemporary Thailand, the gap between hegemonic and cultural con-
structions of urban modernity and lived experiences of city life sets up
a fundamental tension in the daily lives of rural-urban migrants. Young
women moving into Bangkok confront seductive images of consumption-
oriented lifestyles, yet their ability to achieve these desired *thansamay* standards is constrained by their low-wage, low-status employment."[43]

Among other adjustments women have to make in adapting to city life
is losing their provincial dialects and learning the "official" Central Region,
urban dialect in order to communicate with people in the city and avoid the
social stigma attached to being a *dek baan nok* (country girl). Needless to say,
the transition to living and working in an urban setting and adapting to a
new way of life is not smooth for women from an agrarian background.
Noy found it hard to adjust to the pace and the anonymity in a megacity of
10 million people: "Life is not as nice in Bangkok as it is in the provinces.
In my hometown, there is no need to rush or hurry to do anything, but in
the city you have to make money. People in Bangkok don't know each other
and don't really care, but at home, people are a lot warmer and friendlier,
because there's not much else to do."

All the women expressed nostalgia for their "simpler" lives in the country and missed the smaller, close-knit community of village life—which
helps explain their need to build a similar community of closeness within
the factory. At the same time, though, they seemed to have dissociated

themselves from their rural origins as they immersed themselves in a new life in the city where their personal identities became intertwined with a productive identity structured around factory employment. Anne, for instance, found it difficult to deal with the pollution and congestion of the city and said she preferred life back in her hometown where "the air is cleaner." Yet she was ready to point out the downside of rural life: "Even though we have plenty of food to eat, we have no money to spend." Having worked at F1 for seven years, Anne had never thought of leaving and planned to continue working because of the steady income.

"Nonmilitancy": Adaptation and Accommodation

One afternoon in the canteen, the factory bell rang to signal that lunch was over, and as Patcharin rose to leave with her co-workers, she turned to me and said, "Well, we've got to get back to our cages now." Patcharin's remark revealed an awareness of her exploited and oppressive situation as a low-wage worker in a dead-end job. She had been with the factory for twenty-five years. The fact that her four co-workers chuckled lightly and smiled in unison at her remark, as they got up to leave, reflected both acquiescent and accommodating behavior on the part of older, longtime workers.[44] The older women I spoke to felt grateful that they were gainfully employed and looked upon their situation in "relative" terms: in other words, they regarded factory work as better than many other occupations and, even though they felt they could not do much to change or improve their working situation, generally seemed satisfied with their lives. Because they displayed considerable agency and autonomy over their lives, it is appropriate to characterize the women as being more accommodating than acquiescent. They might blame themselves for having been "born poor" (*kurd phen khon chon*), for being too old and uneducated, but they believed in the factory system as a way out of poverty and felt that the only way they could improve their lot in life was through hard work and motivation.

In addition to accommodating and acquiescent behavior among the women, the absence of state intervention in the enforcement of labor regulations, the workers' general lack of knowledge about these laws and their rights, their fear of speaking out, and a material existence that left them little or no time outside of the factory setting can explain the situation of "nonmilitancy" at F1. Tiano asserts, "The feeling of powerlessness over oppressive conditions can lead to an immobilizing sense of alienation that is anathema to activism."[45] These women were not unaware of their exploitation, but they felt powerless to do anything about it and thus conformed to the complacent woman assembler stereotype. But their subjective situation led not to a sense of alienation from work but to a combined feeling of alienation, commitment, and loyalty that they developed toward factory work, which had become their only means of survival. For the most part, the women enjoyed their work stability and had no desire to look for other employment.

In her study of Malay women workers in Japanese factories, Ong discovered that the daily exercise of power by male foremen and supervisors was a key element in enforcing worker discipline. The foreman's authority lay in his discretion to determine which individual woman qualified for special rewards or punishments. In most cases, low wages (for piecework) operated as a powerful mechanism for increasing productivity. But Ong also found that factory discipline suppressed social interaction among the women.[46] At F1, on the other hand, the daily routine of working alongside one another brought the women closer together, both on and off the factory floor. The character of social interaction among them was rooted in their long work histories and generated a camaraderie that helped them cope with their situation—but also inadvertently resulted in social conformity and worker compliance. Women's relations within the factory therefore acted as an effective social mechanism of control over labor so that their collective social consciousness was characterized by accommodating and nonmilitant behavior. Women were mindful of the relatively less favorable conditions at other factories and harbored an earnest appreciation for the more reasonable conditions at their factory, and this explains why F1 workers avoided "causing trouble" so as not to disrupt production and put themselves or their fellow workers at risk.

On the whole, passivity and docility were qualities reinforced by F1 workers' sense of belonging, fostered by the less controlling factory environment and their acceptance of the paternalistic attitudes of the factory owner. Relatively decent conditions of work and pay and the manner in which the employer chose to treat his employees fortified the workers' commitment and loyalty to the factory. At the same time, assembly line production meant that women working side by side every day, under the same harsh conditions, developed strong personal bonds with their coworkers and, in some instances, with their supervisors. Gradually, the monotony and repetitive nature of the tasks drew women closer together, providing a sense of camaraderie as they helped one another get through the long workday. Moreover, a pleasant *social* environment helped alleviate the many negative aspects of the working environment. Kaek enjoyed the company of her co-workers so much that she was able to "forget" about the volume of dust she was inhaling, while Waew, who suffered from a weak immune system and was prone to illnesses, reported that working at the factory has made her "healthier and stronger."

In short, women's collective social identities can be defined in terms of their own perceptions of work and their interpretation of their situations. Although the women consider themselves to have adapted well to their working conditions and their living situations, their stories convey the many difficult and undesirable factors they confronted when making these adjustments to factory work. Wage work became an integral part of almost every facet of the workers' lives, not just a means to an end. Women developed an emotional attachment to the factory and to one another, even though their opportunities for socializing were limited to lunch and dinner breaks at the factory and social gatherings on their days off. The small but tightly knit groups of friends created within this constricted scope of personal relations led to the creation of an intimate work setting that, in turn, strengthened their dependency on the factory. In the case of F3 and F4, women who lived in factory-provided dormitories not only developed a physical attachment to their place of work but formed very close emotional attachments to their roommates.

Benign mechanisms of control over labor generated the illusion of physical and social mobility when, in actuality, there was no freedom of movement or possibility for advancement except in the rare case of an F1 factory worker being promoted to floor supervisor. Women insisted that they were usually "left alone," and the sense of having a degree of freedom during work led to a disciplined and compliant workforce. In addition, a voluntary system of overtime pay, which women workers depended upon to make ends meet, manipulated them to work beyond their regular working hours and provided another reason for their loyalty and complacency. Meanwhile, however, upward social mobility was out of reach, since pay raises were minimal and had little overall effect upon improving women's standard of living.

Wage employment, as well as women's personal convictions about marriage and children, inherently shapes the nature of the social relations in reproduction. Confinement to one geographical location and work setting limits the opportunities for meeting people outside of the factory. Knowledge of a friend's financial difficulties or marital problems may influence an unmarried woman's decision to stay single. Concomitantly, married women who desire large families usually end up with only one or two children because of the financial burden associated with child rearing.

Time constraints further inhibit possibilities of mobilization and resistance as the pace of work and the number of working hours leave few occasions to reflect upon their work and lives. Although a woman may believe that she has personal freedom, what she can and cannot do is determined not only by her wages but by the amount of time she spends at the factory. After work, there is little energy left to do much more than stay home to rest. Another major reason for staying at home rather than going out is to refrain from having to spend money.

Work and wages thus limit leisure. Because their waking hours are spent almost entirely at the factory, many women prefer to stay home and recuperate during their scarce time off. Their social activities outside the factory are limited to getting together occasionally or perhaps visiting a temple. For the most part, they simply do not have the time, especially when an average day starts at 5:00 or 6:00 a.m. and ends at 10:00 p.m. As Porn said, "The factory is where I spend most of my time. Home is where I sleep." In fact, many women said that they wouldn't know what to do if they were given too many days off from work; away from friends and a familiar social environment, they found staying at home "lonely and boring" and preferred to be at work, where they can at least be with their friends. Kuh went so far as to admit that she missed having lunch with her friends on days when the factory was closed.

The working hours associated with factory employment therefore created a strong economic dependency for women. Women feel that the day goes by "very fast," since they work *plern plern* (gradually). Many were surprised when they reflected on how many years they had been employed in the factory: "I've been working here for *that* long?" one woman exclaimed after realizing that it had been over twenty years. Others simply said, "I enjoy working and so the day goes by fast." "I don't like being idle and not doing anything because that would be so boring," said Maam. For Ouan, "it doesn't feel like it's been twenty years, but then, I realize I got married and had a child while I was working here, so it does seem like a long time." Lada, who had been at the factory for more than thirty years, declared that she would continue to work until she was no longer physically capable.

In short, low wages and long hours trap women in an unending cycle of daily survival that fails to improve their living conditions and that causes many women to stay on without realizing how many years have elapsed. Overall, the many factors that shape women's accommodation to factory work and their adaptation to life outside of the factory are embedded within the structure of production and deeply intertwined with the pace and nature of work.

2

Resistance and Worker Rebellion
The "Militant" Women

The stories of women in this chapter reveal a "militant" consciousness evolving at a time when the textile industry was at its height in the early 1990s. Economic prosperity meant greater profits for factory owners and greater exploitation for workers. Workers in manufacturing industries were often subjected to various direct and forcible forms of control, paltry wages, and truly horrible work conditions, prompting a surge in labor unrest in the form of spontaneous and sporadic outbreaks, wildcat strikes, and protests at medium and large factories throughout the urban industrial zones outside of Bangkok. Workers were able to gain the support of workers' groups and nongovernmental organizations (NGOs) and agencies during this time. It is important to keep in mind that the workers at Factory Two (F2), like the women at the Hara factory, had been working under oppressive conditions for several years before they started to do something about their situation. This prompted me to look into the reasons behind the women's struggle at this factory and raise questions regarding worker militancy. What triggered mobilization and active resistance among these women factory workers? What was their path to militancy?

My findings suggest that both the degree of exploitation (in terms of hours and pay) and the relationship between the factory owner and the women workers play a large part in shaping the women's collective consciousness. The degree of exploitation, however, is only one among many factors that generate and shape resistance; the likelihood and possibility of worker mobilization also depends upon the women themselves, upon their shared experiences on the shop floor, and upon what the factory does and does not provide for its workers.

In contrast to workers at F1, which had no history of protest, the workers at F2 had reason to rebel. I examined their struggles through retrospective accounts of their experiences of labor militancy, and discovered how the women's vested commitment in those struggles came to shape and define their personal and social lives on and off the factory floor. The factory became the setting where women collectively bonded as they became increasingly unhappy with their work conditions and began to question their situation. At the same time, their stories reveal the highly oppressive forms of control over labor and uncover those mechanisms employed to dampen women's individual and collective struggles. For the handful of women who led the struggle against their employer, their lives no longer revolved around work but instead revolved around union organizing efforts. Their experiences of militancy and activism thereby came to shape and define every facet of their lives.

The Women at Factory Two (F2)

Between September and December 1998 and from September to December 1999, I conducted in-depth interviews with six women from Factory Two (five of whom had been dismissed for their union activities); one woman employed at the factory who was head of the workers' union at the time; two women who had been laid off from PF, the parent factory of F2 and F4 (located in the export processing zone of Rangsit, in the outlying district of Pratumthani); and four women from different factories located in the urban industrial zones of the Central Region where unionized textile factories are strongest. The women at F2 had worked for an average of eight to ten consecutive years since the factory opened in 1987. Due to the vast amounts of data generated in the narratives of each of the women, I have selected a core group of six militant women to be the focus of this discussion. The six women not only were the leaders of the workers' union at F2 but were the only workers I had access to because most of the women involved in mobilization efforts at the factory had been fired for their union activities and had left the city or found employment elsewhere. Because many of the women currently employed at F2 had not been involved in actions that led to the establishment of the factory's first workers' union, the few women I interviewed were able to provide vivid and detailed retrospective accounts of their experiences, which enabled me to learn about the hundreds of other women at the factory who were involved in the struggle at the time. Interviews with militant women from other factories, some of whom were also union leaders and who were personally acquainted with the F2 women, showed that they shared similar experiences.

Sripai was twenty-nine years old and came from a large farming family of ten brothers and sisters in Lopburi province. She completed the sixth grade before coming to Bangkok and, after taking continuing education classes while she was employed, later received her high school diploma. Sripai initially worked at F2's sister company, F4, until she and eighty-one other women were relocated in 1987, when F2 opened. She worked at F2 for seven years but was fired in December 1994 for her union activities.[1] Sripai got married five years later to a union chairperson whom she met at a labor rally.

Saneh was twenty-eight years old, single, and is also from Lopburi province.[2] Like Sripai, she also participated in continuing education classes (on Sundays) while she was working at the factory until she completed the ninth grade. Saneh had decided in 1986 to come to Bangkok on her own to look for a job and found work in a sweatshop, sewing clothes.[3] Her older sister was working at a women's undergarment factory at the time. The sweatshop employed about ten people, paying only 300 baht (US$12) a month, but it provided food and shelter. A relative in Rangsit referred her to F2, and Saneh started her first day of work there on April 4, 1988, at 73 baht (US$2.92) per day. She rented a place near the factory and worked at F2 for ten years before being dismissed for her union activities.

Like Sripai, Pik also came from a large farming family. She finished the sixth grade and then came to Bangkok with her older brother when she was seventeen to help look after his young children. She soon moved in with her older sister, who was working at a large textile factory in the Rangsit industrial zone. Pik recalled her first time in the big city: "I didn't think much about working in a factory then because I had other aspirations. I always wanted to be a *dek pump* [a gas station attendant]. I thought, what a great job! All you have to do is run up to cars and fill them up with gas and you get to stand around all day. But there were no vacancies at the gas station so I went to work at a restaurant as a waitress for about a month and a half." Pik wrote to tell her father about her job as a waitress and how she made 700 baht (US$28.00) a month, not including tips, and always had food to eat and a place to stay. Her father objected to her job at the restaurant, however, so Pik found work in an electronics factory.

But she found the assembly line there unbearable: "It was very difficult because you had to keep up with the moving belt and I couldn't and I had a supervisor who was constantly yelling at me," she recalled. She stayed on that job just for one day and then left for F2 on October 1, 1988, where she found the work to be "a lot better! Plus, I made good friends," said Pik, "so I stayed." She worked at F2 until she was fired in 1998.

Nay, thirty-one years old and single, also received her high school diploma after taking night classes during her employment at F2. Nay had come to Bangkok in 1988 and first got a job as a waitress. Her older sister, Prayao, who was working in Bangkok, later recommended Nay to a furniture company, and Nay worked there for four months, saving up all the money she made. She was paid 1,000 baht a month (US$40 in 1988). When her sister heard about job openings at F2 and encouraged Nay to apply, Nay wasn't interested initially because she was enjoying her job at the furniture shop: "It was so laid back there, and I had a lot of freedom. It was a very easy job because all I had to do was embed jewels into wood and coat it with lacquer. But I applied to F2 anyway and got accepted." She started work at F2 in October 1991. The minimum wage then was about 100 baht (US$4.00) per day, but Nay received only 85 baht (US$3.40) for the first four months of her probation period. When she started work there, F2 already had a union (formed by Sripai in 1990). Nay recalled her admiration for Sripai and Saneh and said that the two women inspired her to become involved in union meetings. She soon became a union member (in 1992) and got involved with the workers' center, acting as director, and in 1994 was elected chairperson of F2's workers' union. She was fired along with Pik, Saneh, Soey, and Taan in 1998. In 2001, Nay got a job at F4 but was laid off and started working for a women's foundation center with a labor scholar. Nay is at present employed at an electronics factory and continues to be affiliated with the workers' center.

Soey, thirty years old, came from a farming family of five and worked at F2 for nine years before being dismissed for her union activities. Soey first came to Bangkok alone at the age of nineteen and found work at an ice-cube factory in Prakanong. That job was physically too demanding, and she left after six months. Her next job was at a factory that produced gloves, but her hands were allergic to the material. She then found work in a textile factory but left to become a live-in domestic maid for a wealthy household where she earned 1,200 baht (US$48.00) a month. She stayed for only three months: "It was torture. I was the only one there and I had to do everything in that house and I never had a day off. I had to get up very early and be at their beck and call all day. It was very exhausting." Soey left the city and returned home to her family but shortly thereafter applied for work at F2, where her younger sister was working. Soey started at F2 in 1990 during a very turbulent time. She had been on the job for only six days before the factory owner shut down its operations: "I didn't know why the employees were filing a grievance against the factory owner, demanding welfare and other benefits. I didn't know what was going on then, and that was when I started to learn," she recalled. Soey too stayed at F2 until she was fired in 1998.

Taan, at twenty-one the youngest of these women, was also fired from F2 for her union activities.[4] Taan vividly recalled the day 700 women decided to stop work and marched into the office demanding that their wages be issued on time. "No one would come out to pay us, so I and other union representatives stood around and waited. At 5:00 p.m. they issued our paychecks, and the problem was resolved." The very next day, management put up a sign announcing the dismissal of twenty-four workers—all the union leaders and union representatives. "The factory provided no grounds for our dismissal without compensation," said Taan. "We knew that we had done nothing wrong, so we refused to take the white envelopes." When they came to work the following day, management barred the twenty-four women from entering the factory. "We went straight to court and ran around all morning trying to submit our grievance to the provincial office and the small courts to find a way to negotiate with the factory," she adds. A few days later, at the end of October 1997, the six women put up their names to represent the F2 workers, and "this is how we—Nay, Pik, Sanay, Sripai, Soey, and I—became leaders of the F2 Workers' Union." Taan, living at home with her family about two blocks from the workers' center, now volunteers her time as a coordinator for the workers' union and makes a living as a street vendor selling miscellaneous items at a local market.

The Workers' Center

At F1, the factory became the solid foundation on which women's personal and social lives were built; they felt a deep attachment to the factory, often calling it "their second home" and co-workers "their second family." At F2, however, although the factory indeed became the setting where women bonded and came together, the real base of their "activist" lives was outside the factory, at the workers' center, officially known as the Young Christian Workers—Rangsit, Thailand (YCW-Rangsit). The workers' center was integral to women's successful mobilization efforts and continues to be a major support network and base for F2 women and for workers from nearby factories in the Rangsit industrial zone.

Simply called "YC" by the women, the workers' center became the only space where they were able to gather, and it came to play a central role in the lives of F2 women, especially during the time of their struggle at the factory. Women would stop by in the evening when they finished work or after their late-night shifts. Women would stay up past midnight talking, discussing, and planning their activities. It was the one place where workers could come for moral support and vent their problems and frustrations. Many women spent their weekends at the center, cooking their meals there, and for those active in running it, the center was their home. At the time of my fieldwork, Soey, Taan, Sripai, and Sripai's four dogs were living there. All my hour-long interviews took place at the workers' center, which is located within walking distance of F2.

Young Christian Workers was founded in Laeken, Belgium, in 1912 by a "socially conscious group of young people, including Madeleine De Roo, Fernand Tonnet, and a radical young priest, Joseph Cardjin," who wanted to see young workers improve their working and living conditions. A strong and energetic network of young workers' groups started to emerge; in 1925, the organization adopted the name Young Christian Workers and—as the movement spread rapidly across Europe, reaching Africa, the Americas, and Asia by the early 1930s—International Young Christian Workers (IYCW). Its first international council opened in Rome in 1957 after a world rally of 32,000 young workers from around the world, and in 2000, it celebrated its seventy-fifth anniversary at a gathering in Brussels of its Tenth World Council, a meeting that Pik and Sripai attended. The IYCW describes itself as "an international movement of young workers for young workers, run by young workers."[5]

The International YCW has regional coordination offices throughout the Asia Pacific Region (ASPAC-YCW) with regional chapters located in Indonesia, China, Thailand, Sri Lanka, India, and Pakistan. Its activities are directed toward raising awareness, training, strengthening solidarity networks, and lobbying for workers' rights. The YCW movement in Thailand, supported and funded by the IYCW, is primarily involved in struggles for better working conditions and worker protection at factories. The organization operates in two outlying areas of Bangkok, in the districts of Rangsit and Paknam, where it is made up of two categories of young workers: "temporary and contract workers" and "the unemployed." F2 workers fell under the category of contract workers. YCW-Rangsit essentially serves as an organizing context and support center for young women employed mainly in the clothing, electronics, and toy factories in the Rangsit industrial zone. Through the involvement of F2 workers, the YCW-Rangsit group succeeded in establishing the F2 Workers' Union. Through a joint effort with the larger trade union movement, a labor dispute between F2 workers and factory management was won in court and the YCW continues to campaign for a national daily minimum wage of 180 baht (US$7.20), for protection and security of unemployed workers, and against the layoff of workers. The YCW Rangsit chapter recently launched a group savings fund—based on social entrepreneurialism and headed by Sripai—to assist workers with their personal finances.[6]

Located in a rundown, poorly maintained, and mostly abandoned housing development area in the Prathumthanee district of Rangsit, the center's two-story building was in very poor shape at the time of my visit and, as I discovered, not the most comfortable place to sleep. The women were receiving overseas funding (from Europe) to pay for rent and utilities and a monthly stipend to run the center, but no funds were provided for building maintenance. The townhouse has a garage area out front (where the women wash their clothes and hang their laundry), a kitchen, two bedrooms on the top floor, and one bathroom on the mezzanine floor. The ground floor is the common area which the women use as their office space. Several plastic and wooden bookshelves lining the walls are stacked with documents, files, and photo albums of the group's outings and rallies. In one corner are two desks, two chairs, a fax machine, two phones, and a typewriter. The women usually gather, hold their meetings, and do their paperwork in the common area. The center's director is required to reside in the building and is in charge of receiving phone calls and coordinating meetings. I found the center always bustling with workers coming and going, and several women usually slept there on nights when their meetings ran late. All in all, as a social space for workers, the center serves to reduce the alienating experiences that result from the labor-intensive nature of their jobs.

Objective Realities and Women's Lives in the Factory

Factory Two (F2) was established in 1987 by a Thai Chinese businessman whose family is Thailand's largest textile manufacturer. The factory employed around 800 women and produced brand-name clothing—Nike,

Gap, Reebok, Adidas, Timberland, and Gymboree—for export to U.S. and European markets.[7]

Working Hours and Wages

Working hours and wages at F2 were the same as at F1: Mondays through Saturdays from 8:00 a.m. to 5:00 p.m., with overtime hours from 5:00 to 8:00 p.m. (or up to midnight, depending on the volume of work available), and overtime on Sundays from 8:00 a.m. to 4:30 p.m. Workers were paid a minimum wage of 157 baht (US$4.24 at the 1998 rate of 37 baht to US$1.00) per day on a biweekly basis. Unlike F1, F2 paid no annual wage increments, yearly bonuses, or other special benefits.[8] Permission for a leave of absence had to be obtained from the personnel office. As at F1, there was no job mobility, although a woman could be assigned to work at different stations. Workers were allowed a one-hour lunch break at noon, but there was no dinner break for those working overtime (OT) until 8:00 p.m. Only workers working until 10 p.m. or midnight were allowed a half-hour dinner break at 5:00 p.m. Unlike F1, F2 often delayed or intentionally postponed the payment of wages. The factory provided no dormitory facilities but did provide commuter vans that transported workers back to their homes. These vans, however, operated much like public buses, making only certain stops.

Before unionization, daily life for women at Factory Two was very much like that at F1: routine, fast-paced, and monotonous. Most F2 women also had had many consecutive years of employment, performing the same task seven days a week, 353 days a year, fourteen hours a day. Sripai recalled what life was like during her first few years at F2: "I would get up early in the morning, walk to work, work late into the evening, and come home. This was a routine that would repeat itself day after day. I finally began to feel really bored and felt like nothing had gotten better since I came to Bangkok. At the same time, I was discovering many things at the factory. My supervisor would call me names like *kwai* [buffalo] which baffled me because my own parents never called me that."[9]

Because of the export boom in the late 1980s and early 1990s, women were often "forced," albeit indirectly, to work overtime hours from 2:00 to 5:00 a.m., for which they were paid 5 baht (US$0.20) an hour. Unlike F1, where overtime was "voluntary," at F2 the factory would lock its gates prohibiting anyone from leaving the premises. According to the women, management would order the commuter vans not to come by until after a certain time, forcing workers to stay at the factory since they relied on the vans to take them home. Security guards were required to walk around with rifles over their shoulders which visibly intimidated the women. "Sometimes the manager would come out and pretend to pull the trigger in front of us," they told me.

Work Environment and Working Conditions

Sanitation was very poor at the factory—there were only six *suam* (toilets) for the 800 women, and they were so filthy that some women refrained from using them altogether.[10] An inadequate sewage system caused them to overflow and forced workers to climb across wooden planks in order to use the facilities. The factory had an ill-equipped janitorial staff, which forced some women to spend their own money for basic cleaning items such as disinfectant, mops, and brooms. When one of the workers won a small lottery prize, she donated money to purchase detergent and bar soap. Such gestures suggest that workers at F2 had no desire to leave the factory but simply had to attend to certain things themselves. Sanitation was never a concern of management, but it very much affected the women who had to use the facilities. Thus even before the workers' union was formed, the women at F2 always made an effort to improve their working environment but could not take care of many things that were simply the responsibility of the factory. The canteen area, for instance, was unsanitary and even hazardous. As Soey, a former employee and union member, recalled: "The factory had a *samosohn* [food coop] which was in bad shape: the roofs would leak in rain, and the entire eating area would get flooded. Most other places had two installations for their cafeteria to keep out flies, or even had air conditioning, a place to nap, and a place to wash your clothes. But at F2, we didn't have an area even to wash dishes, and there were flies everywhere."

Furthermore, no clean drinking water was available to the workers; the water that was provided came from the same pipe as the water in the toilet area. Workers who got thirsty had to consume the dirty water (since no food or drink was allowed on the shop floor), though many chose to tolerate their thirst until the day was over. Sripai recalled that her "saliva was thick as rubber" by the time she got home.

Another issue was the factory transportation, which the women considered to be "a reckless endangerment to their life." According to Pik, "The vans stopped on the other side of the busy street instead of in front of the factory gates, and the drivers were always on stimulants. I would get off the bus at an earlier stop because there was less risk of dying! There weren't enough buses for all the workers. The only time there were plenty of buses was during the boom years when the *nai jarng* [factory boss] would readily provide transportation for everyone."[11]

Managerial negligence of basic safety equipment and procedures was also commonplace: smoke detectors without batteries, untested fire alarm systems, and the absence of factory fire drills. The work area's poor roofing caused large pieces to fall from the ceiling; one worker reported that a large falling slab struck a woman, almost breaking her neck. Cracked and punctured walls allowed rainwater to leak into the cafeteria and work areas, posing the risk of electrocution from the electric sewing machines; workers had umbrellas propped over their work stations on days that rained heavily. A poor ventilation system allowed hot and dusty air to circulate throughout the work stations on the open shop floor. To protect themselves against the dust, the women had to buy their own protective face cloths because the ones provided by the factory were too thin. No first aid kits or basic medicines such as aspirin and other painkillers were available. A woman who cut or pricked herself was simply told to dip her injured finger into the sewing machine's oil and continue working.[12]

Women working overtime without a supper break would often sneak in food in order to have a bite while they were working. Soey explained, "We had no breaks for supper unless you stayed until 10:00 p.m.; then you were allowed a half-hour break at 5:30. Because we were hungry, many of us had to buy food packed in small plastic bags during lunchtime and stuff them around the elastic waistbands of our uniforms. We would even take in bags of rice which would sometimes fall through our pants onto the floor." It was impossible not to get hungry considering that their last meal had been at noon.

Clearly, paltry wages, long hours, and a poor work environment were permanent fixtures that women at F2 faced on a daily basis.

Management and Worker Relations

The general attitude of employees toward the employer indicated the kind of treatment that workers were subjected to within the workplace. Line production supervisors at F2 were mostly women and, like supervisors at F1, were former workers who received a monthly salary and were required to be present at all times to oversee work on the shop floor. At F2, however, supervisors constantly reprimanded the workers as they paced up and down the assembly line and were openly hostile toward the women, adding pressure to an already intense working atmosphere. Sripai, a slow worker unable to keep up with the work pace, was verbally humiliated on a daily basis by her supervisor. The women kept referring to a lady in the personnel department who would yell obscenities at workers "all day long." And according to Sripai, not only were women routinely subjected to verbal abuse from the line supervisors, but there were instances of women who were being sexually abused by male office managers. All in all, the workers were treated very badly, with the exception of the few who were favored by certain foremen. Women who talked with co-workers during work were regarded as disruptive and promptly moved to another section of the department. Soey recalled that she was always being moved around from one production line to another: "They kept moving me because I talk a lot, especially to the people working next to me. Why shouldn't we be allowed to talk freely while we work? We would usually talk about family life, our personal lives, and about problems at the factory."

Pik noted the condescending attitude toward workers: "When clients came to the factory, they would be taken around for a tour, but they would all be speaking in English so workers would have no idea what they were talking about. Often times, I felt that the management looked down at us as if saying, 'Do you know who this is? The director of so and so bank.'" Daily acts of verbal abuse generated feelings of bitterness and animosity among the women toward the factory. Pik likened their constant dealings with the factory management to "*dek thaloh kan* [kids fighting with each other] and neither one wanting to give in." Bum, a woman from another factory, described the relationship between workers and their supervisors and employer, and discussed workers' feelings toward both types of authorities.[13] Like Pik's, Bum's remarks were indicative of the kind of opinions women had come to develop as a result of their experiences on the factory floor:

> The supervisors were former workers too but because they receive a monthly salary, they feel that the *nai jarng* [boss] is their boss, but for workers, our feeling for the *nai jarng* is different. The *nai jarng* always postpones our payment, so how can we be anything but hostile? The supervisors are sometimes unhappy with things but they wouldn't dare say anything because they obey orders blindly. Some floor supervisors have started to tone down their foul language, but it shows us how poorly educated they are, using their emotions all the time, to yell and scream.

For the most part, women at F1 projected a more "cultivated" understanding of their supervisors, who were also more respectful to the workers, but at F2 the women openly disliked them. As noted in chapter 1, how employees related to management could be assessed by the way they referred to their bosses. At F2, women spoke of the employer as *nai jarng* instead of *seya* but referred to the employer's father as *seya*. It was their way of making the distinction between a boss who was caring and compassionate and one who was not. As Nay elaborated, "His father, *seya yai*, at least saw some human value in his workers. For example, at the other factories his family owns, *seya yai* tried to intervene and refused to lay off the older workers. But because his children are now running the business, they have become harsh both in their thinking and in their behavior toward workers." It was not uncommon for factory workers to have respectful feelings toward the founding fathers (*seya yai*) but to harbor feelings of outright mistrust toward a son (*seya lek*) whom the women found to be "ruthless and coldhearted" and preferred to call *nai jarng*. "They no longer have any compassion for their workers," women would often remark.

Sulin and Wilaiwan reiterated the usual sentiment toward *nai jarngs* everywhere: "Employers do not treat us as human beings. They see no value in us workers who have given our blood and sweat, and have devoted years and years of our lives so that their factory can prosper!" Bum described the marked shift in workers' feelings toward the *nai jarng* as he began to implement changes that affected them directly: "We used to look up to the *nai jarng* like a father figure because we could talk reasonably with him, and now we don't know who has taken over. The *nai jarng* once rented a place to give us a canteen area and then one day they moved the canteen up onto the fifth floor and told workers to move up there. We refused to because our lockers were on the first floor so we protested and simply didn't go up to the canteen and that upset him a great deal."

In the smaller, family-run factory where Prayao worked, the *nai jarng* treated workers according to their seniority and their ability to meet production quotas. Prayao described her experience as a senior member of the workforce: "The *nai jarng* would be strict with the younger workers but not with the older ones like myself. They paid overtime according to law, but because I was able to meet their set quota for the day, I would get 200 baht, and with overtime I would receive 297 baht. Otherwise, they would give you the daily minimum of 162 baht, and a supervisor would come around to pressure you."[14]

The forms that labor discipline takes can depend upon the type of manufacturing establishment and the size and structure of the production process. Paternalistic management was more common in Japanese-owned factories, such as in the toy factory where Oy, a former F2 employee, was working, and where certain tactics governing labor discipline played a large role in shaping women's perceptions of work. Oy informed me that at her factory the management used a "suggestion box" in lieu of a labor union; workers could freely write down their demands and complaints and drop the paper in the box. But Pik, Sripai, Nay, and Saneh believed that suggestion boxes were used to discourage workers from organizing or from demanding "anything more" from the factory, thereby allowing stricter regulations—such as the number of times a worker could use the bathroom or get a drink of water—to remain in place. Workers at F1 and at the factory where Prayao was employed, on the other hand, appeared to have no vested interest in increasing their wages or improving their work conditions because they were too busy trying to boost their wages on their own by way of overtime.

In writing about the ideological effects of the labor process in *The Politics of Production*, Burawoy posits that workers' cooperation in their own barbaric subordination was due to their need to survive, which worked very well for management. As Burawoy put it, some workers were "sucked into participating in their own brutalization."[15] The next chapter relates how, in the shift to the piece-rate system at F2, workers willingly subordinated themselves to the labor process, since that was the only way they had "control" over their wages. And because workers were too busy working, possibilities for continuing struggle at the factory diminished.

Meanwhile, F2 women were simply coming to work in a setting where tension, hostility, and animosity persisted between workers and management and where work conditions were becoming increasingly unacceptable. What they had in common were feelings of despair, frustration, and anger as they were forced to tolerate a harmful and unpleasant work environment. Being in the same place at the same time and subjected to the same conditions eventually brought women together to consider the possibility of collective action. It was during this period that the women started to think there had to be "some kind of law" that could protect them from such abuses. The deplorable, and worsening, conditions of work, along with the initial efforts of a few women—namely, Sripai, Saneh, Nay, Pik, Soey, and Taan—triggered activism at F2. A workers' labor union, led by Sripai, was formed in 1990.

The Struggle for Unionization

Largely because of existing gender biases that both women and men held at the time, only about 200 women (or one-fourth of the workforce) joined the F2 workers' union in 1990 when it was first set up. According to Sripai, not one of the eight or nine male mechanics at the factory belonged to the union initially. The men harbored sexually biased assumptions about women in positions of leadership, and it seemed that a majority of the women felt the same way. "Many women at the factory were skeptical about having women in charge of the workers' union and about having me as the chairperson and representative. Even the women didn't trust women as leaders!" Sripai recalled. She added that many married women had to ask their husbands for permission to participate, and "if their husbands said no, the women wouldn't join." Sripai recognized that there was still much gender inequality back then but pointed out that these stereotypes faded in time, as more and more workers began to understand what a labor union was and why it was in their best interest to become members. As F2 workers became increasingly aware of their rights, more joined the union—within four years, about 95 percent of the total workforce. This surge in membership signified the height of the union at F2 and, ironically, took place during the time Sripai was fired from the factory in 1994.

The most turbulent years at F2 came after Sripai was dismissed. She continued to be directly involved in the struggle and the period 1995–97 was a time when Saneh, Sripai, Pik, and their co-workers were openly speaking out against their employer. Before 1995, the factory had been benefiting from the late-1980s export boom in the textile industry, and its workers were benefiting from overtime wages as a result of increased global demand for ready-made apparel. In spite of the poor work environment, the women were getting settled into the pace and rhythm of life at the factory. Much like the women at F1, many at F2 developed close friendships; their continued commitment to the factory came less from the steady workload and regular income than from the feeling of closeness, belonging, and understanding that developed among them as they struggled through the workday under poor work conditions.

As at F1, the impact of the social environment within a factory explained job longevity at F2, where women had typically had many consecutive years of employment since the factory opened in 1987. According to Soey, "The main reason we chose to stay at F2 was because of the family-like closeness we felt with our fellow workers. All of us were in the same plight, but we were able to share this and be a support group. It was a very large number of workers, in the hundreds, and we were all very close. I would know everything about the other workers, who was doing what, who got fired, and so on, and when anyone had a problem, we would confide in each other. So overall, there was a lot of comfort in the same suffering, and we shared it together." Similarly for Saneh: "At F2, we all felt that we could continue living and working under these conditions because we felt lucky that we had work to do, even with the bad water, the hot temperature, poor ventilation, and so on. As bad as the conditions were, we continued working there, and we put up with everything. But it was all of these things combined that made us strike back."

Armed with a practical sensibility toward work, F2 women not only derived a sense of satisfaction and self-worth from doing quality work but found great fulfillment and much comfort in the tight personal and social bonds they developed with one another, even while they were unhappy with their work situation. Bum stressed the importance of having a strong support network: "It has been an unending struggle for me. At least, all of my friends are here and we take comfort in understanding each other and caring for one another. When my father died, my friends came together and went to his funeral. We grew up together here, and we've been through thick and thin. We share the same experiences, and we all know each other so well. How can I give up something like this and leave all my friends and the close relationships I've developed?" It was this close-knit working social environment that helped women cope with many of the negative aspects present within a factory setting. Their struggle was not the kind that is concerned with small daily acts of resistance; rather, it was a collective struggle where women boldly and fearlessly looked out for one another in the face of an unjust working environment and openly defied the actions of management.

Pik offered one telling instance: "When a supervisor yells at someone and calls her 'a stupid, clumsy animal,' we'll come together to stand up for her because if one supervisor was calling a worker 'stupid,' then she was saying that all the rest of us were stupid too. After we set up our labor union, we became very aware of our very basic rights as workers, and we looked at ourselves in a way we never did before." Saneh recalled one incident that provoked her to express her indignation: "It was the day when the drainage and ventilation system in the toilets broke down. Sewage flooded the bathrooms causing the stench to seep in and permeate the entire factory floor. The smell was so bad that no one could continue working. So I stood up and told everyone to stop working until management took care of the problem. We all sat still for two hours amid the stench until the problem was attended to—albeit very poorly. The floor supervisor simply sent the housekeeper out to buy some air deodorizer and spray it all over the place, which made the stench even worse." Saneh's actions mirrored an incident that took place in the Lowell Mills in Massachusetts in 1836. Harriet Robinson, a Lowell Mill factory worker, wrote about what she witnessed at the factory in the days leading up to the unprecedented textile strike: "One of the girls stood on a pump and gave vent to the feelings of her companions in a neat speech, declaring that it was their duty to resist all attempts at cutting down the wages. This was the first time a woman had spoken in public in Lowell, and the event caused surprise and consternation among her audience."[16]

In spite of the deplorable work conditions and ongoing labor violations at F2, the women insisted on staying. When asked why none of them left, they simply said that they believed the same problems existed in factories elsewhere. Pik offered an explanation on behalf of her colleagues: "If there is a problem, you should try to deal with it, and so we did it here because we *were* here. The money can't be that good somewhere else, so why not think about resolving the issue rather than avoiding it?"

This no-nonsense attitude came to embody and personify the mind-set of the women throughout their struggle at the factory. One day, Sripai and Pik discovered during their lunch break that the overtime wages they were making were lower than those women were receiving at adjacent factories. When they came across graffiti stating that the factory was cheating its workers by paying low OT wages, a small group of workers, starting with Sripai and Pik, began to mobilize other workers, and a core group of thirty-five women led what they described as an "underground" movement at the factory during the early days of their struggle. (Sripai said that most of the women in the group were single, because the married ones had families to attend to.[17] She estimated that about half the workers at the factory were married.)

As Sripai recalled, they started by seeking help from a workers' union at a sister company and were urged to take immediate action against their employer. A formal grievance required at least 350 signatures, however, and the women knew that many of the workers would be reluctant to sign on for fear of losing their jobs; those with low educational levels and the older women were afraid they would not get employment elsewhere. Nonetheless, Sripai and her thirty-four co-workers started "spreading the word" by handing out small leaflets to workers regarding factory violations. Over the next two years, Sripai and the women in their *tai din* (underground) movement "quietly and carefully" sought out ways to inform the other workers at the factory, and remarkably, they were able to avoid suspicion by management. "We did this right under their noses and no one [from management] had any idea who was behind all this," Sripai recalled delightedly. "We waited until we got a good sense of what percentage of the workforce would join us. Once we estimated that approximately 80–85 percent of all the workers were with us, in February 1990 we got all the signatures ready and submitted our grievances to the employer along with all the evidence we had obtained to prove management's wrongdoing." In the end, almost all the workers at F2 came together as a group with a common goal, and the first workers' union was up and running in 1990. According to Sripai, the people at the factory who did not join forces with the workers were mostly factory staff and office personnel.

The strongest bonds were formed among the thirty-five women who patiently and painstakingly coordinated their efforts. For these women, mobilization was simply a practical matter: in order to get the signatures they needed, they had to find a way of informing other workers about the facts of their situation, and the only time they had to do that was during the workday. Given their unwavering persistence in light of the myriad problems they were facing, they not only believed that they were capable of effecting change; they firmly believed that they *had* to effect change and were determined to do so. The core group thus developed a deep, emotional bond with one another and a strong personal commitment to themselves and to their co-workers. For Soey, Pik, Nay, Sripai, Taan, Saneh, and the other women who took part in unionization efforts at the factory, their "golden years" occurred at the height and success of their struggle against the employer, as opposed to "the golden days" at F1 which, for those women, was a time of high overtime work and wages, and all the material benefits that accrued.

After the union was formed, F2 workers continued to file complaints and grievances, but their problems rarely received any serious consideration. The union leaders said that they were the ones who ended up taking care of matters that were really the responsibility of management, such as reporting problems to the personnel department and requesting that items such as disinfectant, detergent, and brooms be purchased for the housekeeping staff. Nevertheless, the women also started to familiarize themselves with the labor laws, the courts, and the legal system, and they made real efforts to educate their co-workers about the law by regularly distributing anonymous leaflets until more workers were able to come together for meetings during lunch breaks and after work.

The unlawful dismissal of union leaders, following a salary dispute with management, marked the beginning of the next turbulent period of struggle and the start of what the women referred to as *kra toon jitsam-nukh* (the act of raising consciousness) at F2. In 1997, the factory not only dismissed twenty-four women for their union activities but also stopped production, took away workers' rights, and rescinded all concessions previously negotiated with the union.[18]

"The Making of an Activist"

"You must keep in mind," said Sripai, "that the union at F2 started from scratch. A few of us had to go out there to seek help on our own, educate ourselves, and we were motivated to do it. It was a very active, very hectic, and very exciting period for us because we saw the real strength and solidarity in our unity."

Sripai's statement speaks to how worker consciousness evolves specifically from workers' own experiences within the workplace. In *Manufacturing Consent*, Burawoy examines why industrial behavior is often assumed to be independent of externally derived consciousness. He found that the consciousness workers bring with them into the factory—i.e. "imported consciousness"—only narrowly affects the way workers respond to production relations. He concludes that the labor process at one factory is "relatively autonomous...[and] creates its own characteristic dynamics." I discovered, from my interviews with women involved in leading militant struggles at their factories, that women's actions were very much influenced by an internally derived consciousness, individual and collective, which was observed or passed on to them by the experiences of other women with whom they came into contact within the factory. As Burawoy points out, "The behavior of workers is in accordance with the organization of the labor process and largely independent of any precapitalist consciousness they carry with them."[19]

The stories of Sripai, Nay, and Soey; of Thom, a younger, second-generation worker at F2, who was head of the union at the time of my interview; of Wilaiwan, a worker at a ceramics factory; and of Bum, a worker at another textile factory—all can illuminate the way worker consciousness occurs internally and is not necessarily "imported." Their retrospective accounts expand upon what authors John French and Daniel James describe as the factors that "shape the process by which some women *do* become activists as well as how those women *experience* that transgressive activist commitment."[20] These were women who came into the factory knowing practically nothing about workers' rights or what a labor union was. But beginning to question their wages and work conditions while also coming into contact with union activities that were going on at other factories ignited their curiosity and subsequently drove them to become involved themselves. The deplorable factory conditions, verbal abuse, and low wages, along with the serendipitous discovery that they were being cheated out of their overtime wages, prompted Sripai and her close friends to feel strongly that they had to do something: hence Sripai's relentless commitment to effect change at the factory not only for herself but also for her co-workers.

The Story of Sripai (former worker at F2)

Sripai is the eighth child in a large family of ten children from Lopburi province. She was seventeen when she finished the ninth grade and started working at F2 in 1987. After a few years, she said, she never came close to what she had expected from a factory job: she never had enough money to spend on herself; she never made enough to send home; and there was never a penny left over for savings. Of course, F2 did not have a workers' union when Sripai started working there:

> I didn't know what a labor union was, nor had I ever heard of the terms *sahaparb* [union] or *sithi* [labor rights]; I didn't even know what "labor rights" were. I would get up early in the morning, walk to work, work late into the evening, and come home. I finally began to feel really bored with this routine and felt like nothing had gotten better since I came to Bangkok. I didn't know that as a worker, there are laws to protect you.
>
> At the same time, I was discovering many things from my experience at the factory. We were being subjected to all sorts of mistreatment. The factory would lock us inside in order to force us to do OT work for which we were paid 5 baht (US$0.20) an hour. Because of the heavy volume of work orders coming in at that time, we were often forced to work overtime from 2:00 a.m. to 5:00 a.m. Then one day during our lunch break, my co-worker Pik and I stopped by the stall of a woman selling noodles outside the factory. A bowl of noodles back then cost 5 baht (US$0.20). We frowned and said to the lady, "Oh Pah [aunt; older woman], there goes our OT money for the hour!" The old woman was surprised and remarked, "Why, my daughter makes more overtime than you do. She gets 15 baht (US$0.60) an hour." Pik and I then started to become suspicious. And then we came across graffiti in the bathroom stating that the factory was cheating its workers by paying low overtime wages—graffiti that coincided with the remark that *pah* had made about her daughter's overtime pay.
>
> Shortly after this incident, I befriended a woman, Miao, in my production line at work. Miao had apparently had prior working experience, and she had a close friend who was employed at the textile factory located just across the street, on property that belongs to the same owner as ours.

Miao's friend was a committee chairperson of the workers' union there, and she was aware of the unlawful practices at F2 and wanted us to do something about them. One day at her work station, Miao took out a piece of paper and wrote a small note saying that she was planning to visit her friend over at the other factory to inform their labor union of the problems at our factory and was wondering if anyone was interested in coming along. On the bottom of the note, she circled the part saying "but we would have to sneak in past the security guard at the gate." That note was passed on to me.

This was the first time I had ever heard the term *sahaparb raeng ngarn* [labor union]. Being young at the time, however, the only thing that interested me was the part of the note that said "you have to sneak in past the security guard" because it aroused a feeling of risk and adventure. I felt like "Wow! This sounds so exciting!" So I decided to tag along with Miao, though I didn't even know who we were supposed to approach when we got there. Five or six other women joined us, and we did manage to sneak in past the guards, since our uniforms in the two factories were almost identical.

The unionized workers at the other factory listened to us and recommended that we form a labor union at F2 if we wanted to improve work conditions. In order to form a union, however, we had to get together 600 workers and persuade 350 to file a grievance. We had to make a list of our demands and submit the list along with 350 signatures.[21] I didn't know what a grievance was. When we left and got back to our factory, we immediately called for a meeting with as many workers as we could get word to. Unfortunately, we managed to get only thirty-five women together, because the others were afraid of being fired. My small group of friends and I feared for our lives initially because there had been several recent incidents of union leaders in the area being murdered. Not long after that first meeting, the employer found out about our get-together. He blamed Miao for organizing it, and she was forced to quit her job, which left only me to take charge of this effort.

In helping us, the women at the other factory regularly followed up on what was going on at F2; they urged me to read about the labor laws and invited me to come along with them to labor meetings and to organizing events. So I began to follow them around—why go home and do nothing? I figured I might as well do something productive with my time, and I gradually began to understand the functions of a labor union and the many things to which workers were entitled.

I soon realized that I needed a support group of women from F2, as a starting point, so I got a few friends together to meet after work. At first, no one wanted any part of it. They told me how useless and impossible a union was, saying I was "silly" to think that I could go against an employer. I was even criticized by my own family and my siblings, who all called me a "dreamer." I was backed by only two or three close friends at work, and so this small cohort decided to take matters into our own hands. We began to write up small leaflets containing bits of information on the labor law and such exclamations as "They're using you like animals!" "They won't pay OT according to the law!" We distributed the leaflets at work by placing them in front of the sewing machines in such a way that they were not visible to office staff and supervisors. But for workers at F2, news, gossip, and rumor "spread like wildfire." Initially, many of the workers who read the leaflets misinterpreted their meaning: they thought that the writer was calling them *kwai* [stupid buffalo]!

One day the employer found some of the leaflets and immediately increased the OT pay for workers—but only to 10 baht, still 5 baht short of the prescribed 15-baht rate. Eventually, women at F2 finally started to understand what was going on and began to like the idea of forming a union, and gradually, more workers decided to join us. By that time, we had to come up with new ways to distribute the flyers. One time, we disguised our handwriting and scribbled information on stickers that we put up all over the factory. We did this over a period of two years until we got information out to our fellow workers about the factory's violations.

We finally managed to collect the 350 signatures needed and proceeded to file grievances demanding a cleaner working environment, additional toilet facilities, and clean drinking water—demands that we won. The employer closed down the factory for nine days during this period, and we took the opportunity to set up a labor union in 1990. I was later dismissed, in December 1994, for taking off more than thirty days to help organize workers at one of F2's subcontracting factories in a rural province. I took my case to court but lost.

The Story of Nay (former worker at F2)

Factory Two had just organized the first workers' union when Nay started working there in 1991, having worked previously at a restaurant and in a small furniture factory. F2 was Nay's first assembly job. Recalling the first time she saw Sripai and Saneh, Nay talked of how she was instantly drawn to the two young women: "I always saw Sripai and Saneh going in and out of the meeting room. When I saw them I thought, 'Wow, these two women walk around with such confidence and smarts.' They really struck a chord with me. I really admired them and started looking up to them." As Sripai and Saneh spoke at meetings, Nay constantly heard other women mentioning the term *sahaparb*: "It got me wondering what they were talking about. What is this *sahaparb* they're referring to? What is it? What does it do?"

Nay became curious and interested in this new and unfamiliar environment of worker organization. The other women told her stories of Saneh and Sripai, of how the two women sacrificed themselves by giving up overtime work and their lunch breaks in order to go and negotiate with the manager, and how they were simply committed to making life better for workers. "I didn't know anything," said Nay. "I only knew how to work. There were already a lot of problems at F2 at the time, such as the reduction in overtime wages, but I didn't know what I could do about it because I had to work." Yet she believed that the few women causing a stir with management had good intentions, and so as soon as she passed her probation period, she started getting to know some of the union members. Nay regarded F2's labor union as very strong, even before she became a member.

The Story of Soey (former worker at F2)

Like Nay, Soey became a union member "without even knowing what a union was. I didn't know why the employees were filing a grievance against the factory owner demanding welfare and other benefits. I didn't know what was going on, but I started to learn."

Soey's introduction to labor unionism came about initially through her sister, who "explained things to me. She told me that workers at F2 had no medical benefits and no other benefits like bonuses. There were all these problems the entire time I was there." Soey resumed work in 1992. By August 1993 she had become head of the Workers' Union at F2 because she was already an active unionizer: "I was always attending meetings and learning things on my own. I was constantly asking questions. My friends at other factories would explain to me how their rights were taken away by their *nai jarng,* and I began to learn more about the exploitation of women. So, little by little I learned about many things. I found out, for example, that according to law, every factory must have a *kana kamakarn* [committee or group] to discuss safety issues in the workplace, where both factory owner and employees would get together and talk—and there was such a committee when we were there. And there was the issue of a first aid kit because the factory didn't have even aspirin in the medicine cabinet. The cabinet was full only when clients came to visit."

The Story of Thom (worker at F2 and head of the Workers' Union)

Thom was single, twenty-five years old, and the union representative at F2 when I was interviewing there. In October 1990, her older sister was working at F2's parent company and told Thom that F2 had reopened and was hiring. "I didn't know what *sawatikarn* [worker benefits] meant because there was no such thing at the sweatshop townhouse where I worked. And at the time, I didn't think about such things because there was a lot of overtime work, which meant more wages." It was only during the signature petition drive that she learned about Sripai: "She was letting workers know that we were being cheated with regard to overtime wages." Thom soon became a watch guard for the union and learned that having a union would enable workers to file grievances and make demands. She stayed at the famous *mop* (demonstration) of nine days, during which she and a group of co-workers approached major newspapers to expose their plight:

> I still didn't fully understand what all the commotion was about, but then the factory increased our wages to 90 baht a day, and we got more benefits. The union leaders would tell workers when to refuse OT work; they explained to me that the more we refused, the more we would be able to demand from the factory owner. It worked, and we won our demands. It was the leaders that brought these *sawatikarn* [benefits] into the union and into the factory, and it was the union leaders, especially Sripai, who sacrificed heavily by risking their lives in order to make all of our lives better. This was when I learned that Sripai, who had a bad leg, would dodge cars on the highway just to run across to the other factory to get information, so that she could educate us about all these things. If you only knew how committed Sripai and Saneh were. I feel very grateful, because they did everything for me. My job now as union chair is to continue protecting workers' rights at the factory, and if I get fired, I just hope that the demands we've won will remain. To this day, my goal is to protect workers and their rights; otherwise, I wouldn't be a part of the union.[22]

The Story of Wilaiwan (ceramics factory worker)

Wilaiwan was a small woman with a strong, forceful personality. She was forty-three and came from a farming family in the northeastern province of Khon Kaen. After finishing the fourth grade, Wilaiwan came to Bangkok for the first time in 1976 with her sister, who knew the driver of the owner of the ceramics factory and recommended that she apply there. She had been working at that factory ever since she was nineteen. At the time, there were only 200 workers. According to Wilaiwan, the monthly pay was good; the factory provided dormitory facilities; and overtime enabled Wilaiwan to make more than 1,000 baht a month by working seven days a week from 7:30 a.m. to 7:30 p.m. It seemed a lot of money, and she decided to stay.

The working situation was poor, however. Aside from the long hours, pregnant women were fired, there was no minimum wage, and payment of wages was inconsistent. Some older women, who were aware of the labor violations, came to give the other women advice. Among them was Sulin, a longtime worker and a worker representative. This was when Wilaiwan first learned that there was something such as labor rights that protected workers. Under Sulin's guidance, the ceramics workers submitted a grievance for the first time in 1981, which led to the establishment of a workers' union. "The women still knew very little of the labor laws," she recalled, "but they knew how to protest. The workers seized the factory in 1981 to demonstrate against the owner. The workers sounded the alarm button and told everyone to come out at the sound of the bell. The male electricians even joined us by turning off the machines. We camped outside the factory gates for fifteen days, and the machines were stopped for two full weeks, until the factory finally agreed to provide rice and overtime on Sundays."

Wilaiwan later became president of the Omnoi-Omyai Labour Council/Union Area Group, which is the oldest of the area labor councils. At one time she was also elected president of the Women Workers Unity Group (WWUG), a network of progressive women labor leaders who organize around important issues for women workers. Today, Wilaiwan is president of her local union, works a daily job in a garment factory (as required by Thai labor law, since only full-time workers can have status as labor leaders), and has been the elected chairperson of the Thai Labour Solidarity Committee, which comprises over fifteen major labor federations, geographically based labor councils (the union area groups), and labor NGOs. All her organizing work occurs at night and on weekends.

The Story of Bum (textile factory worker)

Bum first came to Bangkok from Chaiyapoom when she was sixteen. She had heard on the radio of a factory opening in Nakorn Pathom and applied for the job. A van came to pick up a group of people from her village. The factory turned out to be a frozen poultry processing plant that exported to Japan, and Bum worked there for six years. She knew nothing about the labor laws and only later discovered, through a friend employed at a textile factory, that there was something called overtime. Bum immediately took sewing lessons and left the poultry plant in 1987. Not knowing what a union was, she was told by a co-worker at her new job to become a union member; otherwise, she would be regarded as a "black sheep." After that, she learned a great deal about the labor laws and attended larger meetings with labor groups, which exposed her to other labor activists and union leaders. She got to know the *klum yaan* (workers' zone groups), which made her very aware of problems at other factories, and she began to learn about the law.[23]

One day, an older woman got up and called for workers to *yudh amnard* (take over) the factory. Bum was taken by surprise and, in a "rush of adrenaline," got caught up in the struggle. In 1989, she became union chair, pointing out that "if workers wanted something, they had to fight for it."

The foregoing stories are those of activists in the making, stories of women who came into contact with other women who were involved in some form of struggle, and of women faced with contradictory experiences at work who believed they could do something to ameliorate their situation. The significant efforts of a few courageous women such as Sripai, Saneh, and Sulin had an empowering effect on their peers. Close personal and social contact among them developed into genuine friendships that were fortified by their common struggle. Women looked out for one another and went out of their way to share and communicate their knowledge about unionization, their rights, and the law. Newer workers who came into contact with a more experienced worker, such as Sripai or Sulin, would pass on what they learned to other women around them.

My findings suggest that at F2, the worker consciousness that led inevitably to industrial action was produced internally in the factory and consequently altered relations on the shop floor. Thom and Nay came into a factory that had just set up a labor union. Their "militancy" was created and shaped by their own observations of other workers, by overhearing conversations other women were engaged in, by being exposed to a new language, and by slowly familiarizing themselves with what was happening at the factory and around them. Like Thom's and Sripai's, Nay's initial involvement grew out of a sense of adventure and curiosity, and the realization that workers themselves were capable of improving their conditions. At the same time, Nay wanted to learn something new, since she had nothing "better to do" than perform her tasks. When Thom came into direct contact with women who were already well versed in labor organizing, her involvement came not only out of curiosity but out of a deep sense of admiration for a few co-workers who were actively struggling on her behalf.

She downplayed her own position as chair of the workers' union at F2 out of respect for the women who had led the struggle before her, regarding her elected position as an opportunity to continue their legacy.

Nay's illuminating account of her involvement in the labor struggle at F2 demonstrates just how difficult it is for women workers to organize effectively and successfully. Her story indicates the spontaneity of a labor movement which, in the case of F2, came about during a tumultuous period of political unrest in Thailand. The stories of Nay, Thom, Wilaiwan, Bum, and Soey attest to the essential part played by chance meetings, coincidence, luck, and timing in the variegated intersections of a woman's working history. Activist women were often encouraged by former activists among their peers who needed someone to follow in their footsteps and to pass on the knowledge they had acquired. As former union leaders were dismissed or forced to step down, there was an undeniable need for others to carry on the struggle. Workers' consciousness, harboring its own sources of inspiration, came about through various personal contacts and connections. All these factors came together to shape the way the women thought and acted as individuals and as a group of politicized workers. These were women who, in their retrospective accounts, spoke of having started from "not knowing anything at all about workers' rights." Overall, their divergent experiences with regard to forming a union enabled them to develop a more critical perspective and a wider outlook on their situation as workers.

Personal Sacrifices as Integral to Worker "Militancy"

After the workers' union was formally set up at F2, the factory attended to several of the workers' demands such as improving sanitation, adding more bathroom facilities, and providing clean drinking water. It also stopped its practice of forcing overtime work (through lockups), thus allowing women to leave the factory after regular working hours if they chose to. Following their successful efforts in establishing the first workers' union, the six women and several others who played key roles in the struggle became increasingly involved in organizing activities at their factory. These women often gave up their overtime hours and pay in order to hold meetings after work. Nay recalled, "Pik, Sripai, Saneh, Taan, and I would go in to work like everyone else, but we would leave promptly at 5:00 p.m. to gather and talk about our ideas and problems. At the same time, we all shared an interest and a fervent desire to learn and be educated, to know about our rights as workers and to know about the law and so on. So after our regular working hours was the only time we could meet and learn about things. We also reached out to people who were able to teach us by establishing contacts with various organizations."

Soey added: "We had to sit down and talk about the problems at F2 and plan on what to do next, what to say to the *nai jarng* and so on, and we all had to coordinate the work and divide the work. If no meeting was scheduled, of course, we would work overtime, but we never made as much money as the other workers. I didn't think much about it because I did it for the union. But we were borrowing money all the time because we never had enough." For Wilaiwan, having a labor union made living and working at the ceramics factory "a bit more bearable for the workers," and she felt that her personal sacrifices were "well worth the effort. There is overtime work here which is good for the workers," she said, "but as representatives of the labor union, my colleagues and I were constantly banned from overtime work. So we had to give up a lot. The most I could make in a month was 4,000 baht, while other workers were able to make 5,000–8,000 baht or more."[24]

Many of the women relinquished what little extra income they could make (such as overtime pay) to finance their collective struggle, especially during the initial stages of their militancy.[25] Their personal sacrifices were integral to the workers' struggle during this period of labor unrest. Worker consciousness, in this respect, led to an unconditional commitment to their fight for improved wages and working conditions. With the workers' union in place, the militant women at F2 consistently employed a wide range of tactics to put pressure on management, almost on a daily basis. For the most part, they would discuss problems and coordinate their plans during the workday, using their lunch and dinner breaks to hold their meetings or confront management. Once in a while, they would march into the personnel office and demand to see what was being done. Their ongoing efforts both inside and outside the factory left them with little leisure time. According to Soey, she and several other women were so committed to the workers' center that they "couldn't lead a normal life"—in other words, a life free of the stress and frustration of having to deal with problems at the factory.

Saneh took time out from work to attend continuing education classes that she believed would help "to advance their cause in the long run." Like Saneh, Nay stated that their sacrifice was "not only personal but very much a social one." She stressed, "We were actively seeking out help by ourselves, and this is how we developed a better awareness about our situation. We built up this fight while everyone else was working overtime.

But this was not only a personal sacrifice but a sacrifice for our fellow workers, since we were all subjected to the same conditions, only we wanted to do something about it." Nay felt that most of the workers in the Omnoi-Omyai industrial zone were not actively involved in unionization efforts because they "just don't understand the law and would not know where to go for information." From the vantage point of her own experience, she believed that the women themselves needed to realize that "this is not the way things ought to be." Since her dismissal from the factory, however, Nay said that she was worried only about herself: "Now that I'm out of work, what am I going to do? I can no longer fight for the common good when I can barely take care of myself."

Women at F2 were all working hard to support their families and were often separated from their children and displaced from their rural communities. But the families of those women who were committed to organizing efforts suffered the most since their daughters were unable to spare their paltry wages after having to give up overtime work. Soey received no compensation as a labor union representative and chair and was unable to send money home because the wages she made were barely enough to sustain her living expenses, and any extra pittance was used for union organizing. In desperate financial hardship, she often had to borrow money from friends. But, like Nay, Soey felt that it was a sacrifice she had to make in order to be fully involved as a union member, and she promptly reminded me during one interview that it was a sacrifice she wanted to make, not something she was forced to do. Soey and the other activists were convinced that their efforts were for a worthy cause, and they found their experiences to be very empowering. Nonetheless, women such as Nay and Soey were caught in a bind and had to juggle these dual obligations, forcing them to rely on assistance from relatives and friends who were working in the city. Evidently, the "militant" women's lives revolved around union activism; their commitment to the struggle, which they considered to be of urgent importance, transcended any obligations they had to their immediate families.

How Activism Shapes Women's Self-Perceptions

At the same time, women's active involvement in union organizing challenged traditional notions about women's marginal roles in what had typically been a male domain. In postwar São Paulo, authors John D. French and Mary Lynn Pedersen Cluff noted, "Women workers were often discouraged from participating in political and trade union activities by disapproving parents, husbands, or boyfriends."[26] This was true for some of the Thai workers, such as Soey and Sripai, whose parents and siblings were not supportive of their involvement in the workers' union. These women eventually kept a distance from their families by refusing to share with them their ongoing union activities and by keeping discussion about their lives at the factory to a minimum.

At the same time, the militant women held negative opinions about men, rarely giving them the "benefit of the doubt." As at F1, only a small percentage of the workers at F2 were men, most of them technicians and shipping loaders. Male workers were regarded by the F2 women as "selfish and cowardly and especially when it comes to union activities." Soey was eager to point out "women's fearlessness" in relation to men: "Men don't want to have any problems. They only do things in their own self-interest, like getting promotions at work, so joining a union would not be in their best interest and they just don't seem to understand why women have to come out and demand their rights like this."

Female labor leaders were regarded by scholars and activists in support organizations—such as the Friends of Women Foundation, the Women Workers' Unity Group, the Thai Labour Campaign—as being markedly "more sophisticated and progressive" than their male counterparts. Panr, a woman who was working for the Friends of Women Foundation, commented on the different styles of public speech between Wilaiwan and Sulin, two older activists who came out to voice their support at a demonstration outside a ceramics factory. The few men who were on the podium were unable to express their anger in a way that captured the crowd; their speeches were repetitive and incomprehensible at times, whereas Wilaiwan and Sulin appeared calm and spoke clearly and more eloquently than their male counterparts. The two women had their own distinct styles of attracting the audience's attention, qualities that reflect their many long years of activism and their knowledge of the law. Panr concluded with some delight that women were far better than men as activists and as public speakers: "It's the women who get the job done because men *mai mee nam ya* [men have no substance]!" There appears to be marked gender discrepancies between men and women in regard to organizing and militancy, owing largely to the overwhelming proportion of women in the local workers' export zone groups that represented manufacturing industries—such as textiles, electronics, toys, and food processing. Not only had many women become union members, but several were union leaders and representatives. Correspondingly, women outnumbered men at rallies and demonstrations, suggesting perhaps that worker consciousness is rooted, in part, in the feminization of labor in export manufacturing. Concentrations of female workers in this sector created fertile conditions for the unionization of women, an experience which, in the case of F2, transformed their identities.

The experiences of F2 women came to shape their perceptions about themselves, about other workers, and about the nature of factory production. The women noted how their demeanor and interactions with others had changed, and their thinking and outlook on life as well. Their involvement in collective action essentially transformed them individually and came to embody who they had become, as was clearly evident in informal exchanges. The F2 women's assertive, no-nonsense attitude was a characteristic absent from my encounters with women at F1, who were more reserved and polite in their tone and manner. Among her peers, Saneh was known for her bluntness, outspokenness, and strong personal character, qualities discernible to the women around her. Nay, in her narrative, mentioned how her activism significantly altered the way she "carried herself" and interacted with others, and how her experiences drastically changed the way she thought and spoke. "Let's just say I wouldn't have been able to have the kind of conversation that we are having now," she added with assurance during one of our lengthier interviews. At the time of the reelection of F2's union chair in 1994, Nay recalled, a supervisor acknowledged a change in Nay's behavior: "She told me how *hua khaeng* [hardheaded] and confrontational I had become, and she told me how my transformation was like *khao dum* [black and white], given how coy and obedient I was when I first got here." Nay's involvement in labor activism and her knowledge of the law and labor rights gave her confidence and self-assurance. No longer shy and submissive, she too considered herself "hardheaded and confrontational" because she felt so strongly about workers' rights. Likewise, Pik was rather proud of the way she was regarded by those around her: "Workers even started to place bets on us, especially on me or on Sripai, because we were very well known for our aggressiveness at labor seminars." The women projected a knowing awareness of the transformation in their own personalities and looked back at their former "selves" with a sense of achievement and maturity.[27]

On her path to becoming a union leader, Soey was a constant presence at labor meetings, and in 1992 her colleagues chose her to be the *tua tan njuad* (representative) of her production line because they knew how committed she was to their struggle. Soey, who got to know Sripai and Saneh only much later, described herself as less experienced than her two friends. Moreover, "I actively participated in many union activities and I understood some things, but I'm not someone who can talk as forcefully and as eloquently as Pik or Nay, especially when directly confronting the factory owner. I'm more afraid and not as aggressive in negotiations." Yet Soey soon became the director at the workers' center while she was working at F2, and her newly appointed position along with strong support from her co-workers made her feel more confident and allowed her to become more outspoken: "Being director of the workers' center gave me an opportunity to speak out more, and it felt good because we all encouraged and supported each other."

F2 workers' successful efforts came from an active determination to learn about their rights and from their ability to internalize events around them and to share their acquired knowledge with their co-workers and friends. For Pik, Sripai, Saneh, Taan, Nay, and Soey, their struggle for better working conditions and pay at F2 was a tremendous learning experience. Their attitude and demeanor, evident in their speech and dialogue, reflected their general outlook about the world around them while also revealing a great deal about how they saw themselves.

Lydia Kung captures eloquently the meaning and significance of the factory setting for the women whose lives become very much a part of it: "Factories are the setting in which women come into contact with persons and activities previously unknown to them. What they experience there sets them apart from women employed in restaurants, shops, or banks. On the basis of women's common experience in the factory, then, it seems reasonable to ask whether new forms of consciousness or identity about themselves as workers, as one occupational group with shared interests, have emerged."[28] It follows then that women in one factory may encounter a set of societal and economic circumstances entirely different from those of women in another. The structure of the workplace environment, women's different multiple experiences within the factory, and their personal and social relations are all factors that lead to such different outcomes. As stated earlier, it is not always the case that low wages and deplorable conditions provoke resistance, because resistance itself has a history of its own inception interspersed with the multiple narratives of its subjects.

Women's Perceptions about Factory Work and Unionization

Given their extensive experience and regular interaction with an array of women's groups, F2 women were generally aware of the conditions of women in other occupations. When asked to compare their own working conditions with those in other factories, Pik considered that workers at an electronics factory had a much harder time because they were required to keep up with a moving assembly belt and work at such a rapid-fire pace. Pik knew this from the firsthand experience of her one and only day on the job at an electronics plant: "You can never take your eyes off the moving conveyor, and this strains your eyes a great deal. And you have no business running to the bathroom unless you get a pass! That was just insane and the work itself was impossible." Pik felt that even the higher wages at the electronics factory did not make up for the amount of work that was required and such physical restrictions as not being allowed to use the bathroom.

With their understanding of how work was structured in other factories, Nay and Pik were quick to share their thoughts on the issue of management tactics and why many large factories were not unionized: "There may not even be a need for labor unions in some factories because of the kinds of things given to workers. Factories that distribute annual bonuses, for example, are least likely to have labor unions. These are the factories that provide other perks such as group vacations, sporting events, even taking employees out to dinner. In such factories, workers are *im tua* [satisfied enough], and the reasoning on the part of the employer would be, 'I give them so much already, what more could they want?'"

Nay and Pik believed that workers who are conscious of their rights within the workplace are less likely to tolerate a work situation where such basic provisions as drinking water are absent. "Nothing can change a conscious worker," they would say. "It all has to do with the individual worker," Pik stated matter-of-factly. "A worker who doesn't have knowledge of labor laws would never know what she is entitled to." Nay wished she could "turn back the clock" given the tremendous amount of knowledge she had acquired from her involvement in the struggle: "Knowing what I know now, I would be able to deal more effectively with certain issues. But it was a learning experience, and now I'm thirty years old, more mature and grown up, and a lot wiser, and just too old to be involved to the same degree in the factory and its politics."

When asked if they would go back to work in a textile factory, the women said that even if they needed to, no one would hire them, because of their reputations. "There is no way I can go back because I publicly cursed the factory owner," Pik laughed. They added that they would return only if they were really desperate and had no other choice, but even then, the women maintained, they would obviously be working in a different frame of mind: "Because of our experience, we can no longer just sit idle and work without thinking about our rights." To my surprise, Nay was later hired by F4, the factory located just across the street from F2, through her connection with a young woman who worked there. She landed a job in the Packing and Finishing Department, where her task was to trim off excess threads from the clothes. "Perhaps Nay is not as notorious as I am!" said Pik, who pointed out that the blacklisting of union leaders was common practice.

According to Pik, the conditions were better at the parent company because of "healthier" management-worker relationships. Nevertheless, Nay was ready to present a long list of problems when I interviewed her shortly after she started work at F4: "The toilets there are worse than the public restrooms because no one takes care of them. There are no cleaning solutions or anything, just a housekeeper who takes out some of the trash. I have to close my nose and mouth because the stench is unbearable." It was frustrating for her to see that none of the workers, not even the union representatives, took any action, although they had an independent union. But Nay was intent on keeping a low profile:

> I miss the good old days at F2 because if there were ever any problems, we would try and fix them. But here, nobody seems to follow up on anything, and a lot of workers have no motivation to come outside and learn things on their own or to gain experience. I don't understand how the workers can just let work and health standards get to this level. The labor union chairs at least should realize that they would not be doing it just for the workers but also for themselves, especially with regard to basic health and safety.

Nay's involvement in the struggle at F2 had undoubtedly provided her with a critical eye toward her working situation and left her upset about the conditions at F4 and disappointed with the workers' union at the factory. Nay's remarks about F4 illuminated the variable nature of worker consciousness and highlighted how the social relations in a particular factory setting can differ markedly between unionized factories.

Oy, a former F2 worker who had been dismissed for her union activities, provided insight from her own experience at another factory where she was subsequently employed. Coming from a strongly unionized garment factory to a large, non-unionized toy factory, Oy suggested that perhaps "some women are not meant to be activists." When asked to compare the workers at the toy factory with the workers at F2, she was quick to point out marked discrepancies: "Because there is no labor union here, you are dealing with a totally different group of workers. The social environment is very different from that of F2. The women here have other concerns like going out to the mall or to night clubs, [and] . . . they have their own social environment that is nothing like my experience at F2. They see their conditions here as decent enough when, in fact, they don't realize that there are so many unlawful practices going on." This remark shows how "militant" women perceive themselves as different from and more knowledgeable than the average factory worker. When F2 women were asked what they did in their free or spare time, they replied with a terse "What free time?" They rarely stayed home to rest, since in addition to working full-time at the factory, they were always on the move, constantly involved in some kind of organizing activity. F2 women became so consumed by an ongoing battle with their employer that their lives, on and off the shop floor, revolved almost entirely around their mobilizing efforts.

Sripai emphasized that one's own motivations are necessary to ignite struggle and maintain a commitment to change:

> There was a period of real struggle at F2, but even then a lot of people didn't want to become involved because it was risky, and furthermore, you can't just create an activist worker because you can't really *create* someone. That person must have reason to act and must have had the experience and the incentive to seek out help on her own. Union leaders must have experience because you're dealing with a *nai jarng* who already has so much artillery on his side. Union leaders must actively go and seek out knowledge, go out and seek assistance, and educate themselves about the law to become more knowledgeable, so that they can be ready to respond. New leaders need to go out and "fuel their fire," so to speak, and constantly be encouraged, and this is a headache for former members like Pik, Saneh, and me because we have already had this kind of personal experience and wisdom, and there is no way we can just "give it" to these younger women.

Similarly, Oy highlighted how frustrating it was for her when she first started working at the Japanese-owned toy factory, because most of the women around her "didn't have a clue" about labor rights. She pointed out that "having a stable job with a steady income" was one overriding factor that made workers generally content with their situation. Given the long hours and harsh working conditions, however, Oy often had the urge to speak up to let her co-workers know about certain problems, but she found her efforts to be futile: "The women shrug and turn away. Frankly, they just don't want to listen, even though they know what a labor union does. I've come to realize that it's better not to say anything at all because they would label me as someone who *roo dee* [knows too much], and they wouldn't understand anyway because they haven't gone through what I went through at F2. There are no benefits here, unlike at F2, so it was very difficult for me to accept all the restrictions and regulations at first. The only thing that kept me going was the overtime work that was available."

To Oy, it seemed that the workers at the toy factory harbored a certain resentment toward the idea of organizing, despite being fully aware of the functions of a labor union, since their factory was located in the highly militant industrial zone of Rangsit. Sripai's and Oy's narratives suggest that the collective experience of women at F2 was the main factor in developing a consciousness of workers' rights, and affirm that their activism had come to shape their perceptions about unionization and factory work.

When asked what they had gained from their involvement in union organizing, Wilaiwan said, "Experience and a lot of knowledge." With only a fourth-grade education, being involved had allowed her to meet with other workers, participate in seminars, and attend lectures and workshops. She highlighted her experience as a "learning process":

> It's like being in a classroom except it's a "classroom outside the classroom" kind of learning experience. We get to learn the laws we need to without having to bury our heads in books we wouldn't have time to read. We learn on our own, too, so it develops us personally. We get to support other workers and help give advice as well as participate in their meetings. This isn't an experience you can buy with money, only with time. It's a learning process, and maybe I don't get anything material out of it, but I'm able to help other people.

Sripai's involvement in union organizing had changed her perceptions of women in other occupations:

> I used to think that secretaries and those department store saleswomen, who get to wear nice clothes and nice uniforms and work in air-conditioned places, all have good jobs and are well-off and comfortable. But I think that appearances can be deceiving. I never knew how much money women in these occupations make, but once I started working for the labor union at F2 and started getting information, I learned about their salaries and about the kind of work they have to do, such as having to stand all day smiling to customers while receiving little pay and no benefits. So these people have hard times too.

Sripai's remark about the relative situation of working women in other occupations is a striking indication of how worker consciousness can generate empathy and solidarity with other workers, especially on the part of women who have been intimately and thoroughly involved in all aspects of activism. Armed with information about various occupations, she realized that even "office women" and "salesgirls" do not fare any better than factory women. Sripai's observant comments tell us that worker consciousness goes well beyond the factory level. The knowledge she acquired on her own during her many years of struggle at F2 had given her a newfound understanding of work, making her more compassionate and sympathetic toward women in other occupations. After her dismissal, however, Sripai (unlike Pik and Saneh who now work for the Thai Labour Campaign) has turned down job offers from NGOs and women's foundations because, she said, "there's nothing I can do to help workers if I myself am no longer a worker."

Other unionized workers whom the F2 women came into contact with on a regular basis at the workers' center were just as inquisitive and perceptive as Sripai. Cheep is a woman in her early forties who works in a food-processing factory that exports frozen chicken to Japan. On a visit to the workers' center one evening after her shift, Cheep sat down to chat with other women who were present. Curious about work in textile factories, she asked Pik what work was like for women assemblers. Their casual exchange was striking because the questions she asked Pik were the same questions I had asked women during my initial interviews. Cheep wanted to know what kind of clothes the workers assembled, how long it took to sew an item, what each task involved, how many hours women worked a day, and what their wages were. I also learned that several of the women who gathered that evening had had the opportunity to travel to other countries to speak at conferences.

Aside from union organizing activities at the factory, women frequently dealt with the labor courts and became very knowledgeable about labor laws and legislation. While updating me on a pending court case regarding bonuses, Pik pointed out that workers who were actively involved in some form of struggle at the factory knew "the tricks of the trade" because they had made so many court appearances: "We are all so familiar now with the kinds of tactics lawyers plan to use in court, especially their verbal threats and intimidation, and we handle it pretty well each time. We're the ones who are calm and poised in that courtroom."

Several former F2 workers who had been dismissed from the factory had been engaged in an ongoing effort to help the workers' union from the outside, especially in grievance cases that had been taken to court. This gave them an opportunity to learn about the ins and outs of the legal system, which in turn enabled them to take on opposing counsel. They had little expectation of winning at trial, however, and were always prepared mentally for defeat. One time, Sripai was excited to share news of a friend's "victory" in the courtroom and told me how Dun's ability to express herself had shocked the judge and the defense lawyers, leaving them "all speechless." The fact that the judge was a woman was not relevant, for in other court cases where female judges presided over labor cases, they ruled in favor of the employer.

Thanks to their varied experiences outside the factory in a multitude of settings—in court, labor outings, factory sit-ins, campaigns at NGOs and research foundations—Pik, Nay, Sripai, Saneh, Soey, Taan, and the other dynamic women at the workers' center always had a story to tell or an adventure to share. Their stories almost always included admiration and praise for a worker or a group of workers, suggesting that a unified camaraderie hovers over their common struggle against the employer.

From Militant Worker to Labor Activist

Women's retrospective accounts of their experiences helped uncover some of the factors that contributed to resistance and worker rebellion at F2. In spite of the deplorable work conditions and ongoing labor violations during the first few years of their employment, women stayed on because they had become accustomed to the routine and derived a sense of satisfaction and self-worth from doing quality work. They found special comfort in knowing that everyone around them shared the same plight. The factory indeed became the setting where women bonded as they became increasingly unhappy with their work conditions and began to question their situation. Poor work conditions (disregard for safety and sanitation, lack of proper facilities, low wages, enforced overtime work) and a harsh working environment (verbally abusive staff, postponement and delay of wages, restrictions on eating, drinking, and talking) eventually led to dejection, confrontation, and resistance among the workers.

Believing that conditions elsewhere were not likely to be much better, a handful of women decided to do something about their situation, and their lives were forever changed. For the women who led the struggle, their lives no longer revolved just around work but completely around their organizing efforts. Suddenly, life outside the factory was about meeting every day at the workers' center, regularly attending labor workshops and seminars, and seeking out information and support.

Meanwhile, the strong personal and emotional bonds they developed were with close friends who were co-workers and fellow organizers. Women devoted whatever "free" time they had to establishing contacts with women from other factories, learning about labor laws, and holding meetings. Several women used what little cash they had to finance their struggle, even as they gave up overtime pay and relinquished their personal obligations to their own families. In contrast to the emotional and physical sacrifices that F1 women made for their families and kin, the personal sacrifice women made at F2 was on behalf of their fellow workers. At the same time, the new experiences they accumulated outside the factory enabled them to develop a more critical perspective about their situation, profoundly changing the way they related to the world, and shaping their perceptions about factory work and about themselves. The knowledge they acquired about the law, about women in other occupations, and about their rights as workers provided them with a strong sense of agency and empowerment. Worker consciousness was thereby shaped by women's collective experiences at the factory and the experiences they shared during their struggle.

Post-F2 Activities and the Continuing Struggle

Having been fully involved in unionization efforts since their dismissal from F2, Pik and Nay expressed their intent to help mobilize the workers at F2's subcontracting factory, but they were concerned about the lack of financial support and resources. As Pik explained:

> The only problem is that we need to survive too. We haven't been getting anything from the work we've been doing. Nay and I, for example, just finished collecting so much data for this research foundation, but we were never reimbursed for our efforts. We spent all day analyzing and summarizing data for a labor scholar, and the only thing we managed to accomplish is having this respected and well-known scholar get our stories out to the public, and so we do this willingly. I'm still out of work, and one of these days I will probably have to scavenge for food from the trash!

Nay, who was eventually hired back to work at F2's parent company, F4, tried to talk to some of the workers there about the labor violations in the factory: "The union leaders are very weak here. They just have a nice labor union office, but there's nothing in it. A leader should be someone who is devoted and motivated, willing to learn and to genuinely help workers—like me. I have done everything that I can, and it was a real sacrifice, and although I'm not expecting the same level of commitment and dedication from someone else, just a little bit more of it would be good."

Pik talked about collective efforts at organization which were always carried out with a genuine concern for the welfare of other workers yet also benefited them by providing new learning experiences:

> The reason why all these brand names have been so loyal to F2 is because the work here is of such high quality. We were very meticulous workers, and we knew that we did very good work. But during our organizing, we decided not to boycott these brands because we feared that other workers somewhere else would be out of work. So what we did was write up letters explaining the working conditions at F2, and with some help we got our letters sent out to all the factory's big-name clients, and this tainted the factory's image. Once the clients were made aware of the situation, word got back to the factory, and it worked. We have done everything we could, and we struggled against all odds to get what we wanted. We started to attend labor conferences to speak out and learn new things, and it was a good way to survive because we were able to bring back leftover food from the conferences.

As at F1, the sense of pride and satisfaction that F2 women developed about the quality of their work gave the factory a loyal clientele, and the women wanted to use the factory's dependence on its brand-name clients to their advantage as a tool in their organizing efforts. But how did the women come to learn about these strategies? Over the period of their militancy, F2 women came into contact with other labor activists, lobbyists, union leaders, academics, and researchers who were very helpful in providing support and guidance to the workers, inviting them to attend seminars and meetings. Through their counsel and advice, the women learned how workers at other factories organized, campaigned, and demonstrated and began to apply similar tactics in their own situation. The six leading women also maintained a close working relationship with their legal aide (who was in charge of their case at trial), and through his contacts and references they were able to get in touch with an even broader array of individuals and organizations.[29] In an interview with Pik, Saneh, Soey, and Sripai, I asked what they thought about the academics and scholars they came to know throughout the course of their struggle:

> *Ajarn* [professor] Jai, for example, is an academic. People like *ajarn* Jai can probably help us in broadening our views because they are able to look at a

larger picture of things, providing a broader view within which our smaller struggle is taking place. Most of the time, women workers can only *experience*. That is, they can only see their immediate problems such as physical needs and are unable to look beyond their own immediate needs. A scholar or academic, on the other hand, is able to look at the problem and situate that problem within a broader framework, whether it be social, economic, or political, and is able to educate us and make us understand these linkages, what connects all of this together, and how this web is entangled and interrelated so we can understand the problems on a broader and more complex, deeper level than just looking at it simply as "employers and the state are bad" and so on.

So, in sum, these people are able to connect and paint a larger, more complete picture for workers to visualize because, for example, financial institutions—how do they play a part in labor? How do they affect labor unions? What is the link? We would not be able to figure out or even think that there was such a link or connection. So we can always go to them for advice. And a center such as the Arom Foundation helps us a great deal because they've been doing it for a long time. The kinds of information they have and the research they've done make it very useful. And if there is a *mop* taking place somewhere, the scholars at this foundation can be like a channel or a mediator for us. They're like a fundamental voice of the workers and the demonstration.

Though careful to stress the importance of their own working experiences, the women attributed part of their maturation and personal growth to the contacts they developed outside the factory with other labor activists, academics, and researchers; for example, Sripai was also encouraged to attend labor meetings and organizing events by co-workers, lawyers, and NGO activists. Their eloquent reflection upon this aspect of their unionizing experience poignantly speaks to the breadth of social life for F2 women, whose involvement presented them with a vast range of new knowledge and introduced them to an entirely different "world" outside the confines of the factory and even outside the boundaries of their struggle. The women were able to build more support networks, make new friends, and these new learning experiences deepened their consciousness as workers and as citizens. This kind of conversation could not have taken place with F1 women, precisely because they had not had the same kind of experiences.

Armed with these experiences and the knowledge they had acquired, it is no surprise that former F2 women were eager to see their efforts continue and were intent on creating a support network for a new generation of workers. After their dismissal, Pik and Nay had to find other ways to make a living, and for several months they were selling miscellaneous clothing items on the street. Meanwhile, the women used the workers' center as a place to hold meetings and as a support base where they would get together to talk over meals. They continued to help coordinate labor activities and help workers file grievance forms and petitions, advising workers, on the basis of their own past experiences at F2, how to deal tactfully with factory personnel, explaining what they could and could not do, and suggesting how to go about their negotiations. Pik and Saneh took on projects with research foundations one of which involved the arduous task of interviewing workers who had been laid off at a large factory in the area and spending countless hours filling in survey questionnaires for workers who were not proficient in reading and writing. They also helped create questionnaires and regularly assisted workers in filing complaints against their employers.

Following transformations in the production process and the layoff of over 600 workers, the former F2 women do not expect things to be the way they were during the successful period of their militancy, but they would like to see workers continue to fight for their rights within the workplace. After their dismissal from the factory, the six women had dedicated themselves to their mobilizing efforts (filing grievances for workers, disseminating information to workers), and they divide their time between holding union meetings, mobilizing workers, and organizing protests. Activist women who were able to find employment at other factories have had a hard time adjusting to a new work setting where worker organization was absent.

The Weakening of Worker Solidarity at F2

Following the 1997 financial crisis, women began to witness the rapid decline of their strength and solidarity as the economy faltered, as work orders began to wind down, and as workers grew increasingly worn out physically, mentally, and emotionally. Passages taken from their interviews provide a snapshot of the factory women's retrospective look at "the good old days" and their assessment of the current state of the workers' movement. Here, Nay was nostalgic about her experiences in the demonstration of '97 when the women at F2 decided to mobilize and join forces with the workers from one of F2's subcontract factories:

> We picked up the workers at the subcontract factory in Korat and brought them into Bangkok so they could join the *mop* [demonstration] at the Labour Ministry. I wanted to be with them, so I decided to take two days

of my vacation time to be with these workers. The day ended in negotiations. The officials came to sign the documents, agreed to reinstate all the
workers, including even those on probation, and have them begin work on
December 1. But on December 1, they wouldn't let anyone into the factory,
so the workers started another *mop*, this time right in front of factory gates.
So the chair of one of the workers' zone groups [*klum yaan*] and Sripai went
back over to support the workers. F2 workers were very worried about the
situation in Korat, so we collected 50 baht each to get a bus to go see our
sisters at F2's subcontract factory. On the morning of December 3, workers
from all the unions in the *klum yaan* came together to help the subcontract
workers by collecting a total of 10,000 baht.[30] So three large factories came
together to talk about the situation and decided that it would be best to
bring the *mop* into Bangkok.

We came up with a very clever and very organized plan for the demonstration, which was to take place in front of the Parliament House. We
made the clock tower at the Sunday market our meeting point and arrived
there at 9:00 p.m., arousing the immediate suspicion of the police because
there were so many of us. But the women were still separated into small
groups that pretended not to know each other until all of us got there.

The timing was not great because His Majesty the King's Birthday (also
National Father's Day) was coming up on December 5, and the police came
to request that we please cancel our plan, in the light of the forthcoming
celebration in his honor. We went to camp out in front of Parliament House
anyway and proceeded to discuss what we should do. We slept in group
shifts so that about 100 women were present at the site at all times. I took
ten women with me, and everyone divided up the tasks. The thinking was
so quick, especially among the older women who ran the show. It was
amazing. After December 5 we decided to meet again. And remember, organizing and putting hundreds of women together is not an easy task. This
time we camped outside the Ministry of Labour, and the *mop* lasted until
December 20.

Nay's recollection points to the kind of worker solidarity that existed
throughout the Rangsit industrial zone at that time. Workers were well
organized and motivated, had strength through numbers, and were serious about their cause, chipping in and pooling money to help their fellow
workers. Their determination to help their fellow workers plunged them
into new experiences that were as exciting and adventurous as they were
dangerous.

Nay had fond memories about workers' spontaneity, inventiveness, and
resourcefulness during this demonstration, recalling in detail how they
had chartered a bus to a province they had never been in before, how they

were able to mobilize hundreds of women effectively, and how, despite many obstacles, "everything all seemed to come together." More important, this was the first time that the women received exposure through the mass media in a television broadcast. And it was the first time their struggle took them away from the factory and into the public arena and put them in direct contact with the state, thus elevating their playing field. Here they were, demonstrating in front of Parliament House and the Ministry of Labour and dealing with local authorities and the police. Their experiences at this demonstration marked the high point for the F2 workers' union. Nay continued:

> We organized ourselves so well during this long demonstration, getting up and taking night shifts to be on guard and on rotation. And because there were a lot of workers that gathered there, we took the opportunity to educate other workers about their rights and about the labor laws. By that time, we had managed to mobilize ourselves very effectively, and F2 workers were well known and were regarded as the most outspoken, hardheaded, and well-organized group in the entire industry, particularly in the industrial zones of Omnoi-Omyai and Rangsit. We had a huge workforce, and we managed to act together as one voice looking out for one another's interests. It got to the point that when there were strikes or protests going on at another factory, the workers from F2 would immediately go over to support and encourage them in any way possible.

But she also recalled the rapid decline of worker solidarity that soon followed and how F2 workers were left feeling betrayed and abandoned: "When our factory went on strike, no one ever came to help us, and we were left to our own devices. There is no real unity or solidarity in the Rangsit zone today. F2 workers were left feeling that we'd wasted our time and energy on a cause that never matured, and we all felt vengeful and hurt."

Back in the heyday, the women at F2 had been known for their unity, their militancy, and, most of all, their unrelenting support for workers at any factory. But that was not reciprocated. Taan believed that any factory with a labor union wanted either to get rid of it or at least to weaken its strength. She recalled how management would intentionally create problems for union leaders, in one case sending a message to workers that having a labor union "doesn't make anything better." "Sometimes union members and their representatives ended up feeling so powerless and defeated," said Taan.

In reflecting upon their own making of history at F2, Sripai recalled her experiences and spoke about her ongoing relation with the younger generation of workers:

> I suppose you can say that we were the last group of activists because we just couldn't *create* activist workers to replace us. You can't just *create* someone. That person has to have the experience and learn all the ropes on their own, just like I did. The women felt that once we left, the quality and the strength of the union at F2 was just not the same anymore, because the workers and union members were not the same, and later, their ways of thinking started to branch out in other directions. In other words, there was no continuity, which was very problematic. The new generation does have good intentions of wanting to do something and to be effective, but they are still novices. Compared with us, they have very little experience in how to deal with employers.

Sripai pointed out that the decline of the workers' movement in F2 was, in large part, a direct result of strong leadership and the void that was left when these strong leaders were no longer around: "Women became too dependent on the few of us who were the heart and soul of the struggle." On the basis of her extensive experience and her strong commitment, Sripai indicated that the emerging generation of activists would face a greater and newer set of challenges. She believed that an activist had to be "on the inside" because that was the only way to understand thoroughly, fully, and completely the intricacies and dynamics within the factory—the understanding necessary in order to mobilize and organize effectively.

The women who remain at F2 are mostly older women with lower educational levels, and younger women with a sixth- or ninth-grade education who feel increasingly discouraged and disillusioned about unionization. Thom, a subsequent union chair at F2, often came to Nay and Pik for advice and sometimes asked them to accompany her to meetings or seminars. But Nay and Pik said that they usually declined because they believed that the best way for Thom to learn was for her to "be on her own": "We want Thom, who is young and inexperienced, to go out and get her own experience. We have already done our part, and it would be countereffective for us to attend these meetings, because if we were to say anything, we would be intimidating and, in effect, silencing the newcomers." The dependency of younger workers on older, more experienced workers and their need for constant guidance and direction actually held back the real impetus needed for a struggle to materialize.

Nay reflected upon her accomplishments as a union leader at F2 and conveyed to me her opinion of the younger generation of workers at F4, where she occupied a more "marginal and invisible" role now that she was back in the factory setting: "None of the workers at F4 seemed to have learned anything from their friends at F2, but it's not the workers' fault because these workers don't have a whole lot of knowledge to begin with. But I'm very proud of myself because I was able to achieve this much at F2, such as giving workers cleaner toilet facilities—so clean they can eat and sleep on the bathroom floors!"

Pik too stated what she thought about the current generation of workers at F2 and generally felt that they were not as motivated as the women in her day: "These *dek loon mai* [younger generation members] are not doing anything. We try to train and teach them and guide them, but it's like training a toddler to walk. They're all beginners again, and they don't seem really interested in doing anything. We really don't know how to help them." When I asked Pik whether she thought it was because they simply did not have the time, she retorted, "It's certainly not that, because they *have* the time. They have all the time in the world." She continued to stress the value of "real passion and commitment" that a worker must have for her struggle. Like Sripai and Nay, Pik was critical of the new generation of workers at F2, especially in terms of workers' commitment to one another and to their union.

The former activists harbor a certain cynicism not only toward the employer but also toward workers, labor leaders, and contemporary workers' unions that no longer seem to be seriously invested in the struggle. The women feel that workers no longer believe in making the effort because their spirit has been dampened and morale weakened by ongoing and endless battles against "ruthless employers" in a time of economic recession. Since 1997, hundreds of workers have intentionally been squeezed out from F2, and, indeed, the post-1997 environment may have something to do with these transformations (elaborated in chapter 3). The 100 or so women left at the factory no longer have strength in numbers, and former workers point out that women are more afraid now of losing their jobs. Aside from the massive layoffs of workers from the factory, Nay feels that union dues have become a deterrent for workers to join: "The union has had to increase their annual membership fees because they don't have enough money to cover expenses, and it's impossible not to spend money on travel because union reps constantly have to attend meetings, seek assistance from NGOs, and organize labor rallies." Sripai adds that at F2, the fact that "the union itself has done very little to support the workers' cause" explains its dwindling numbers there. According to Sripai, union leaders can only collect 3,000 baht in monthly fees, and "they spend that money carelessly. When they need to go somewhere, they take a cab! In our day, we didn't even know how to hail a taxi, let alone ride in one." Sripai believes that union leaders need to change their outlook and their way of thinking.

Meanwhile, the factory itself was trying to figure out ways of getting rid of the workers' union but held back because it needed a union as "a front" for its clients and its public image. According to Nay, "The factory is keeping its labor union 'only for show,' like a puppet on a string, when it's actually trying to weaken the union and keep the union under its control. It's a very sad situation at F2 right now because back when we were active, the union was at its strongest, and F2 workers had a lot of clout." Since their successful and very public demonstration in 1995, however, the employer at F2 made it very difficult for the workers in an effort to wear out collective and individual struggles and weaken F2's independent union. The factory began to employ "new" and oppressive mechanisms of control over labor, such as deliberately shuffling union leaders and members around in order to prevent them from coordinating with the other workers, and pitting workers against one another (with the shift to piece-rate work, discussed in chapter 3). Even though the postponement of wages was one among many factors that provoked union activism during the early days of workers' struggle at F2, wage postponement became a common tactic used to frustrate workers and weaken labor solidarity in the post-crisis period. In many ways, old forms of control over labor were reintroduced and implemented to stymie labor unrest following the shift to piecework.

As union chair, Thom, who was often demoted by the production manager, stated that she felt a gradual rift among the workers who experienced these tactics firsthand. Moreover, her daily confrontations with management caused many workers to feel that all she wanted to do was "sit in an air-conditioned office," and she admitted that some workers would no longer speak to her. Sripai added that strikes and demonstrations organized at F2 had backfired because "conditions have been made worse by a vengeful employer!" She wondered how workers could go on tolerating this kind of treatment and hoped that workers would "come to realize that they need to continue to fight for what is theirs."

I met up with Sripai a few years after she had left her post as director of the workers' savings fund and after a brief stint at an electronics factory.

She is at present working for an import/export furniture company. I asked her what she thought about the state of worker consciousness today. Upon reflection, she offered the following explanation:

> If I were to compare the state of worker consciousness (*jitsamnukh khon ngarn*) then and now, I would say that my generation of workers didn't know much about our rights, but workers today have had more education. So I feel that workers today have a greater awareness in general but don't really understand their rights, and this could be because of OT work and just the fact that they are working more hours and making less money than we were and therefore have no time to think about their own rights at work. For the older generation, once we learned about our rights, we became genuinely interested in wanting to know more and to find out what we could do to improve our situation. Even though workers today may be more aware of their rights under the law, I think the situation for workers is a lot worse than before, much worse. And there weren't as many factories in Thailand back then. At F2, none of the workers I knew of had respiratory problems. There were reports of some at F4, because workers had been working there longer. But workers today die every year from hazardous working environments, from black lung and other industrial poisoning. Back in my day the air was better. We never knew of workers dying in such numbers as they are today.

Sripai's remarks vividly point to the increasingly difficult situation workers face in the climate of globalization, where workers across free-trade zones throughout the developing world are competing with each other for jobs but are not represented and protected. Meanwhile, the factories they work for regularly violate labor laws, prohibit workers from unionizing, and can fire workers without warning or compensation. This situation is detrimental especially to working women, who have to take on more jobs and work longer hours and are forced to survive on less income and fewer resources. Possibilities for mobilization and resistance are impeded by more oppressive forms of control, and this global "race to the bottom" has transformed the production process of local factories and, correspondingly, affected the relations in production.

Concluding Remarks about "Militancy" and "Nonmilitancy"

Although the women from F1 and F2 came from very similar backgrounds and were engaged in the same occupation, their individual and collective experiences at their factories produced very different interests, concerns, and dispositions. Whereas one group became politicized and immersed in a struggle for workers' rights, the other group was constantly overwhelmed by a struggle for survival and directed its energies toward a more "comfortable," albeit very limited, engagement with life outside of work. Observing workers who exhibited either militant or docile behavior reveals that one group of workers was more "class conscious" than the other. My findings indicate that, as Tiano says, there are "diverse forms of consciousness reflecting various structural influences."[31] It is therefore necessary to look at the complexities and differences in the structure of the production process that shape women's consciousness.

The stories of F1 and F2 women imply that activism has to come from within the factory and from the women themselves. The degree of exploitation is only one among many factors that kindle the kind of worker consciousness that may lead to worker militancy. There were many instances that gave rise to worker militancy at F2, and there were as many factors that explained worker accommodation and acquiescence at F1.

In writing about the ideological effects of the labor process in *The Politics of Production*, Burawoy came to understand that there was something about the labor process that "generated a certain complicity of the workers in their own subordination."[32] The stories of the F1 women provide a profound and rich insight into the reasons behind their compliance and acquiescence. Women's interpretations of work reveal the many reasons why some women workers "manufacture consent" more readily than others. Women at both factories internalized the nature of work and the monotonous rhythm of assembly work. In addition, they all duly adjusted their living conditions to their low wages. They differed, however, in the ways they came to react and relate to how that work affected them. Women at both factories chose to accept factory work as a legitimate way to earn a living, but one group chose not to accept the conditions under which they labored, and they fought to ameliorate those conditions. Their struggle became as all-encompassing as the stability of work became for women at F1.

For women at both factories, job longevity was attributed to a close-knit work environment where the factory setting not only produced but defined their social relations. Poor work conditions notwithstanding, women preferred to remain at the same workplace, where they had made friends, rather than leave and "start all over" in a new setting. The processes that shaped worker consciousness were thereby contingent upon objective conditions (structure of the workplace environment), factory history, treatment by the employer, women's differential experiences within and outside the factory, and the dynamics and social interactions developed among the women themselves. As Susan Tiano conveys in her assessment of worker consciousness, "a woman's sense of 'the system' may extend beyond her work site to include her assessment of gender relations, the labor market, the economy, and the state. The relevant distinction in women's orientations toward the system is their beliefs about its fairness, responsiveness, and capacity for serving their interests." Tiano labels this parameter "system affinity" and contrasts women with a positive regard for the system with those who view it negatively.[33]

In the case of F2, women were brought together on the basis of the politics of workplace experiences: that is, the problems they faced together at work. Their conscious dispositions arose out of common interests and the recognition that something had to be done to make their demands heard. In this regard, it is essential, when looking at women's struggles against capitalism and their resistance to globalization, to understand the underlying material conditions in which they find themselves. F2 women were unified first by their shared experiences of oppression as low-wage female workers and subsequently by a shared commitment to struggle against a disliked capitalist employer.

The two factories differed quite dramatically in the sense that controlling mechanisms at one factory fostered acquiescence and accommodation, whereas objective conditions at another provoked worker discontent and rebellion. At F1, control was maintained by providing workers with fairly decent working conditions along with mutual and cordial relations between management and workers. Dependence on overtime work and pay and paternalistic work arrangements fostered loyalty and worker commitment while enabling the factory to profit from maximum labor productivity. At F2, on other hand, poor work conditions and a harsh working environment eventually led to worker discontent. Hence two currents of worker consciousness can be identified within these two different work settings. Worker consciousness started to transform and change following the 1997 economic crisis, however, when worsening conditions of work and pay compounded with fear and economic hardship differentially affected workers at the two factories. At F1, women started to question their conditions at the same time that the factory was up for inspection. At F2, the crisis led to a diminished workforce and caused the remaining employees to become less outspoken, more reserved, and more fearful in voicing their demands as they tried to hold on to their jobs.

The stories of women presented here demonstrate that worker consciousness is multidimensional and must be contextualized and examined within its localized and particular configurations. The next chapter shows how marked shifts in the production process along with certain structural changes at the factory level transformed these two currents of worker consciousness following the 1997 crisis.

3

Workers in the Post-Crisis Period

The financial crisis in East Asia, triggered by the collapse of the Thai baht in July 1997, prompted many large employers to close down their factories and outsource production to smaller, non-unionized, subcontract factories as a cost-cutting measure. Massive layoffs of women in export industries resulted.

A large part of the financial crisis was a direct result of sustained infusion of foreign capital, or "hot capital," during the early to mid-1990s, which primarily went into currency speculation, the stock market, and the real estate and financial sectors. Lured by the prospect of quick and easy profit, owners of large manufacturing establishments, including those in the textile industry, became major players in stocks and real estate, investing the earnings from their companies. Subsequently, the lack of continuing investment in the productive sectors of manufacturing, especially in labor and new machinery, caused a slowdown and stagnation of Thailand's export sector. By the late 1990s, major export manufacturing industries were laying off large numbers of their workers.

In 1998, many textile and garment companies closed down, displacing hundreds of thousands of workers from the manufacturing sector, a significant number of them women.[1] At one textile factory, nearly 5,000 women, most of whom had been employed for ten or more years, were laid off in the month of July alone because a new labor law, scheduled to take effect in August, mandated high worker compensation for longtime employees. Although factory owners often cited "poor market conditions" as the primary reason for shutting down and for the dismissal of workers, they still wanted to run their businesses and saw the "crisis" as a great opportunity to lower production costs while maintaining profitability. Having received a US$17.2 billion dollar bailout package from the IMF, the Thai state was obligated to abide by the usual loan conditions which gave large and medium-size factories a green light to lower labor costs even further as the cost of living and the inflation rate rose. Consequently, labor laws and regulations were relaxed, causing common violations in regard to worker protection–related issues such as wages and job security.

A changing production environment following a period of economic crisis had implications for women in both factory settings, F1 and F2. In the context of recession and a weakened economy, new mechanisms of control over labor not only forced women to work longer hours but acted as an essential tool to circumvent labor law, rupture a strongly unionized workforce, and stem labor uprisings.

The changing nature of production was characterized by the shift away from the assembly line and overtime system of work toward a "new" regime involving a piece-rate work system.[2] The implementation of this system not only worsened structural conditions within the factory but also created tension and animosity among workers: the competition of individual women for piecework inhibited their socialization and solidarity while encouraging individuation and self-interest. Workers were forced to work as much as they were physically capable of doing (while "voluntarily" forgoing bathroom breaks, eating, and sleeping) in return for subsistence wages.

Studies in the research literature on women and development which see women as trapped in an exploitative situation sometimes fail to look at women's responses in times of crisis and recession, when employment opportunities disappear and the norms of passivity no longer apply. I explore these issues by examining the changing structural conditions of work and living, the outsourcing of production from the urban to rural areas, and the practices of factory owners. Entrenched in an economic slump, women who were dismissed from the jobs to which they had devoted most of their lives confronted a harsh and unwelcoming territory. How did factory workers respond to worsening conditions of work and pay as they faced an uncertain future? How did the behavior and attitudes among militant women in unionized factories and among nonmilitant women change? Given the increasingly difficult circumstances facing workers within the industry as a whole, what was the impact on worker consciousness and collective action?

The actual experiences of some workers from both F1 and F2 make it possible to examine how new forms of managerial control, along with worsened structural conditions of work, produced rebellious responses, and also to take account of conditions that generated a more fearful and compliant workforce. The reduction or elimination of the overtime system exacerbated exploitative conditions within the factories and created a rupture in the unity and cohesion of organized labor in what had previously been militant industrial zones. At the same time, latent forms of mobilization among women in non-unionized factories in Bangkok and the surrounding industrial provinces had fewer opportunities to become manifest. Female textile factory workers faced more intensive forms of exploitation even as possibilities for organization become more difficult. In addition, more factories were outsourcing their production to smaller subcontract factories in outlying provinces, and since most subcontract factories are unregistered and tend to operate outside labor regulations, workers there faced harsher work conditions and lower wages, combined with threats of dismissal if they challenged those conditions. In essence, factory owners became empowered by the crisis, while state support for workers' rights diminished.

The East Asia Crisis

Foreign direct investment (FDI) in the form of "hot capital" (portfolio investments and loan funds) started to flow into Thailand in massive quantities in the mid-1980s and accelerated in the 1990s, with heavy investment coming from Japan. Between 1985 and 1990, about US$15 billion of Japanese direct investment poured into Southeast Asia, and by 1996 about US$48 billion in Japanese FDI was concentrated in the countries of Indonesia, Singapore, Malaysia, Thailand, and the Philippines.[3] Foreign capital also came from countries within the region such as Hong Kong and Taiwan. And by the early 1990s, foreign capital was flowing in from Europe and the United States as well. A large part of the financial crisis was thereby a result of speculation in property in the form of portfolio investments, where returns were based on real estate values rather than increased productivity and economic efficiency in manufacturing or service industries. These investments went into currency speculation, real estate deals, and credit expansion.[4] Further, there was an increase in consumer spending which added to unprecedented growth in retailing, finance, and telecommunications. As Walden Bello and others summarize:

> While Thailand's trade policy and investment policy in the non-financial sector continued to be marked by a significant degree of protectionism, its drive to attract portfolio investment and bank capital led it to engage in a fair degree of liberalization of its capital account and its financial sector....Issues of stocks and bonds by private entities were, however, not the only or even the primary channel of capital flowing into Thailand. Loans to Thai private financial institutions as well as non-financial entities were gladly advanced by international banks....Overlooked in the borrowing spree were the potentially disastrous consequences of borrowing short-term and at relatively high rates of interest to lend or invest in activities, such as real estate financing, that were long-term in their return.

Economic "short-termism" played an even larger role in the subsequent bursting of the Thai economic bubble generated by these activities:

> The inflow of foreign funds escalated with the establishment of the Bangkok International Banking Facility (BIBF) in 1993. The BIBF was a system in which local as well as foreign banks were allowed to engage in offshore international banking activities....Two years after the facility began, BIBF loans came to $41.1 billion in 1995 and reached $49.1 billion by January 1997....Among the prime beneficiaries of the BIBF bonanza were Thailand's finance companies....The finance companies, as well as the banks, made their profits basically though arbitrage. The result was a financial *walpurgisnacht*, as finance companies went on a borrowing spree and foreign portfolio investors seeking quick and high returns bought shares in local finance companies....Thus, foreign capital, partly intermediated by Thai finance companies and banks, found [its] way to the speculative sectors, such as the stock market, real estate, and the creation of consumer credit....Of these activities, investment in real estate was by far the favorite of foreign and local capital. So attractive was investment in real estate that some finance companies not only lent to property developers but...diversified into real estate speculation....With the property sector being so hot, everybody knew that it would sooner or later be hit with a glut....Most of the loans and investments began to go sour, very quickly, in 1996, as the extent of the glut in housing began to hit home....The crisis of Thailand's real estate and financial sectors unfolded within an economy whose pillars were fragile in the first place.[5]

Consequently, in August 1997 the Thai government accepted a US$17.2 billion bailout package from the IMF, which was offered to help stabilize the Thai economy. Since recipient countries must pay back most IMF loans with interest, states are forced to create the condition for selling their labor at the lowest cost possible in order to remain competitive. This caused large and medium-size Thai factories to transform their production processes while it forced the state to weaken labor regulations, worker protection, and job security in order to favor multinationals and business owners who were in a position to earn foreign currency. In effect, the state and its institutions adopted a hands-off approach by giving leeway to companies and factory owners rather than monitoring and regulating factory production. The state became increasingly reluctant to enforce labor laws, so that workers' rights suffered. Capitalists, not the workers, were seen as the key to lifting the country out of recession. Consequently, the financial crisis resulted in massive layoffs in export manufacturing, the auto industry, and the banking sector.[6] According to the Labour Ministry, a reported 2 million people were unemployed by the end of 1998. Of this number, approximately 320,000–335,000 were industrial workers (more than 150,000 of whom were women). About 4,960 workers (10 percent) from the PF's workforce were laid off during the month of July 1998 alone.[7]

Having lost their jobs in factories and on construction sites, men and women were returning to their villages. According to NGO estimates, "An average of five migrants had returned to *each* of the country's 60,000 villages by December 1997."[8] Hoping to absorb the hundreds of thousands of laid-off workers, the government tried to open up industries in rural Thailand, which led to the expansion of subcontracting factories in outlying provinces. In the past, the agricultural sector had usually absorbed surplus labor during times of industrial recession, but this was no longer the case since agricultural production in Thailand had significantly declined. Research conducted by Ramkamphaeng University indicated that the majority of laid-off workers were older women, 90 percent of whom had families and were primarily responsible for them. According to this report, rampant layoffs often targeted longtime workers because doing so enabled the employers to cut off these workers' relatively high wages and avoid compensation payments. According to Jaded Chouwilai, statistics released by the Ministry of Labour and Social Welfare showed that among the 1.2 million unemployed nationwide at the end of 1997, only 44,753 (21,746 women and 23,007 men) received financial assistance from the Welfare Protection Fund under the Labour Ministry.[9]

"Poor market conditions" were cited by factory owners as the primary reason for closing down their operations and for the dismissal of workers. But in reality, in order to cut costs and remain competitive, the owners were simply moving their production out to local and regional areas where wages were lower and where labor was not unionized. This shift in production was characterized by the establishment of subcontract factories and the piecework system (*rabob rahb mao*) that came to replace the former assembly line system of work. At the same time, Junya Yimprasert and Peter Hveem point out that since 1997, many of the Thai and foreign-owned clothing manufacturers that had opened up factories in Cambodia, Laos, Vietnam, and China, have moved back into Thailand, driven by new state policies facilitating a more open economic climate for investment and trade.[10] Consequently, Thai and foreign-owned contract factories in Thailand have been able to hire cheaper migrant workers from neighboring Burma, Cambodia, and Laos. In the northern province of Tak alone there are over 200 garment factories that employ female migrants from Burma. Like Thai factory workers, migrant workers report that they are forced to work long hours, are paid by the piece, and are not always paid for overtime work.[11]

For the most part, the piece-rate payment system resulted in a wage lower than the minimum wage set by the government. David Harvey notes that "competitive pressures and the struggle for better labor control led...to the rise of entirely new industrial forms...with a whole network of sub-contracting and 'outsourcing' to give greater flexibility in the face of heightened competition and greater risk. Small-batch production and sub-contracting certainly had the virtues of bypassing the rigidities of the Fordist system and satisfying a far greater range of market needs, including quick-changing ones."[12] Outsourcing of production by textile manufacturers within Thailand was a clear indication of this new pattern of industrial networking and expansion in the name of market competition. In the Thai context, it entailed the geographical relocation and dispersal of a factory's operations to non-unionized areas in outlying industrial provinces. This transformation is similar to that of the automobile industry, described by Beverly Silver, where Japanese auto producers "chose to depart in significant ways from the Fordist style of mass production....Japanese automobile producers established a multi-layered subcontracting system that simultaneously allowed them to guarantee employment to (and establish cooperative relations with) a core labor force, while obtaining low-cost inputs and flexibility from the lower rungs of the supply network."[13]

In Thailand, subcontracting production has always existed in sweat-shops and in at-home work via a piecework system, but only recently has it been extensively integrated into the production process of large manufacturers, as in the case of the apparel industry. Not only a cost-cutting measure for employers by way of reduced minimum wage rates in the provinces, subcontracting also allowed employers to evade labor regulations, thanks primarily to the non-unionized workforces in these geographically isolated areas.[14] Local capital mobility from urban indus-trial areas to rural areas was largely precipitated by domestically owned companies that manufactured apparel for multinational companies. Rural provinces became the new outsourcing zones, and subcontract factories made up the new sectors of production, where work arrangements en-abled employers to exert direct and indirect forms of managerial control over labor. The subcontract piece-rate system enabled Factory 2 to elimi-nate the overtime pay system while extracting more productivity out of workers and paying less for their labor. The factory would set a daily tar-get for the number of finished pieces, and the subcontractee would be re-sponsible for certain sections of production and be paid by the number of finished items. This system of production made the workload more stress-ful, since fewer employees were expected to perform more tasks. Putting workers under more pressure to finish pieces in a very limited time forced them to work without taking breaks to use the bathroom, eat, or drink, which in turn led to health problems such as kidney failure and urinary tract infection. Physical exhaustion caused some workers to cough up or vomit blood, and many suffered from repetitive strain injuries.

It is important to note that although subcontracting employment may be viewed as a "temporary" form of employment due to the high burnout rate and other variable factors, many women seek to make this new form of employment a "permanent" one, especially in a volatile job market and "unstable" economy.

F2's Subcontract Factories

After 1998, F2 dispersed a greater proportion of its production to its two subsidiaries while it laid off almost 80 percent of its core workforce, drop-ping from 800 down to 150 workers at its original location by 2001.[15] One subcontract factory, SF1, employed around 400 women, and the other, SF2, around 600.[16] Both factories are located in the northeastern provinces, in Korat and Ubon Ratchatani respectively. SF1, which has an ordering relationship with Nike, subcontracts parts of its large orders to SF2, an indication of the flexibility and adaptability of peripheralized production processes.

I was told by Pik that F2 had had some twenty subcontracting factories during the peak period, which enabled the factory to take in "all kinds of orders no matter how large." But having shut most of them down, F2 became reliant upon its two remaining subcontract factories and could handle only "two to three brand labels at a time." The decline in the total number of F2's factories, as precipitated by the market, did not reduce labor productivity but did, in effect, allow management to command higher productivity via unlawful means of control and coercion. Nay reported that both SF1 and SF2 were hiring more workers to keep up with high overseas demand for ready-made apparel but had not been paying workers' wages on time. She discovered that the women at SF1 and SF2 were making 150 baht (US$3.57 at the 1999–2000 rate of 42 baht = US$1.00) per day on average, a rate 12 baht (US$0.29) short of the minimum wage, and were subject to a great deal of abuse and misconduct by management. Working conditions were described by an employee of SF1 in a 1999 phone conversation with Nay:

> All benefits such as year-end bonuses and diligence pay which workers are entitled to, other than the basic salary, have been rescinded. Workers are forced to sign a factory-issued document before taking sick leave or leave of absence, stating that "she will take X number of days off without pay." The factory does not provide mandatory health benefits even though it automatically deducts social security fees from workers' salaries, forcing workers to pay for any medical services out of their own pockets and seek reimbursement from the factory. Hospitals would refuse to offer treatment, claiming that the factory had not paid its dues. The factory refuses to pay for the two sets of uniforms and two pairs of shoes required for each worker, forcing workers to purchase them with their salaries.[17]

Much like the conditions at F2 before unionization, the subcontract factories had no operational fire alarm systems, constant water leaks from the rain, and poor roofing. The factories had an insufficient number of toilet facilities for the hundreds of employees, and they lacked ventilation and purified drinking water. They provided no dormitory facilities, even though they are located in desolate and hence potentially dangerous areas. Neither factory offered adequate transportation for their workers: a smaller van came to replace the large bus that had been used to transport workers when the factories first opened, and the number of vans declined.

Both factories forced women to work overtime by ordering the pickup vans not to come until after a certain time, and anyone not willing to stay was called into the office and threatened with dismissal—a situation much like that mentioned in chapter 2, where factory pickup vans were ordered not to come until workers had completed their overtime workload. At the subcontract factories, however, workers had no other way of leaving the premises *except* by factory transportation.

Pik and Nay hoped to help the women at F2's subcontract factories set up a labor union but found that the workers were too fearful of losing their jobs. Furthermore, their geographical isolation prevented them from making contact with other labor unions and workers' groups for the assistance and information they needed in order to mobilize. Nay attributed lack of worker mobilization at these factories also to the provincial background of young workers: "Their primary concern is to make money," she said.

In essence, subcontracting production in the apparel industry represented a new form of enslavement of low-wage, female laborers who were physically and psychologically induced to produce as much as they were capable of in return for subsistence. Factory workers were turned into "new slaves" in a production system that coercively forced them to work as much as possible for less than minimum wage and in the absence of any form of job security. Thus the "extraction of absolute surplus value"[18] was no longer limited to the commodification of human life in occupations usually associated with sexual or criminal exploitation but expanded to industrial workers in the periphery whose entire existence became commodified and rendered "disposable" under the piece-rate system of production.[19] Women were selling not just their labor power but also their bodies, their health, and their well-being in the effort to produce maximally and meet a quota that provided less than the minimum wage.

Worsening Conditions at F2

From 1998 on, women at F2 witnessed a return to pre-union conditions of work and continued to labor under such deteriorated conditions: cracked walls, absence of safety measures (no fire alarm system or emergency lights, locked emergency exits, an electricity controller that occasionally exploded), dirty toilets, and the constant stench of manure from a nearby farm that permeated the work area. Being confined inside a solid block building with poor ventilation made the work environment "unbearably hot, dusty, and stuffy." The factory no longer provided clean and cold drinking water, and workers were now earning their wages by piece-rate for whatever they could produce.[20]

Harvey's illumination of a labor market structure in a period of high market volatility, heightened competition, and lower profits can be used to describe what was happening in Thailand as well as throughout export-producing countries in East Asia in the post-crisis period of economic recession. Harvey explains the intricacies of flexible employment arrangements in a competitive global labor market:

> The potential costs of laying off core employees in times of difficulty may, however, lead a company to sub-contract even high level functions...leaving the core group of managers relatively small. The *periphery* encompasses two rather different sub-groups. The first consists of "full-time employees with skills that are readily available in the labor market, such as clerical, secretarial, routine and lesser skilled manual work."...The second peripheral group "provides even greater numerical flexibility and includes part-timers, casuals, fixed term contract staff, temporaries, sub-contractors and public subsidy trainees, with even less job security than the first peripheral group."[21]

Even though Harvey develops a world systems perspective of global labor market structures, whereby flexible accumulation within the core is facilitated at the expense of the periphery, there are marked parallels between Harvey's delineation of flexible employment arrangements at the macro level and the intricacies of the subcontracting arrangement at the local firm level. In my conversations with workers I discovered that in the case of F2, the core workforce consisted of the more skilled workers at the original factory location, while the workers at F2's two subcontract factories made up the peripheral group of workers. All were full-time employees, but neither group had job security. The core F2 workers considered themselves "more skilled" than the neophytes at the subcontract factories who, they said, performed "very simple" tasks in contrast to the more "complex and meticulous" tasks demanded at F2. Workers at F2 attributed their skills to their extensive training and experience on the job: "We have been doing it for a longer time—sewing, that is. The subcontract factory accepts inexperienced women who are poorly trained." Moreover, these inexperienced new workers had become disposable human commodities that could easily be replaced, considering the high unemployment rate, under a factory system that offered no employment contracts or worker protection.

As Pik recalled the volume of work that was coming in during the massive layoffs at F2, she inadvertently described some distinct features that differentiated the two classifications of workers: "One time, F2 received an order for 300,000 pieces, which were immediately sent out to the subcontract factories, but all the final stages of inspecting and repairing the items were done at F2, because the workers are considered to be more skilled. With a huge order like this, subcontract workers were expected to complete 300 pieces a day. A quota was first set at 150 items just to make sure that the workers could do it, and then they increased the number of pieces until workers got used to the pace and could produce 300."[22] There seem to be perceived differences in skill and ability on the part of F2 workers whose "new" tasks are highly exploitive, not only in terms of quantity but in terms of quality by way of the difficulty and precision involved in inspecting and repairing assembled garments. Under the new arrangement, however, F2 workers were also subcontract workers, since they too were paid by the piece. Thom offered a sample of the kind of work allocation F2 managed for its two subcontract factories and for itself: "If F2 received an order for 10,000 items, they would keep 3,000 items at the factory and disperse the remaining 7,000 to SF1 and SF2. Before these two factories opened, F2 would take in everything. We received 100,000 orders once, and the overtime pay per hour was 31 baht. Those days are long gone. Now the factory gives workers the 'option' of setting their own wages. You could choose to do 100 items for 30 baht, 40 baht or even 15 baht, depending upon the type of order that comes in."

Thom's description denoted the highly flexible and spontaneous nature of work allocation, which lay within the complete discretion of management but also within the discretion of workers, who were given the option of determining the type of work they wanted to perform, which in turn determined the wages they would earn for the day. Pik compared the structure of production at F2 during the "export boom," when there had been up to ten production *njuads* (lines) of production at the factory, with the transition to the piece-rate system as the factory reduced the size of its workforce: "Back then, one *njuad* had about thirty workers and each *njuad* had to finish 300 items per day as required. Each worker had a specific task: one worker would line the pockets, another would sew in the collar, and someone else would sew on the shirtsleeves. But once the number of workers was reduced, the tasks became condensed, leaving one worker to perform more than one task: sew in the sleeves and then the collar, which is very difficult to do."

With a single worker eventually performing the same amount of work as five women did before, according to Pik, these *njuads* decreased steadily over the years, from thirty to only two *njuads* of production. As a result, the volume and pace of work kept the workers from having time to eat, drink, or use the bathroom. One woman said that if someone really needed to use the restroom, she would "literally run to the restroom and back to her work station." Moreover, this system has fostered tension and animosity among the workers, as individual women compete with each other to see who could do the largest batch of work and thus receive the highest wage. For instance, a worker may be paid anywhere from 12 to 40 baht ($0.29–$0.95) per 100 pieces, depending upon the degree of difficulty of the item. This system of production thereby had some very significant implications for the relations between workers and the possibilities for worker mobilization. As workers competed with each other individually for piecework, cooperative work relations greatly diminished.

F2 workers were no longer able to rely on high overtime wages, since they were assembling by the piece, and work orders were being dispersed to the subcontract factories. Meanwhile, this system of production at F2 proved physically harmful to the women. As Pik related, "Some women suffered from bone frailty [*kra dook suaham*] that was due to the heavier workload. And because there were fewer workers, women were faced with more tasks while their wages were being pressed down as workdays decreased and working hours lengthened per day. Physically, workers' bodies just couldn't take it, and this is why there was such a high burnout rate." Indeed, there had been several cases of women voluntarily leaving the factory because of physical exhaustion, in addition to the factory's own layoffs, the cutback on overtime, and wage violations (postponement of wages or refusal to pay wages).

What is important to emphasize here is the phenomenon of labor turnover that resulted from excessive physical demand, which had not been a common occurrence at the factory prior to the crisis. A "temporary" workforce of "full-time" workers emerged as a direct result of the new structural conditions imposed at the factory. With this system of production, the *nai jarng* essentially deprived workers of attending to their immediate physical needs while at the same time squeezing the most out of the fewest number of workers. This is an excellent example of overt exploitation disguised as a covert mechanism of control over labor, which results in a higher degree of exploitation but a lower potential for worker resistance. Workers were no longer selling just their labor power; they were selling *themselves*—that is, their health and their well-being—to produce maximally while being meagerly compensated. At the same time, because they were competing with other commodified and disposable bodies, they no longer had the power to strike or demonstrate. As the former system of assembly line production was replaced with piecework, workers were concerned with short-term survival, not long-term careers at the factory. Meanwhile, employers were no longer obligated toward their workers, since workers existed only for the number of pieces they could deliver. An owner not responsible for the health and well-being of his workforce does not see the need to provide employees with food, rest, or drink.

These conditions were not unlike those described by Chawkieng at the Hara Textiles sweatshop where she worked in the mid-1970s:

> Back then I used to work from 7:00 a.m. to 6:00 p.m. because it was a piece-rate job. This meant we were all turned into enemies [*saat tru*] against each other because our wages for the day depended on how much work we were able to take on. So every morning there was a race to get to the factory to see who could be the first to choose the best batch of work, which meant less or more money for the day. And we would work without looking up once from our work stations, 11 hours straight. Because back then, you could make up to 100 baht a day, and when the newcomers saw that other women could do it, they wanted to do it too. The work environment then was such that taking time out to eat meant a lot of money out of your pocket, and during that time I had three children to feed.

At Hara, however, the employer provided rice for his workers during their lunch break (even though the rice was not edible), but at that time there was a high demand for workers in export industries. In the recent situation, workers were easily disposable and replaceable, especially since a large majority of women were unemployed. Nonetheless, Chawkieng's account illuminates the competitive nature of piecework, which operated against cooperation and worker solidarity. Similarly, Prayao, whom I have categorized as a "militant" worker, described the brutality of piece-rate work at the small factory where she was employed:

> There are a few girls here that work themselves to near death just to make the maximum possible a month. I don't know how they do it. There's this one girl who works so much she makes 10,000 baht a month (US$230) to help pay off her family's debts. She wouldn't sleep because she would work until 5:00 a.m., and she's so skinny because she wouldn't eat. She would work nonstop from 8:00 a.m. to 5:00 p.m. and from 10:00 p.m. to 5:00 a.m. and continue again from 6:00 a.m. to noon for any rush orders [*ngarn leng*]. A few women work like this, and I don't understand how they can. If I could work like that, I would.

This new form of "enslavement" is detrimental to women's health and well-being, yet it seems that women such as Prayao would nevertheless subject themselves to such a punishing situation, if they were physically capable, to receive higher wages. The pace and intensity of work is not unlike the situation faced by women workers in post–WWII São Paulo, described by French and Cluff as follows: "In one factory section, women were having difficulty meeting the base piece-rate quota, because management was running the machines at too fast a pace. Moreover, women were constantly threatened with suspension by foremen for failing to meet quotas and were criticized for not being able to carry out the heavy work demanded."[23] At the factory in São Paulo, operated on a piecework system, women were forced by direct coercion and intimidation to work at too fast a pace and were expected to meet daily production quotas. The piecework system was set up differently in São Paulo because the women were not given the same financial incentive (i.e., the option of choosing the more difficult and higher-paying items or of setting one's own daily quota) which "motivated" the women in Thai factories. Either way, it appears that the working environment to which women were subjected in labor-intensive industries had not changed over five decades. For F2, this structure of production was more cost effective and worked much more efficiently than a system that subjected workers to direct forms of control, such as the one that had been in place during the early days of F2's operation.

Thom considered this piece-rate system of production to be a very unfair and uneven process for labor because it created resentment and hostility among the workers, since the rates were not the same. She said that this system was "so out of control" that it made workers "crazy" and "exhausted" and at the same time created such an atmosphere of greed that the women fought over the work orders. Those who could cope "worked themselves nearly to death" trying to make almost the same pay they had once earned for overtime work. In addition, the very rapid pace at which they had to produce resulted in many defects in some items, and the workers were penalized individually. Some defects are unavoidable, but the factory's imposition of fines and penalties to hold the workers personally responsible for defective items increased the pressure even further. A monetary fine would automatically take from a workers' wages 81 baht (US$1.93) for every 400 baht (US$9.52), and workers were forced to sign a contract accepting this arrangement. These monetary penalties are especially hurtful given the reduced wages at F2, and they caused elevated levels of stress and anxiety for the women. Thom provided a breakdown of the wages that workers were paid in the piecework system: "We would receive 12 baht [US$0.29] for every 100 pieces, which is about 120 baht [US$2.90] for 1,000 pieces, and that is a lot of production for very little money. Today, they even cut out the overtime, so I took the rest of the day off to run some errands, and then I have to start again tomorrow and work until 8:00 p.m. Our most recent order was for 100,000 kids' jackets, which we just completed."

Pik, who regularly met with the remaining F2 workers at the workers' center, expressed her concern about the women who were working "without getting any sleep and walking around like zombies." Pik recalled one afternoon when more than a hundred women collapsed from exhaustion and were taken to a nearby hospital. The activist women believed that the conditions of work at the subcontract factories were much worse even than what they were at F2 before the establishment of the first workers' union, and they did not feel optimistic about workers organizing to demand changes at these factories. Sripai believed that employers used divisive managerial tactics to hinder the formation of labor unions or to weaken existing unions, whose strength rested upon unity among its members.

According to Nukul Kokhit and Wanee Thitiprasert, some unions did not dare confront management for fear that the employer might turn to other subcontract factories and sack noncompliant workers.[24] Remaining F2 workers lived in constant uncertainty and fear of losing their jobs and therefore continued to labor under harmful and stressful conditions. In many ways, in the context of worsening structural conditions, the workers were subdued and effectively "disciplined" by the shift in the production process. Still, such harsh physical conditions of work provoked a collective sentiment of fearlessness among some women, who would engage in spontaneous acts of rebellion, even though their actions were no longer comparable to the traditional "militant" labor tactics they had used in the past. Rather, their actions against the employer were directed primarily toward their working conditions and were limited to walkouts, work stoppages, and, in rare instances, quitting.

Nay and Pik found that a few acts of spontaneous retaliation did arise when workers could no longer take the abuse, especially when already fatigued women were forced to work additional hours at short notice. Pik relayed such an instance: "The women were very much aware that they were being taken advantage of, so they would simply refuse to work late. When the day was over at 5:00 p.m., they would all get up together and leave the factory. This happened on a few occasions at F2, but it really all depended on how the women felt and how they reacted at that particular moment."

In an interview with the regional director of the AFL-CIO headquarters in Bangkok, Phil Robertson recalled visiting factories in Cambodia and the high levels of exploitation of young girls aged 16–18 who were working in shoe factories. These girls faced constant physical and verbal abuse by factory owners and supervisors and would "gang up" to fight back. Robertson described an instance of spontaneous worker rebellion: "A girl was called into the office and was forced to sign a document. When she refused to sign, they called in the male security guards to intimidate her, but the other workers stopped what they were doing and surrounded the office until their co-worker was released." Such spontaneous acts of rebellion were instances of worker reaction to an immediate situation, however, and did not signify any long-term commitment to organized struggle. In Cambodia, where factory jobs have become plentiful and workers have "nothing to lose," such spontaneous outbursts usually stem from a sense of fearlessness among young workers, and also from complete physical exhaustion on the part of women who have no legal or institutional outlets to turn to.

State Complacency

William Robinson posits that "an analysis of the power of the capitalist ruling class must take into account the state and the political process. . . . With regard to globalization and the transnational capitalist class, this means ensuring the reproduction of global capitalist relations of production as well as the creation and reproduction of political and cultural institutions favorable to its rule, *central among which is the state.* . . . Under globalization, I suggest, the capitalist state has increasingly acquired the form of a transnational state."[25] In the national context, key domestic capitalists act within the framework of the transnational state in a capitalist global economy and its practices are put into place at the factory level. Pasuk Phongpaichit and Chris Baker indicate that leaders of the Thai textile industry were key players in lobbying the government for changes in its industrialization strategy in the early 1970s. Until the 1970s, domestic capitalists showed little interest in export manufacturing, but as economic growth slowed in a global recession in the late 1970s, exporting seemed a favorable option, and employers organized to put pressure on the government to improve export production. As the authors note, the Association of Thai Industries, formed in 1967, became more active, and, in 1977, along with the Thai Bankers Association, petitioned the government to form a regular government-business standing committee to discuss economic policies. This marked the beginning of a mutually interdependent working relation between the state and capital. Capitalist employers were able to exert influence and control over government policymaking, and by 1978, they were successful in persuading the Bank of Thailand "to give preferential credit on textile exports," and the Ministry of Finance "to grant refunds on taxes and tariffs levied on inputs." Subsequently, textile and garment companies from Japan, Hong Kong, and Taiwan relocated production to Thailand, along with other labor-intensive segments of high-tech industries such as semiconductor production and computer assembly. In the mid-1970s, a minimum wage, machinery for dispute settlement, and social security law had been introduced. The Thai state has had a long history of union suppression that accompanied foreign direct investment and the expansion of local manufacturing industries. Phongpaichit and Baker indicate that throughout the 1990s, the government continued to prevent a revival in labor organization by conceding to businesses while suppressing labor. In 1991, the state legally banned public sector unions.[26]

Under directives of the IMF during the administration of Prime Minister Chuan Leekpai, immediately following the financial crisis, foreigners were allowed many investment privileges in the nonfinancial sectors of the economy. The state was also directed to keep interest rates high in order to discourage foreign capital from leaving the country, and to cut back on government expenditures in order to achieve a budget surplus. Bello and his colleagues stipulate that Thailand's rapid growth during the mid-1980s to mid-1990s was accompanied not by industrial and technological deepening but by multinational corporate investment, which left the country with a large reserve of cheap, "unskilled" female labor that was quickly absorbed into the country's export manufacturing industries, particularly in textiles and electronics. In the aftermath of the crisis, "Thailand's manufacturers took the easy way out: relying on ever cheaper labor, . . . reducing the size of factories to contain production costs and inhibit unionizing, and farming out more and more production to temporary workers, contract workers, and migrant workers." Hence, the trend toward casualization and subcontracting resulted in the increase of temporary and subcontract workers outside the Bangkok area, especially after labor disputes or unionization efforts at factories.[27]

Although the Department of Social Welfare and Labour Protection inspected companies for labor violations, they often underreported their findings, seldom held companies accountable, and penalized only a small fraction of those that seriously violated labor legislation (especially in regard to wages and work conditions). With over 2 million people out of work following the crisis, large numbers of urban industrial workers participated in rallies and demonstrations in support of workers' rights in the drafting of the country's new constitution. Because workers were not provided with the proper channels to express their grievances, they often had to resort to militant forms of action in order to make their demands heard. But "organized action continued to be hindered by the fragmentation and rivalries in the labor force."[28] Consequently, a riot erupted at the Sanyo Auto Plant which ended in the arrest of hundreds of workers.

Even before the crisis, the Thai government had "paid little attention to policing the labor law, and provided scant protection for unions against management aggression," as Phongpaichit and Baker indicated. The result was an upsurge of labor activity in the early 1990s which fell "in line with the growth and growing importance of the urban work-force. In 1992 and 1993, more workdays were lost to strikes than any year since 1976."[29] These are the two significant periods I document in this book: the Hara factory demonstration in 1976 and the militant labor activities that took place in the Rangsit industrial zone, led by women at F2 during the early to mid-1990s. But the implementation and enforcement of even minimal labor regulations continued to be weak and inadequate. According to Junya Yimprasert and Christopher Candland, large corporate manufacturers and their subcontractors in Thailand were required to abide by corporate "codes of conduct," defined as a "set of labor standards to which producers were expected to adhere."[30] Manufacturers that had codes of conduct, however, were often unable to provide any protection for workers, "largely because enforcement [was] voluntary and generally internally monitored. Information on cases of violations is kept within the company." Moreover, corporate codes of conduct did not "guarantee workers' rights to form unions."[31] During a tripartite conference in 2000, the deputy director of the Labour Protection and Welfare Department admitted that "official authorities have been very lenient with many manufacturers and would go to investigate the plants only if there was a request."[32]

Meanwhile, as they did in the mid-1970s and early 1990s, labor leaders continued to organize and to seek support through NGOs and other informal channels to help protect them from repressive laws and antagonist forces, but they were facing increasingly more difficult circumstances. Thitiprasert, for instance, says that many workers did not receive compensation without appealing to courts and that many labor unions did not have leaders strong enough to make effective appeals on behalf of the workers.[33] Many union leaders were subjected to death threats or dismissal, and were prohibited from entering factory premises.

In short, complacent legal and political institutions empowered factory owners to use the crisis and recession as an excuse to consolidate more gains and to extract more work from workers for less cost. State authorities were not only complicit with employers but tried to persuade employees to make compromises with their bosses. In essence, legal complacency benefited capitalist employers, who presented themselves as the best way to "save" the state from recession. Citing the case of one such factory in Rangsit, Yimprasert asserts that this is a "good example of the lack of concern on the part of state authorities and their indifferent attitude on labor dispute cases in general."[34] Various forms of local corruption also caused a significant reduction in the protection and welfare of workers.

What Was Happening at Factory One

The *rahb mao* (piecework) system did not come into place at F1. The only imposed condition of work at F1 was the reduction of overtime work on weekdays and the elimination of overtime work on Sundays, but these changes were due to a significant decline in work orders from the company's overseas clients. They were big setbacks for the workers, however, who could no longer make as much extra income from overtime. The women said that even when there were huge work orders, management refused to let them work on Sundays, in order to avoid paying the double wage; instead, they squeezed the workload into a six-day work week with some overtime. Women reacted by intentionally working at a much slower pace so as to have the work spill over into Sunday overtime. This collective act of manipulation by the more accommodating F1 workers might be compared with the similarly desperate acts of rebellion at F2, except that at F1, the women were working to defend their wages rather than acting against a physically intensive production process. In a sense, this signifies relevant forms of resistance on the part of the women: that is, the cutting down on an essential aspect of the production process that the women had become highly dependent upon. In a collective effort, the women figured out a discreet way to subvert the assembly line in order to take back the wages that had been "taken away" from them.

Silver distinguishes between overt acts of resistance, whereby actors openly challenge exploitation, and hidden forms in which actors engage in subtle forms of resistance.[35] In his study of the *maquila* industry and women workers employed in the *maquiladoras* along the U.S.-Mexican border, Devon Peña found that a significant proportion of workers informally participated in the struggle against work speedup at their factories.[36] So, while workers at F2 engaged in direct forms of protest such as strikes and demonstrations to demand higher wages and fewer working hours, women at F1 were slowing down production in order to extend their overtime hours and increase their wages.

My initial interviews with the women at F1 took place just one year after the July 1997 devaluation of the Thai currency. The effects of the crisis were particularly severe as inflation rose, following the IMF financial bailout, while wages remained the same, forcing many women to cope with higher costs of living. Women had to make cutbacks on household spending by trying to purchase cheaper products in the market. Sri from F1 said that after the factory cut down on overtime work, many women had been borrowing money from each other, from relatives, or from loan sharks. The overall slowdown in production since 1997 meant that the women at F1 were working only eight hours a day and thus had more "time off" but very little money to spend in their increased leisure time. As Kuh explained, "Most women *want* to work overtime. We used to work sixteen-hour days when the factory was receiving heavy work orders, and now we are working half that many hours which means that our salaries have been cut in half."

Interestingly, women at F1 wanted to prolong their working hours at the factory, since they suffered drastic wage reductions from the slowdown in production and hence regarded a shortened workday as detrimental to their livelihood. Overt forms of exploitation were not as evident at F1 as at F2, however, perhaps because F1 was a relatively smaller textile establishment and had not had to resort to piecework; apparel exports to F1's major European customers were less affected by the crisis. On the other hand, F2's large multinational clients were able to outsource to other lower-wage countries in their global production supply chain, given that the Thai economy was deemed unstable at the time. F2 therefore resorted to the piece-rate system as a way to cut costs and cope with the crisis, which resulted in more exploitative conditions for its remaining workers. At F1, the decrease in orders from its overseas markets during the crisis forced the factory to cut down on overtime, which was considered by workers to be a fairly "legitimate" move. But since workers had become wholly dependent on overtime work for their survival, and because the factory owner simply expected workers to "bite the bullet like everyone else," many F1 workers became doubly exploited as they took on other jobs to supplement their lower income.

Accordingly, women at both factories suffered by way of longer working hours, while neither factory was acting in the interest of its workers (even though there were no layoffs at F1). In the post-crisis period, worker consciousness was being shaped by these marked shifts in production: harsher work conditions led to alienation and accommodation for women in one setting but to adaptation and manipulation on the part of the women in the other. F1 women had become increasingly discontent and insecure about their situation and wanted to see a return to times when the work volume was at its peak, women were staying up until midnight to complete orders, and abundant overtime pay greatly inflated their wages.

Adaptation and Survival in the Post-Crisis Period

In response to the query of what the women at F1 did in their free time from the factory, especially on Sunday, Tuy said that overtime pay affected single and married women differently: unmarried women could live without overtime pay even though they still had to be careful about their spending. But married women, who generally bore a heavier financial burden, were always strapped for cash and found it very difficult to live without the extra income. Most women preferred to stay at home to rest and said that the "extra time" allowed them to do housework. Yet they maintained that their "lives hadn't changed all that much." I proposed to the women an ideal work scenario: If they were required to work only five days a week, what would they do with the two days off? The women responded that they would use that time to earn extra money.

Many F1 women did take on extra jobs on their days off rather than hold the factory accountable for providing them with adequate wages. Likewise, Leslie Sklair found that in Mexico in the late 1980s, the intensity of the debt crisis forced many *maquila* workers to put in even longer hours to support themselves and their families.[37] Before the crisis, the women in my study never had to worry about taking on alternative jobs; the factory was their only source of income and provided them with the possibility of increasing their wages through overtime work. Their immediate concern with making more money perpetuated their belief that work was the only way out of poverty, and it was this belief that signified a change in women's attitudes. In writing about the similarities between two machine shops that used the piece-rate system, Burawoy notes that workers exerted extra effort once they "thought it was possible to survive under a piece-rate system." There was a causal relation, then, between a worker's willing participation in the labor process and her complete dependency on earning wages, which became her only priority. And as Burawoy indicates, this practical need to earn a living "came to overwhelm all other experiences on the shop floor."[38]

As noted in chapter 1, the system of overtime created a binding economic dependency between labor and wages that forced women to "willingly" work long hours for the high overtime pay. In the post-crisis period, women at F1 all echoed the same sentiment with regard to their lower wages: "When we were making so much money, we never had the time to spend it. But now that we have all this time, we can't afford to enjoy it!" This irony was best summed up by Boonyuun: "I don't know which is better, to have money and be exhausted, or to have less work and nothing to live on."

"Our wages don't even balance out with the cost of living," Khae said angrily. During the crisis, workers' wages did not increase proportionately with the exorbitant rise in the cost of living, which is why women were forced to find ways to make extra income. Puan told me that "one has to *tham jai* [prepare yourself] for anything to survive in this economy." For the most part, women complained that their wages were not sufficient to accommodate the increase in living expenses, especially the inflated prices of basic food staples. As a condition of the $17.2 billion bailout package from the IMF, the Thai currency had been devalued (from 25 to 42 baht to US$1.00); interest rates had been raised; and the price of local labor had been reduced. From their interviews with workers at unionized factories in Thailand, Yimprasert and Hveem report that even though unionized workers usually earn more than the minimum wage, they receive only an estimated 0.4–0.5 percent of the total retail value of the garments they manufactured. Yimprasert and Hveem argued that workers in Thailand do not get paid a living wage:

The minimum wage in Thailand increased only 40 baht between 1994 and 2004, while the currency exchange rate dropped 80–100 percent from 25 baht per dollar to 39–50 baht per US dollar since the economic crisis of 1997. . . . In 2004, Thai workers' monthly salary was US$91–111.80 (US$3.5–4.3 per day x 26 days). Yet the Thai government has refused to increase the minimum wage to the level of 200 baht that the Thai labor movement has been demanding. Instead, it has responded by increasing the minimum wage by just 1 baht in 2004 and 5 baht in 2005 (0.6% in 2004 and 2.9% in 2005)....In Korat province, this total wage just covers basic expenses, such as a plate of rice, a coffee a day, accommodation costs and transport to work for a worker, which together totals 90% of the 2004 minimum wage in that area which is 145 baht per day = 3,770 baht per month (26 working days).[39]

The monthly salary that a worker earned on the daily minimum wage in 2005, then, was not enough for other necessary expenditures such as utilities, food, basic personal items, and money to support their families. It was thus no surprise that workers worked overtime hours, took on other jobs, and were constantly in debt.

In assessing the impacts of NAFTA on the *maquilas*, Sklair found that even though *maquila* workers along the border earned higher wages than workers in the interior, the cost of living and the rate of inflation in the main *maquila* areas were higher than elsewhere in Mexico. At the same time, "one cannot say whether the *maquila* worker is better or worse off than the worker in a Mexican *nonmaquila* factory or in any other occupation" without comparing what a typical *maquila* worker buys with what a typical non-*maquila* worker buys.[40] In Thailand, cutbacks in government spending and the prohibitive cost of food have hurt women workers, whose wages were already low. The usual neoliberal argument in justification of starvation wages is that lower wages in a poor country go a longer way than they would elsewhere, but this does not take into account the prices of the things poor people buy.[41] Taa, who made 8,000–9,000 baht per month (US$190–214) during the boom years, now makes only 5,000 to 6,000 baht (US$119–143) without the overtime in her department. She no longer spends much money on herself and has become more stringent with her earnings. As she explained, "Several years ago, we had lower wages but we made more money because we worked for longer hours, and the cost of living was a lot lower. Today, we have a higher minimum wage but a lot less work, which means very little money, while the cost of living has gone up more than ever."

The majority of the F1 women in my sample admitted the many difficulties they had encountered in trying to make ends meet but nevertheless insisted that they had been able to control their finances and had "adjusted well" to the effects of the crisis. According to these women, surviving in this period of job insecurity was not easy but made them become "more resourceful, independent, confident, and responsible." Such self-described characteristics pointed to women's collective determination to adapt to new working situations in order to cope with the increased cost of living and the decline in wages. Women had simply been forced to face increasingly difficult circumstances beyond their control, and perhaps a sense of false consciousness surfaced among F1 women who had made themselves believe that they should be grateful for having their jobs. In many ways, the ideological effects of the labor market produced ideological effects on the labor process by placing value on individual perseverance, hard work, determination, and ingenuity.

The crisis most adversely affected married women with dependents whose husbands had been laid off from their jobs. These women had to find other ways to supplement their income, such as waking before dawn to prepare food that they could sell. Kuh would get up at 4:00 a.m. every day to prepare food to sell in small bags to her co-workers, so that her twelve-year-old daughter would have pocket money for school. Malee, who had two boys, started selling packaged lunches to supplement her income. Her husband would buy fresh produce from the market every morning, and Malee would prepare the dishes her co-workers had requested the day before.

To save money, Dao would walk back to her rented room around the corner from the factory during her lunch break to eat with her roommate and older sister, both of whom worked at F1. They no longer bought ready-made food or ate out but opted instead to prepare a quick hot meal using a portable electric pan on the floor of their 12-by-8 room. When the factory began cutting down on overtime hours, Dao decided to supplement her income by making a chili shrimp paste to sell to co-workers and other friends. Meanwhile, her roommate and partner, Nong, had been working weekends as a door-to-door distributor of health food products and other miscellaneous items. Both women were obligated to send money home. "Since we've had this freed-up time, I wanted do something worthwhile," said Dao.

Though not subjected to the kind of oppressive conditions that were in place at F2 and its subcontract factories through piecework, F1 women nevertheless experienced as physically demanding the part-time employment during the week or on weekends that added to their already long hours at the factory. But supplementing their full-time factory wages with extra jobs—in multiple occupations, ranging from preparing homemade food to sell during the week to part-time sales for other businesses on the weekends—had become necessary for survival in the post-crisis period.

The high incidence of women working two or more jobs in addition to their domestic duties was becoming commonplace even in industrialized countries such as the United States. Arlie Hochschild points to the rising number of women who had children but were working full-time and cites a study that found working mothers to be most deeply affected by family stress. Like Thai factory workers, U.S. working parents were more likely to put in longer hours on the job because they needed the money, and those who worked in factories were expected to improve and increase their own production levels.[42]

Fear in a Time of Crisis

Malee said that she and her workers were initially "jealous" (*itch chaah*) of women at factories that gave out bonuses, but their awareness of layoffs at other factories had made them feel "lucky" and "secure." F1 did not lay off any of its workers but had reduced the work hours. "Everyone is grateful to *seya lek* [junior factory boss] for letting us keep our jobs," she admitted. This general feeling of complicity and relief pointed to an imbued sense of fearfulness *and* gratefulness among F1 women, whereas a collective sentiment of fearlessness had prompted women at other factories to become more outspoken and risk dismissal (such as in spontaneous acts of rebellion at F2). Women at both factories were well aware of their vulnerable situation in the labor market. They knew of the layoffs of workers throughout the industry, and it was this real awareness that forced workers to harbor such conflicting feelings toward their employment and their increasingly difficult situations. The reactions of workers in each of the two different factory settings were thereby consistent with their collective identity and individual predispositions, as outlined in chapters 1 and 2. F1 women, aware of the massive layoffs of workers at other textile factories, were afraid that their factory might close down and were riddled with anxiety about what they would end up doing. Many women said that if they were laid off, they would not look for another job, given their low qualifications, and would probably return home and start their own businesses. Several women said they would use the skills they had acquired in their factory job to open up their own clothing shops.

For women at F1, the possibility of being laid off was the greatest threat to their livelihood, but they seemed to exhibit a reassured sense of optimism, reinforced by their trust and respect for their *seya lek*, who had not laid off anyone from the factory at that point. F1 was still one of the leading manufacturers of men's underwear in Thailand, and its successful brand label captured a large share of this niche in the domestic market. F1 was thereby able to rely upon continuing local demand for the quality undergarments that were assembled at F1. Even though overseas work orders had declined, the factory's local niche market protected the business during a period of instability in the global market. F2, on the other hand, was completely dependent upon export production for the global market. Because there continued to be a steady worldwide demand for ready-to-wear, brand-name fashion and sports apparel, multinational companies were able to rely on other manufacturers within their global supply chain. Even while F2 was still receiving orders from its major clients, the factory took this opportunity (i.e., a vulnerable market situation) to protect itself by downsizing the workforce and outsourcing production to lower-cost, non-unionized workers in industrializing rural provinces. Yimprasert and Candland indicated that many laid-off workers turned to subcontracting, including women from F2 who, though knowing that they would receive lower wages, felt they had no alternative.[43]

At F1, fear and anxiety in a time of crisis and economic recession produced a more compliant and accommodating workforce, whereas physical exhaustion and fearlessness at F2 prompted high labor turnover and/or retaliation against the employer. At F1, longtime workers still wanted to hold on to their jobs, whereas F2 workers certainly felt the crushing effect of global competition as downsizing, subcontracting, and harsher conditions of work were unleashed on them.

New and Unimproved: Post-Crisis Structural Conditions

Aside from factory closures and the hundreds of unlawful dismissals from factories in the industrial zones, employers had been using loopholes in the labor laws to their advantage. One popular statute, Article 75 of the Thai Labour Protection Act (*maatra jet sib hah*) was passed in 1997 in response to the economic crisis. This statute essentially granted employers the right to implement temporary shutdowns, or cut down factory operations to four or five days a week, but it required employers to pay workers 50 percent of their wages while production was stopped. The stipulation read: "In the event that any employer must stop its operations, either permanently or temporarily...the employer is allowed to pay the employee not less than fifty percent of their wage and at the rate the employee received before the date of notice of closure and for the whole period that the employee is not working."[44]

Before Article 75 was enacted, any employer who wanted to shut down a production line temporarily had been liable for the workers' full wages. With Article 75, the employer could impose 50 percent reductions in wages at any time and for any amount of time, and, more important, could impose these reductions against specific workers or specific units in the factory (such as a part of the production line that strongly supported the union). Many manufacturers used this loophole by temporarily stopping production so as not to pay any wages to workers during those shutdowns. If workers protested and took their grievances to court, however, the employer would likely be found liable to pay the workers at least 50 percent of their wages for those days.

In essence, then, Article 75 was wielded by employers to reduce wages, but it was also an effective weapon against workers who tried to organize, since they could barely live on just half of their wages. According to the Ministry of Labour, Article 75 was adopted for cases of natural disasters, such as floods, which could shut down a factory for a week, but instead, it opened the door wide for flexibility on the part of business owners.

F2 had been abusing this clause since September 1998, when management announced that the factory would sporadically suspend operations.[45] In their meeting over *maatra 75*, Saneh, Pik, Sripai, and Taan accused the F2 employer of "reckless" use of the labor law by citing "poor economic conditions" as a justification to stop production, especially since the factory was benefiting from piece-rate work. Former F2 women were no longer hopeful about the situation, and Sripai pointed out that there had been no progress in dealing with the issue: "Employers' manipulation of the law made it very difficult for workers and their struggle, and employers just hoped to get away with it. And those who were able to react to it were those who know about the law, like the people in this room, but they were not employed in factories. The only thing we could do was to analyze the situation and understand how the law works so that we were better able to confront it."

Factory Two had always used various tactics to weaken and destroy the workers' union, not only by directly asserting their managerial power but also by using the legal system to their advantage. Workers at F2 and at its two subcontract subsidiaries explained that another common tactic used to hinder worker mobilization was "commendation"—that is, open praise for those workers who could keep up with the workload—which had resulted in intensified competition within the *rabob rahb mao* (piecework) system. According to Thom, "Those 'special' workers [*khon ngarn pi seth*] would immediately be called into the office and praised in front of other workers. Meanwhile, women who couldn't work as fast would be yelled at by their quicker and faster co-workers, causing tension among them." Chawkieng had provided a similar description of favoritism at Hara: "In those days at Hara, anyone who was able to use this particular sewing machine was treated by the *nai jarng* like a queen. It was so *tu raed* [ridiculous]. Today, I will train and teach every worker equally to use the machine so that everyone knows how to operate it." At the same time, the higher probability of producing defective items posed an inherent danger for the fast worker, subjecting her to even more pressure and making it difficult for her to seek comfort and relief from her fellow workers.

As Harvey notes, the conditions of consciousness formation and political action change with the "nature and composition of the global working class."[46] For F2 workers, collective resistance was being made more difficult by worsening structural conditions, the decline in the number of workers, and workers' lack of resources to mobilize. On one of their days off, women from F2 got together at the workers' center with former F2 workers to talk about Article 75 and other issues, such as declining worker solidarity at the factory and in the Rangsit area in general. Pik urged remaining workers at F2 to come together like *pee pee nong nong* (siblings), especially since the intensity of the *rahb mao* system was dividing workers. Thom shook her head, noting that *rahb mao* had significantly altered workers' attitudes toward unionization and their behavior toward one another: "Those who can do the *ngarn rahb mao* [piece-rate job] are not the same people I used to know. If we were to tell them about this discussion we're having, someone most likely would go and rat on us to the supervisor and get someone like me in trouble."

Chawkieng likewise had related how workers at Hara were turned into "enemies" as they competed to get the largest batches of work: "'First come, first served' was the factory policy. The woman who was the first to get to the factory was the first to choose from the batches of work, which varied in amount and which meant less or more money per worker. So in the morning, you would see women lined up at the gates like horses at a racetrack, and when the bell went off and the gates opened, we would all run like crazy just like in a race to beat each other to the finish line!"

That production system, in place at Hara thirty years earlier, was similar to F2's recent piecework system, which had disrupted what once was a unitary feeling of solidarity at F2. Worker solidarity and possibilities for resistance were thus effectively hindered as women were forced to compete with one another and to protect their livelihood by acting as "watchdogs" to prevent anyone from trying to disrupt production. Moreover, because women were working excessive hours each day, they no longer had the time to socialize with their friends at work. Further, Pik reported, many of the remaining workers at F2 had started to take "uppers" or stimulants such as the popular drink *krating daeng* (Red Bull) just to stay awake, thereby reducing the energy for mobilization that they might otherwise have had.

Nay felt that the prevailing conditions forced a worker to become "more selfish, independent, and greedier than before" and believed that tolerating the physical abuse of a production system that exacerbated already harsh working conditions was "just not worth the few extra baht." With "new" structural conditions in place, workers were imbued with a "new" consciousness so strongly associated with competition and faster production that they neglected worker solidarity and their own experiences of collective struggle.

This system of production, while actually benefiting only the owner, appeared to function to the advantage of the worker by increasing the perceived possibility of earning more wages. The economic crisis may very well have been an excuse, as argued by militant women, to extract more from labor while providing fewer benefits, thereby signifying the importance of crisis to capital.

Effects of the Crisis on Women Workers

The economic recession, coupled with inflation, caused a process of reverse migration—the movement of family members from the city back to their home provinces. In the Northeastern Region, nongovernmental organizations found that many return migrants had turned to subcontracting employment along with such forms of informal activity as street vending and homework.[47] Thitiprasert notes that the real income of rural families had been reduced by half, owing to the absence of income remittance from their family members working in the city which had forced extended kin to take up informal work.[48] At the same time, the availability of laid-off workers had allowed small, informal subcontracting arrangements in and around the city to flourish.

Chouwilai reported that more than 90 percent of the workers laid off from the parent company (PF) of F2 and F4 were older women, most of whom had only a primary education. These women had worked in the factory since they were in their teens and regarded factory work as a permanent form of employment. Many had been unable to find new employment, given their limited skills and the perception that they were too old to acquire new skills.[49] Like the *maquiladoras* along the U.S.-Mexican border, labor-intensive factories in Thailand tended to favor young women. The disproportionate presence of older married and unmarried women workers in large and medium-size Thai textile factories can be attributed to physical endurance and job longevity. These women were still able to keep up with the workload and were regarded as very skilled, experienced, and hence valuable workers. But even their valued skills and longtime experience could not guarantee them employment elsewhere, since factories preferred to hire newer, younger workers, the assumption being they were more likely to be obedient and submissive. Forced to help themselves, many older laid-off women formed small groups to take in subcontracting homework; others took whatever jobs they could find.

Pah Ouan and Pah Lek, two women in their forties, were among the last group of 5,000 workers to be laid off from PF. Pah Lek briefly worked as a janitor and gardener at a college campus following the shutdown of PF in 1999, and then quit her job to take care of her two young grandchildren. Although she had worked at PF for over fifteen years, she received only 30,000 baht (US$714) in severance compensation and had to borrow money from the bank to continue to finance the house where she and her grandchildren lived—a house situated behind the factory, which had become an abandoned warehouse. Pah Ouan had been working at PF for over twenty years. Jobless for six months after her dismissal, she was forced to reenter the job market when her husband was laid off from his job. She found subcontract construction work out in Samut Prakarn province, work that required her to carry cement bags on the site for below minimum wage: she received 150 baht per day and worked seven days a week with no benefits or protection.

Most of the laid-off women who lived in the area had worked for PF, and many of them had been able to find only temporary jobs lasting no more than two to three months. Consequently, women suffered heavy emotional and financial duress during the crisis period. As Nay recalled:

> It was very hard for many of the women during the demonstrations. Most women at PF's factories are older women with families who had to borrow money at high interest rates and became deeply indebted. Once work

stopped, there was no money, forcing many women to take their kids out of school. And the men were becoming more irresponsible and would refuse to share their earnings, and this caused a lot of family problems for many of the married women. I witnessed a lot of divorces and separations, and some of my own friends even tried to commit suicide. Others simply couldn't stay on to protest any longer and returned home to their families.

According to Nay, the women would come to the workers' center to talk about the problems of increasing pressure from their families. During one demonstration, F2 workers were criticized by workers at other factories for their hardheadedness (*hua kaeng*), which did little to support their struggle—yet when they decided not to go ahead with a protest, they were criticized by their supporters.

As Sripai recalled, "Even before the factory shut down, the *nai jarng* had already moved out all the machinery and even the walls! Basically, all parts of production were physically taken out of the premises, which meant that the *nai jarng* was already well prepared. Then we thought, if the factory is shut down, what good would it do to take over the factory when there's nothing left to take over?"

It was impossible for the women to wage a daily struggle against the employer because they did not have the financial resources or the energy to spend time at a demonstration without any income. And as many workers started to look for other jobs, the number of people at the demonstrations declined. "We were also being harassed all the time, and management simply told some of the workers to leave and find new jobs, so it was hard for us to call these people back," said Sripai. The women were also aware of the risks they took in protesting, such as being physically assaulted or getting arrested. Furthermore, Sripai pointed out, "We all had our own personal problems to deal with—Pik's mother, for instance, became very ill during this time—and our own families to support." As Nay mentioned, married women whose spouses were already out of work found their life more stressful. Married couples suffered breakups as husbands grew bitter and resentful of their spouses' dismissal. They also disapproved of their wives' leaving them on days off to join labor protests. All in all, unemployment, low job security, and women's involvement in struggles against the employer (in demanding reinstatement and compensation) significantly affected familial and gender relations within the household, often leaving women to cope with a double emotional burden and stress both inside and outside their homes.

Many women had not only themselves to support but also children, elderly parents, siblings, and other relatives to care for. Women with children accounted for almost 90 percent of all the laid-off employees at PF. Their dismissal, followed by lack of income, often forced them to take their children out of school, which in the long run would likely result in higher rates of illiteracy among working-class families.[50] Chouwilai cites evidence from the Ministry of Education that 28,632 students dropped out of state-run schools between mid-1997 and the close of 1998, after their parents lost their jobs.[51] These dropouts included the children of many of the 1,200 women dismissed from a large textile company whose employees were ages forty to forty-five and who had worked for six to fifteen years. These women expressed "hopelessness" saying, "potential employers consider us too old and incapable of working efficiently."[52] This was what forced many women, such as Pah Ouan and Pah Lek, to resort to odd jobs that paid lower wages and provided no benefits.

According to Chouwilai, 80 percent of female employees interviewed at PF had been sending money home but could no longer do so. And because their rural families lacked money for seeds, fertilizer, and other farm expenses, and because families in debt were often forced to default on their loans, unemployment in the urban industrial sector became socially and financially detrimental to women and their families in both the urban and the rural areas.[53] Women who returned from the city to their homes were constrained either to enter the informal economy or to reenter the industrial sector by accepting work in the peripheralized, low-paying, non-unionized subcontract factories. And with levels of income remittance declining as a result, older family members tried to enter the workforce as well. As cutbacks in social welfare left women and their families no safety net to fall back on, they had to lower their living standards in order to cope with the rising costs of basic food staples, and to risk their health and well-being in harsher work conditions and more stressful home situations. Meanwhile, those women who remained in the city struggled against constant feelings of hopelessness and despair as they too had to deal with worsened structural conditions of work and pay.

Conclusions

Subsequent to the massive displacement of labor from export manufacturing industries, so-called new forms of control over labor became predominant. Trends in the textile manufacturing sector involved a shift to smaller, subcontract factories and a return to worsened forms of work and pay, as in the piece-rate system, or, in the case of F1, a drastic reduction in overtime hours and benefits. For the most part, many factories were attempting to lower their production costs by decentralizing their operations and moving parts of their production to subcontract factories where they could hire fewer workers to work longer hours for lower wages. The extraction of absolute surplus value, as in the cases of F2, SF1, and SF2, resulted in a situation whereby industrial workers were commodified and rendered "disposable" under the piece-rate system of production and in an environment of massive unemployment.

Surplus value results when labor is paid a much lower price than the price of the labor product itself.[54] The extraction of absolute surplus value denotes a situation where labor comes at absolutely no cost to the owner of production and thus, by definition, the owner of the means of production was absolutely "winning." The rate of surplus value can be raised only by prolonging the working day in absolute terms.[55] But this prolongation is effected by the workers themselves out of economic necessity (i.e., the need to survive) via the setup of such a system of production. Under this regime of factory production, extraction of relative and absolute surplus value oscillates between payment for piecework and the postponement or nonpayment of wages. In the case of nonpayment of wages, a worker will already have given her full labor power and productivity to the factory in absolute terms. And nonpayment of wages was a common violation in non-unionized factories that employed the most vulnerable groups of women, such as rural women and migrant women who worked in rurally based manufacturing enterprises.

Overall, in the post-crisis period, women who remained in factories faced a heavier workload and intensified stress, especially in unregulated, uninspected factories, while they continued to shoulder the burden of supporting their families. The multiple burdens placed upon working women and the constraints placed upon workers in non-unionized factories contributed to a decline in women-led, factory-based protests and demonstrations. At F2, women no longer had the time, energy, or resources to mobilize, given that the factory was paying them less than subsistence wages and subjecting them to a work environment that pitted workers against one another.

It is important to note that the piecework system of production in the apparel industry is commonplace in free-trade zones throughout the world. In Jamaica, for example, women garment assemblers are required to sew 600 pieces per day, and if they fail to meet that set target, they are not paid any wages at all.[56] Jamaican women, too, complained of not being allowed to eat, drink, or use the restroom under such an intensive production system and compared their work situation to that of slaves, in the sense that they sometimes risked working for free. Unlike slaves under British colonialism, however, Jamaican factory workers today are not provided with food, drink, or rest. This form of enslavement can be regarded as "new," and such conditions in manufacturing establishments are becoming more and more prevalent in the rapidly industrializing countries of East Asia and elsewhere.

At F2 and its subcontract factories, the traditional relationship between employer and employee under assembly line production no longer exists, since the employer no longer has any of the social obligations that he used to have toward his employees. Factory workers have become increasingly disposable, flexible, and easily replaceable, and in a sense they are becoming irrelevant to the system of production. Workers risk "working for free" and compete with other disposable bodies on a daily basis. Because workers are selling *themselves* and not just their labor, they no longer have the power to go on strike as they did in the past. In the early years at F2, workers had legal rights within the workplace, and once a handful of employees became aware of these rights, they decided to organize other workers. They fought for the right to set up a union, for the right to use the bathroom, for cleaner and safer facilities; and they fought against verbal abuse and physical intimidation. In other words, workers' social consciousness materialized into a collective effort and led to improved conditions. But in an increasingly globalized world where companies, national economies, and peoples are competing with one another, the possibilities for mobilization are becoming increasingly more difficult. As Sripai stated, "Even though workers today may be more aware of their rights under the law, I think the situation for workers is a lot worse than before, much worse."

Effective strategies of labor unrest in the form of strikes and work stoppages are becoming a thing of the past among workers preoccupied with short-term survival rather than long-term careers in a steady work environment with hope for improvement and increased benefits. Moreover, the trends toward subcontracting, piecework, and outsourcing, coupled with structural adjustment programs and neoliberal trade policies, severely and directly affect women and their families. Although unleashed from the oppressive confines of the factory floor, women find themselves thrust into a new realm of uncertainty and insecurity, forced to rely on the only skills they know. At F1, women had to come up with ways to supplement their income to make up for the wages "lost" through work stoppage or production slowdown. Many women took up odd jobs on the weekends, sold food in the morning, or made specialty dishes for sale. Thus in the post-crisis period, multiple occupations became necessary for survival.

In sum, four major features characterized the post-crisis period as it pertained to women in the Thai apparel industry. First, the transition to a piecework subcontract system of production resulted in heightened competition and individual interest among workers, thereby reducing worker solidarity and cooperation. Second, the nature of the production process itself forced workers to "willingly" work longer and harder in order to produce more, to the detriment of their health and well-being— particularly in the absence of job security, benefits, or safeguards in worker safety and protection. Third, the primacy given to quantity over quality subsequently diminished any sense of pride and self-worth that women had previously attached to their labor, yet subjected them to monetary penalties for defects, thus further limiting their earning power. Fourth, complacent state policies in a context of economic recession and crisis operated to the advantage of the employers, whose actions were not regulated, monitored, or penalized, whereas workers were not accorded legal or institutional outlets for their grievances.

Lynn Stephen, looking at how poor urban women confronted the economic crisis in Mexico with diverse strategies of collective action, found that many women "have learned that they do not need to adopt the same identity or share identical interpretations of their experience in order to act together." Successful mobilization efforts on the part of women have much to do with "an overlapping set of questions regarding the various dimensions of inequality they experience as women," she writes.[57] In the Rangsit industrial zone, laid-off factory women who remained in the city came together precisely as a result of their shared experiences as workers who had devoted many years of their lives to the factory. But many women were forced to abandon their struggle (such as those who had been protesting outside the Ministry of Labour) because of not having an income, though others did stay on to follow up on their grievances, despite their adversity.

Many laid-off women ended up in townhouse sweatshops or in the informal sector; those who remained in their jobs were subjected to ongoing labor abuses. Given the unemployment level of nearly 2.5 million people by 1999, women who had jobs wanted to hold on to them and, to that end, were willing to tolerate intensified forms of oppression and exploitation. As working conditions returned to the days of the Hara sweatshop era, as described by Chawkieng, and to conditions of work described by F2 women before unionization, workers were no longer as fearless and outspoken as they had been. As former F2 workers witnessed a return to pre-union conditions in the very place where they had fought and won their battles, they could not help but feel overcome by the hopelessness of their situation as they continued to fight against their more "powerful enemies." For the most part, women are relegated to supporting each other and supporting other women. "Hopelessness," "frustration," and "despair" are the three words that F2 women used repeatedly to convey their collective sense of powerlessness. In Tiano's terms, F2 women became increasingly alienated because they were "mistrustful of or reject[ing] the system but feel[ing] powerless to change their lives."[58]

Worker consciousness, then, needs to be examined within the framework of a "new" capitalist logic following the massive displacement of labor in an atmosphere of flexibility and job instability. But at the same time, state policies that are complacent and supportive of owners and capitalists rather than of labor need to be analyzed vis-à-vis the rhetoric of globalization—that is, free market ideology. In the case of Thailand, the crisis became the justification for transforming the mechanisms of control over labor, which were achieved at the expense of workers' rights and livelihood.

The interaction between capital and labor constantly changes, as do women's own perceptions of work in both centralized and peripheralized production. Nor do all factories in the developing world operate in the same manner, whatever the similarities in the gender composition of their workforce. What happened in Thailand is the spatialization of production, which goes against the usual logic of industrial manufacturing: rather than a centralized production process, factories are decentralizing their operations. But in today's globalizing world, this phenomenon is becoming common practice, and thus any future inquiry into factory workers in general, and into the global apparel industry in particular, calls for a new research agenda.

In the post-crisis period in Thailand, the spatial relocation of work away from the city, and hence a move of factory production from urban to the rural provinces, means that more workers are able to work within their original neighborhoods. Hence a closer look at reverse migration is called for: especially in terms of the patterns by which workers are displaced from the manufacturing sector, and in terms of the consequences for the rural economy and society as a whole. As the state moves from Keynesianism and Fordism to post-Fordist free-market policies, it is important to look at women's "new" work experiences and the conditions that make them more or less "militant" or "nonmilitant," powerless or fearless. In addition to the economic and political situation, researchers must also consider the workplace and the immediate environment within which worker and social consciousness arises. Corporate-driven globalization encouraged by lax state regulation and weak enforcement of labor laws is not unique to Thailand, but despite their differences, the experiences and struggles of workers at Factory One and Factory Two provide a testimony of women's undeniable strength, courage, and resilience in the face of continuing and, in some cases, more intense exploitation.

Conclusion

Looking Back, Moving Forward

On Tuesday, December 17, 2002, F2 shut down its operations without advance warning to any of its workers. Women coming to work as usual that morning found the factory gates locked. Workers were given no reason why the factory closed. Later that day, workers discovered that the owner had already moved all the production equipment and machinery to another facility and was continuing to produce garments at its subcontract factory. The F2 employer alleged that the Bangkok Bank had filed a claim against the factory and that a court warrant had been issued demanding repossession of all factory assets, including land and property.

The remaining 150 workers at F2, left without pay or compensation, immediately began to file grievances with the Labour Ministry and protested outside the Prime Minister's office. F2 women often expressed their bewilderment that their employer would rather pursue grievances in court, shut down operations, and relocate elsewhere than try to comply with workers' demands and provide the minimum basic needs—which, according to the women, would harness a more compliant and productive workforce.

The situation of factories shutting down at short notice is commonplace and a testament to the extraordinary power of capital over labor: workers are truly disposable commodities and are rendered irrelevant to systems of production in today's globalized economy. Eliminating production lines, firing workers without compensation, shutting down and relocating production to cheaper sites—all have become increasingly common practices in garment factories around the world. Just as goods are disposable in a consumer culture, so too are people at the end of the global supply chain. Childhood is disposable. Health is disposable. Even the environment that people must live in is disposable. In the face of globalization, all nation-states seek to regulate less (in the name of growth and modernization) when they should be regulating more and more effectively in partnership with businesses, labor unions, and communities. And regulation should apply not only to factories but also to the local environmental impacts of sweatshop production.[1]

Pressure groups such as the Clean Clothes Campaign and Campaign for Labor Rights constantly alert us to the worst examples (such as the use of children in sweatshops) but the problem is much more widespread than this. Nonetheless, respect for labor standards is growing, and in some countries the International Labour Organization is actively involved in monitoring factory conditions and ensuring that corporate codes of conduct are applied. Furthermore, to get these procedures in place it takes enormous acts of political will, often accompanied by intense campaigning activities on the part of the groups affected and nongovernmental organizations. With many governments, including that of Thailand, seeking to attract investment and generate trade growth as a priority, however, many factories have been relocated to free-trade zones, export-processing zones, or special economic zones. Thailand is just one example of where even minimal labor standards often do not apply to workers in labor-intensive factories. It is not coincidental that many of the people laboring under these conditions are stateless migrants without formal legal status or access to all the entitlements of citizenship. In short, deregulated zones enable or facilitate the exploitation of the most vulnerable people and those least able to mobilize on their own behalf.

As I write this conclusion, I am tapping away on the keyboard of a new HP Pavilion laptop. I don't know how many sweatshops and how many workers were involved in making the parts for the machine in front of me, so part of the problem is lack of information. We don't often know where our goods come from or under what conditions these modern-day "treasures" are made, but we hope that brand-name corporations that have signed up to codes of responsible conduct really do try to live up to them. But even if they try, many textile factories around the world do not meet the codes of conduct of international brands, meaning that workers will continue to be subject to exploitive and harmful conditions at work. Meanwhile, workers who do mobilize against exploitation are often dismissed and replaced. So what is being done?

The story of the Gina Form Bra (GFB) workers is one excellent and recent example of a successful struggle waged by workers at a local factory against their employers, a struggle made possible with the support of international organizations, consumer and student campaigns, labor advocates, and human rights groups. GFB was owned by Clover Garment, an intraregional firm based in Hong Kong, and employed some 1,600 workers, 95 percent of whom were women. The Gina workers used creative tactics to build international alliances with transnational activist networks, union organizations, consumer groups, and NGO campaigners; theirs was the first labor case to be taken up by the National Human Rights Commission. In 2004, their successful campaign led to the signing of a comprehensive collective bargaining agreement with the GFB management, the withdrawal of all court cases filed against the Gina Workers' Union and its members, and the reinstatement of thirty-seven leading rank-and-file members with back pay in a settlement that totaled over 4 million baht.[2]

In October 2006, however, the company announced that it was shutting down its operations in Thailand and transferring production to its factories in China and Cambodia. By this time, the Gina workforce was down to approximately 1,400 workers. These workers staged a protest outside the U.S. embassy in Bangkok to demand the severance pay the company had promised them. The demonstration was the first labor-related protest since martial law had been imposed following the September 19, 2006, military coup, but the laid-off workers said they were left with no choice but to demand wages owed to them. The workers also called for American consumers to boycott the Gina products, including lingerie for such brands as Victoria's Secret and Calvin Klein.[3] The union chairperson said that the factory cited "unfinished paperwork" as their reason for not specifying a date of payment and also that the company had tried to coerce workers into signing letters of resignation that would have legally prohibited them from receiving their severance pay. Even though that rally was not interrupted by the authorities, the suspension of civil liberties that has followed the military coup, such as the ban on public gatherings of more than five people, will probably make the situation for workers and for worker support organizations more difficult. With a new government headed by a retired army general as interim prime minister, Surayud Chulanont, and military coup leaders who call themselves the Council for National Security in place, there may be more problems with accountability and legal redress, which may mean that workers can expect to face and endure worsened conditions of work and living until there is a return to democracy.

New Targets for Exploitation

When I started research for this book, it was evident that women were a special case for exploitation in the sweatshop economy. But as I write in 2007, new targets for exploitation have emerged: refugees, economic migrants, indigenous peoples displaced by environmentally damaging projects or military action in neighboring countries—anyone who is willing to accept the low wages and poor conditions that exist in all sweatshops in any part of the world because he or she has no choice. And as manufacturers seek out cheaper sites for production, workers in one location can easily be swept aside and replaced with workers in another, usually in places where there are fewer restrictions and less state regulation. Thailand's northern border provinces, for example, are emerging as the new zones for manufacturing production and provide a unique context for looking at sites where factory employment is not so obviously gendered. Women are no longer a special case for exploitation in these borderland regions, because women *and* men *and children* are being hired by outsourcing companies to work alongside one another in garment factories and in other labor-intensive industries. The latest trends in global restructuring will have major implications for both female and male laborers, not only on the kinds of jobs available to them but in the kinds of living and working conditions they can expect.

We need to remind ourselves that the same problems discussed in this book will manifest themselves with different people, since companies are able to move when and where they want to and can thus exploit more effectively. The same processes are being replicated in other countries such as India and China, so it is no surprise that many scholars present a rather bleak picture for workers who labor under an increasingly unregulated free-market system that makes workers' rights and human rights secondary to the needs of capital. We must therefore pay attention to the growing importance of the transnational activist networks (TANs) that are emerging as a new type of strategy for cross-border organizing, consider the potential of TANs to hold accountable corporations and the governments of developing countries, and examine the problems they face and their successes and failures.[4]

New Strategies for Activism and Research

Workers and labor organizations in the West know that outsourcing is a reality in today's global economy and thus recognize the need to link with activist networks and campaigns elsewhere. We must therefore take note of how union strategies and trade unions in North America and around the world are changing. Transnational activism and solidarity are the answers, and the Gina case is one example of a successful international labor struggle.

One effective strategy in the Gina case was for campaigners to target brands that placed the heaviest volume of orders at the factory. The Gap became the first target of campaigners, in part because it has its own independent monitoring agents in Thailand.[5] Only under such pressure did the Gap ensure compliance and act on demands in favor of the Gina workers, playing an important role in demanding and securing the reinstatement of a GFB union leader. Coordination with a local labor organization gave workers the financial support they needed to continue their strike and led to setting up the workers' own union office in 1999.[6] Philip Robertson and Somsak Plaiyoowong assert that coordinated actions at the factory level and the national, international, and global North/consumer nation level are critical for any successful labor campaign. They indicate several factors that led to the Gina workers' victory: a strong and cohesive union with effective communication between union leaders and workers in all stages of production; speed of communication so that information can be passed down to the rank and file immediately in the face of employer intimidation; preparedness on part of the union and its supporters when dealing with the legal and political defense against the employer; clear, authoritative, and well-documented information on the ground; the presence of a bilingual and knowledgeable "midfielder" who plays a key linking role and whose constant contact with the union ensures that local union views are placed at the center of discussions on international strategy; and extension of their activities to new "constituencies" in order to keep the pressure so continuous that the employer sees no way out.[7] Clover Garment decided to find a way out, however, by shutting down the Gina factory and relocating to places where unions do not exist.

Although the F2 women and many women employed in export manufacturing industries in Thailand lost their jobs, some women such as Pik, Sripai, and Saneh were left in a better situation than before. Pik and Saneh went on to become full-time staff members for the Thai Labour Campaign. Sripai became the director for a savings fund; she later found full-time employment as a sales representative for a furniture company and now receives a monthly salary. But most of the women workers, including many former F2 women, were forced to reenter the workforce in low-paying occupations, often in factories with the very same sweatshop conditions that they had fought so hard and successfully to eradicate.

Since workers will often come across the same problems, there is still much work to be done, especially about the conditions of the new sweatshops and with the people who labor in them. What will happen to the next generation of workers who end up in global sweatshops where conditions are as bad as they were for Chawkieng and the F2 women, and where possibilities for mobilization are increasingly diminished? What will happen to displaced female laborers as light-assembly industries move to other countries and are replaced by heavier and higher value–added production such as automobiles, automotive components, and advanced technologies? It was reported in 2005 that the Thai textile and garment industry was experiencing a shortage of about 60,000 workers because of the outsourcing of production and the movement of Thai workers into higher-paying industries such as electronics. But in the end, this "shortage" is just another indication of companies looking to use cheaper workers.[8]

So what research methods are there to continue the much-needed work in this area? Critical ethnography and participatory research methods are crucial because these techniques allow one to observe, understand, and analyze power relations and sites of resistance and thereby offer an argument against the totalizing nature of the current global economic system. Focusing on one particular industry and a particular group of actors in a specific locality was a good starting point for my study of resistance. It allowed me to look at how labor militancy among workers develops and materializes, and also allowed for examination of how social interactions among certain groups of women take place on and off the factory floor. These kinds of in-depth investigations can offer wonderful insights into how ideas for struggle, rebellion, and protest emerge and are passed on from one group of workers to another.

I went into this intensive research project assuming docility among workers at the end of the global supply chain as well as the effectiveness of factory discipline, and I wanted to find out why. As the project unfolded, however, rather than finding factory women dominated and compliant with gender-specific norms, I discovered that they could be adversarial, proactive, capable, hardheaded, outspoken, and "no nonsense" in response to their situation. In addition, my presence as an ethnographic researcher caused my research subjects to reflect on their own situation and, in the process, become more conscious of their own assertiveness. The more militant workers also reassessed the difference they were making advising workers (including males) in other factories, joining NGOs, and aligning themselves with other activist networks. During the initial stages of my fieldwork, the women conveyed to me their distrust of the largely quantitative and technical methods of previous researchers who had approached them. Ethnographic research techniques, however, enabled the women to realize and appreciate that I was making a genuine effort to listen to their stories.

The free flow of communication put the women at ease, and they were more than happy to share their experiences with me, and they did, though being well aware that I was an educated member of the urban Bangkok elite doing work on factory women. They saw me not as someone who just wanted to extract information but as someone who wanted to understand and learn. As such, I contend that only qualitative research grounded in a relationship of trust between researcher and respondents is likely to provide insights into the precise conditions involved. Awed and intimidated by articulate respondents who were able to bring the often dry and detached research literature to life, I came to realize that research had to be adaptable, and I learned that I had more in common with these women than I had expected, in spite of the considerable differences in socioeconomic background. In addition, I discovered that humor could provide strategies against exploitation and hopelessness, that workers used imitation, ridicule, and even pity to rise above the bad behavior of both female and male managers.

The effects on the researcher in this case included a crash course in perseverance and sacrifice, and my experiences in the field led me to focus more on activist movements. Moreover, I sought to highlight that academic research should be relevant to the situation of respondents. Nevertheless, I will continue to stress the importance of drawing on *women's own voices* to convey their dignity and passion and to emphasize that justice has a central place in research.[9] Stories of women textile factory workers demonstrate how the larger global market forces produce very different consequences and reactions in the lives of ordinary citizens. By going out and talking to women inside and outside their work settings, I was able to see how work shapes their social relations and how women build their own personal worlds around it.

In this analysis of women and their responses to the production process, the issue of structure and agency should be noted. As in the work of Anthony Giddens, structure and agency (i.e., experience) simultaneously coexist; they are not just two poles.[10] There are times when workers' agency matters more, and there are other times when structure matters more. Structures of production matter more than the agency of the workers and the managers when they are strategically oriented, but they can prompt the agency of workers who, even under the direst circumstances, will use whatever resources are available. Although many aspects of life may be constrained for both groups of women workers that I studied, women did find ways to assert themselves, albeit not always successfully. Even in F1, the structures that control and the capacities of agents were not mutually exclusive. My research demonstrates that the social relations between female factory workers and between workers and management are reproduced, sometimes in a modified way, through intersubjective exchange and that the "structures of production" are reproduced, modified, or even transformed through the agents in the process.

The insights to be gained from my study are not limited to specific contexts but have the capacity for formal generalization across cultures and in future empirical research. I believe that research should not only seek to draw on the first-order constructs of those studied but also aim to make the knowledge produced (the second-order constructs) relevant and intelligible to those studied. The implication is that the marginalized and powerless actually do not need researchers to speak for them or to speak to them; they just need academic investigations to start and finish with respondents in mind.

In reflecting upon the kinds of social and interpersonal interactions women are engaged in as outcomes of their "militant" or "nonmilitant" experiences, I find that two currents of worker consciousness emerge. The strong bonding among F2 women speaks to their remarkable ability to link their experiences *outside* the confines of the factory to their ongoing struggle and their relations as workers and as activists. The strong personal bonding among F1 women speaks to the collective longevity of their employment at the factory and their history of noncombative behavior. F1 women were not exposed to the world outside the factory to the same extent as F2 women. They were, in a sense, limiting themselves to the safe and familiar spaces of home and factory, whereas F2 women were opening themselves up to the vast and unfamiliar terrain beyond the factory setting. Although the women from F1 and F2 came from very similar backgrounds and were engaged in the same occupation, their unique individual and collective factory experiences produced very different interests, concerns, and dispositions. While women in one group became politicized and immersed in a struggle for workers' rights, those in the other group were constantly overwhelmed in a struggle for survival and directed their energies toward a more *comfortable*, albeit very limited, engagement with life outside of work.

Women's stories can illuminate how Thailand's "economic miracle" was made possible during the boom in export-led production, especially in textiles and garments. But the women who labored long and hard during the period of economic prosperity received none of the benefits beyond those made possible, at one factory, by working longer hours. And it was a situation of hardship and perseverance that the women transformed into one of camaraderie and cooperation, which resulted in the adaptation and accommodation to factory work that ultimately benefited the employer. Meanwhile, at the other factory, women were subjected to maltreatment by a "typical" employer who was trying to get the most out of the workers he hired, and it was this situation that brought workers together and eventually caused them to transform their discontent into a successful struggle. Then the economic crisis abruptly disrupted their lives, forcing women to adapt to and cope with even harsher work conditions under increasingly difficult circumstances, either by finding additional means to earn the equivalent of wages lost in overtime pay or by working longer and harder to earn wages by the piece. Chapter 3 showed how structural conditions in the post-crisis period weakened the strength of unionized workforces in the industrial zone, while workers throughout the apparel industry were left in a general state of powerlessness and vulnerability. At the same time, a false consciousness surfaced among women who felt that they should be grateful for having jobs at all, when so many other women were being fired. In desperate times, women who are trying to survive are less likely to question or challenge the system, because they are just too busy working and simply don't have the time or the energy to organize. Meanwhile, as women are left to fend for themselves, their social commitment toward one another diminishes.

Studies of working women in the countries of East Asia generally find that women's employment is temporary, and they often specify marriage, child rearing, and physical exhaustion as the primary reasons behind women's decisions to leave the workforce.[11] Yet low labor turnover and job longevity were, in fact, prominent features of the workforce in this study among both married and single women. Research into female employment in Mexico and the Caribbean also found low rates of labor turnover among women workers in labor-intensive manufacturing industries.[12] Although the women in my study found factory work to be relatively better than previous jobs they had held, the overwhelming reason for their long employment histories had more to do with the close personal and social bonds they developed at the factory.

Nevertheless, like the women *maquila* workers in Tiano's study, women's "vulnerable labor market status restricted their employment options," forcing many who had low educational levels and only specific skills "to remain on the job for sustained periods."[13] Many of the women in my study worked out of economic necessity as primary breadwinners in their families, supporting their children or younger siblings or elderly parents. Moreover, several women made more money than their husbands who held unstable jobs or were unemployed. Physical exhaustion as a reason for leaving the factory came to the surface only in the post-crisis period, when working conditions simply became too taxing on their bodies.

Textures of Struggle: The Factory Setting and Worker Consciousness

Women's life experiences and their social relations in production illuminate what Burawoy calls "the specificity of the capitalist labor process."[14] Women's responses to their factory employment and to the various forms of exploitation under which they labor show that the development of workers' consciousness is uneven, an outcome of multiple and intersecting dimensions of a woman's experiences at work. As James Petras and Morris Morley point out, "The heterogeneity of the working class" is reflected in "multiple sites of working-class struggle."[15] The nonmilitant women believed that they were an integral part of the company's success: the more the company prospered, the more they would prosper. In fulfilling this role, women accommodated their minds and bodies to the repetitive monotony of work and felt a sense of responsibility to their assigned tasks. At the militant factory, where the women felt used and cheated, the sentiment was that the more the company prospered, the more workers suffered. Women's collective social identities were therefore contingent upon their own perceptions of work and upon how they interpreted their situations.

Themes of consciousness/politicization, ambiguity and uncertainty, and a victim's interpretations of justice and injustice seem to emerge from women's stories of living and working. Sripai said that "if it were not for the horrific conditions at F2, we probably wouldn't be who we are today." The Hara case tells the story of a worker who went public by revealing the injustices at the factory, which resulted in a successful mobilization among the workers and tremendous support from the public and the media. The action of Chawkieng's employer prompted her to "seize the factory," which caused her to be blacklisted and eventually led to the start of her own business.

The stories of Chawkieng and the F2 women activists raise compelling questions with regard to where they were when things began to change and to issues of chance, causation, and responsibility. In their narratives, the women provided detailed descriptions of their particular situations and explanations for their actions. Through telling their stories, the women talked about what happened "to them" or "what could have been" or how they coped with the pathways of hardship in their lives, leading up to their outcome as politicized subjects. There were many intersecting factors that may help explain the complex dimensions of women's perceptions and their changing views regarding militancy and activism. For the militant women, their collective struggle led to a personal as well as a social transformation into union members who came to look upon work and workers in a different light. Their experiences at the factory had become very much a part of who they are. For Sripai and her friends, their struggle was not only a personal sacrifice but also a "sacrifice for their fellow workers."

The stories of the F2 women illustrate how coercion expressed in direct forms (i.e., "old-fashioned" worker mistreatment or physical and verbal abuse) may more readily lead to activism and to resistance than coercion expressed in indirect forms (an institutionalized system of overtime work and pay under fairly acceptable work conditions and amicable relations with management). Yet although tendencies toward union activism are stronger where direct forms of coercion are more prevalent, the point is that both forms of coercion were present in the factory conditions of both groups of women. It is the mix of direct and indirect forms of coercion that leads to specific outcomes. High labor turnover (through voluntary resignations) was not in these cases an indicator of exploitive conditions, because women at both factories had exceptionally long periods of consecutive employment relative to the number of years the factory had been in operation.

The root causes of worker rebellion are therefore unpredictable and have much to do with the individuals involved and the structure of the production process as shaped by the demands of the local and global market. Evidently, there is a great deal of variation in collective consciousness, even among workers from similar social and economic class backgrounds within the same industry. The interplay between the organization of factory work and the organization of women's lives, as structured by wage employment, created conditions either of passivity and powerlessness or of resistance in well-established medium and large factories.

Nonetheless, the degree of exploitation is only one predisposing factor, among many others, that leads to the potential for worker resistance.

At F1, exploitation became almost "communal" in the sense that each woman's whole world (that is, place of work) became her only support system. At F2, there were multiple layers of consciousness, and what came to define and shape collective action was a culmination of the social, personal, and political forces that revolved around factory work and the conditions it proffered. For both factories, long working hours stand out as the most exploitive conditions of factory work, but it was the deplorable working conditions, rather than the long working hours, that prompted the women at F2 to organize. Despite some of the unlawful practices at F1, workers there did not feel threatened or abused, unlike workers at F2, where deplorable working conditions and a poor work environment were permanent fixtures that ultimately provoked reaction.

Moreover, activism was prompted by the geographical setting of the factory as in the case of F2, where workers had the opportunity to meet and mingle with unionized women workers from adjacent factories on their lunch or dinner breaks or on their way to work. Doing so led to the discovery of unlawful practices at non-unionized factories and gave women workers the opportunity to talk about their working conditions. At F1, on the other hand, the confinement of a factory to one geographical location, away from an industrial zone and the presence of organized factories, limited the opportunity for non-unionized workers to come into contact with unionized workers who could potentially share their knowledge about workers' rights and labor laws. Women at F1 were situated within a very enclosed social system with little outside contact, whereas F2 women's work environment allowed for more social interaction with workers from neighboring factories, enabling a different kind of socialization to take place. The workers' center, for instance, was a convenient meeting place for women to hold informal meetings and discuss issues pertinent to their struggle. Still, even though F1 women were not politicized, they were forming strong personal bonds on the factory floor, working cooperatively to ensure that production ran smoothly and efficiently. At the same time, the many factors that shape worker consciousness were constantly changing. Chapter 2 related how F2 women found meaning and self-worth through their union struggle, professing that they felt more "alive" than ever before. But in the post-crisis period, formerly militant workers and the younger generation of workers at F2 became increasingly depoliticized as they faced more oppressive work environments. Even older F2 workers expressed pessimism about the future and acknowledged that their efforts were futile because employers were always "a step ahead."

The women in my study initially viewed factory work as a path to a better life, but many, reflecting on their long years at the factory, came to an overwhelming realization that factory employment had not improved their quality of life. Many women at F1 expressed genuine amazement when asked to figure out how long they had been at the factory, saying that they had never expected to be working there for so many years, but that they had become so accustomed to the routine of work that "time just went by." Wage work was an integral part of almost every facet of their lives. Their working days and hours had created an economic dependency for workers whose lives were centered on a closed social system at the factory. Whatever personal freedom women were able to experience was often defined and circumscribed by the inordinate amount of time they physically spent at the factory. Socializing among the women was limited to their lunch and dinner breaks, inclining them to develop an emotional attachment to the factory. In effect, these time constraints and the women's binding economic ties to their wage employment affected their personal relations, and in the case of F1 the close-knit working atmosphere that women had built for themselves and the feeling of belonging perpetuated a long-standing and compliant workforce. This emotional aspect of factory employment cannot be ignored, especially for those who work at the same factory over long periods of time.

Former textile workers and union activists such as Pik and Nay realize that a lot of women are "fearful of their employers and don't know what to do or who to turn to." Both wanted to offer their peers a *tahng ratr* (shortcut) to justice based on their own experiences. But they were also well aware that the kind of terrain upon which activism can begin had vastly changed since the days of their own militancy, noting that more and more women were facing tighter financial situations and time constraints. "Old-timers like me know what needs to be done," said Pik, "but we really can't do much even though we all know how to articulate these issues. The main problem is that these things take up time, and besides, we don't know how to persuade workers to be like us." Given the unrealistic task on the part of a few experienced workers such as Pik and Nay of helping others become aware of their rights, women workers were often left to their own devices when it came to the task of organizing. Even in industrial districts where the concentration of unionized textile factories was greatest, most workers remained unaware of their rights and continued to be subjected to labor violations. The outcome for women at F1 remains to be seen, although one can reasonably expect to see those workers become increasingly outspoken as they come to believe that they deserve much more from the factory.

Pik and Nay, along with the hundreds and thousands of women who are trapped in this unending cycle of oppression and poverty, know that a whole new challenge lies ahead, and they hope that the next generation of workers will realize, in some way, that any form of organization will have to come from within the factory and from the women themselves. As Nay stated, "It's impossible for us to go out to inform and educate all textile factory workers. From our experience at F2, any kind of action must come from the workers themselves and from *within* the factory. Women have to come to realize that things are not the way they ought to be." The path to militancy, to becoming a conscious worker, may have changed since the days of Nay, Pik, and Sripai, but as long as there are women who labor under truly oppressive conditions, protest and rebellion may still erupt here and there, from within the structural conditions of transformed workplaces. Thus it is essential, when looking at struggles against capitalism in the context of the global supply chain, to understand the underlying material conditions in which women find themselves.

It appears that the prevailing structural conditions for women workers in textile factories in Thailand are getting worse, owing to marked shifts in the production process, particularly since the economic crisis. Moreover, whether or not a factory is unionized says little about the level of workers' consciousness or the degree of workers' militancy. More important factors, such as the history and development of a workers' union and, particularly, the individual characteristics of the women involved in the process must be taken into account. In this sense, an ethnographic study provides a useful illustration of the vast and marked differences between the women workers who became knowledgeable and conscious of their rights and were determined to claim them, and those who accommodated themselves to their occupation and found no reason to question their working and living conditions.

Intimidation or other strategies (including paternalism) on the part of the employer for wielding direct authority and power played a central role in this analysis. Working behind locked gates where security guards carried guns, driven by economic necessity to work long hours for little reward, and living under the constant threat of dismissal for anyone seeking to question the operation of the factory created a situation that involved some degree of "psychological terror." What was remarkable was the resilience of the women who experienced this terror and the very fact that they tried to change the conditions at the factory. What the employer of F2 thought would generate a consensual, fearful, and compliant workforce actually resulted in just the opposite: fearless workers who had nothing to lose and who used every trick in the book to realize their objectives.

My investigation of two currents of women and their consciousness within factory work may have wider implications for the possibilities of mobilization at the national and transnational levels. It is important to consider objective conditions along with women's subjectivities through an exploration of their attitudes and their perceptions of work and living. The urgent need to examine the conditions affecting women's lives today highlights the importance of ethnographic research and analysis. As Neil Smelser pointed out, "No one among us does not recognize the value of descriptive depth, richness of analysis, and contextualization of explanations."[16]

A multifaceted analysis takes into account different levels of control and coercion, social relations and other relationships in order to understand in greater depth the subjective issues of powerlessness and passivity, resistance and rebellion. Women's worlds within the workplace had become very much embedded in their daily lives. For the militant women, their world now contains a sense of nostalgia for their past efforts at union organizing and political involvement. For the nonmilitant women, their world of work will be an ever-present nostalgia for stability and permanence. Women in both groups remember "golden" times for their factories which reflected their particular perceptions and ways of living as reproduced and shaped within the structural conditions of their work environment. While militancy signified being together in opposition to the employer, it also reflected the identity that F2 workers constructed through struggle during their "golden years." Similarly, while the "golden days" of F1 were associated with overtime and higher incomes, nonmilitancy also reflected the identity that F1 workers constructed through work.

Today, amid an atmosphere of massive layoffs and factory closings, long-term strategies of labor unrest in the form of strikes and work stoppages are stymied as workers are offered less protection from the government and are left to cope with short-term survival. The lack of enforcement and implementation of labor laws continues to be an ongoing problem in Thailand and elsewhere, and more needs to done with regard to questioning and contextualizing the role of the state in relation to factory operations. Meanwhile, factory workers are becoming increasingly enslaved, human commodities in a factory system that is no longer accountable to its workers and can easily dispose of them. The current wage structure must also be challenged because it is clear that women are living a hand-to-mouth existence on minimum wages barely enough to support one person.

I hope that my work will demonstrate the importance of focusing on the objective conditions of women's work and will provide new avenues for research. Understanding and assessing localized situations is the first step toward transformation and social change in line with the actual needs of the women themselves. Future research on the new sweatshop economy should continue to highlight the importance of the social and personal relations that are intrinsic to a fundamental understanding of women's subordination and power relations. It is not sufficient simply to state that women do or do not realize they are being exploited; rather, in assessing women's potential for active resistance, it is necessary to look at the individual and collective experiences of work at one particular place. In the current atmosphere of fast-track capitalism, paternalistic factories (as exemplified by F1 and F3) are in decline. It is no longer seen as ideal or even necessary for a factory to provide a minimally tolerable work environment for its women. A factory run on paternalistic lines where the employer saw himself as a father figure may have worked well in the past and did not experience the disruption to output that women at F2 managed to inflict. Nevertheless, it is clear that the employer at F1 was successful in controlling a largely female workforce and in stymieing both unionization and worker unrest.

Case-level studies offer rich, detailed, in-depth analyses and demonstrate that processes of exploitation have many similarities across nations, regardless of their geographical, political, and economic contexts. Ethnographic research, if placed within a larger framework that links the local with the global, can establish complex links between global economic processes and workers' responses. This would be an important starting point for future research on female laborers because it could demonstrate the connections between the networks and flows of capital and the actual state of labor relations in outsourced manufacturing. At the moment, most working women throughout the world are trying to adapt to the larger forces of globalization in order to survive—but ongoing struggles on the part of women workers are likely to continue as long as their working and living conditions continue to erode.

Critical ethnography acknowledges the values and norms of the researcher and deploys ethnographic research methods in pursuit of social and economic emancipation. Ethnographic research, of course, takes time but can provide a vivid and detailed examination of the informal mechanisms of control and women's responses to them which are often overlooked by other methods. New research on women workers in the global supply chain should aim to produce accounts that not only discover but also contribute to changing the power relations in these contexts. For example, Michael Burawoy, in responding to the critique of participant observation as "incapable of generalization and therefore not a true science," develops the "extended case method" to establish better connections between theory and research techniques and increased reflexivity.[17] He urges researchers to document the diverse forms of resistance or struggle that are taking place in order to highlight the totalizing nature of the capitalist system.

It is the recognition of the normativity of ethnographic research that leads us to consider how social research can improve women's lives. The closure of F2 could be taken as a discouraging event after years of struggle, since after all, the accommodating women of F1 are still at their jobs and experiencing relatively good working conditions and wages. Similarly, the success of the Gina workers was short-lived, since the factory has been relocated. It is apparent that apparel production is on the move to the border zones, where stateless migrants provide a willing workforce at lower wages. New research on women's lives and ethnographies of hardship should therefore also explore the experience of migrant women as a particularly vulnerable group. At least the Thai factory women had some form of legal redress for their grievances and some legitimacy in seeking to form a union. Migrant women and men from Burma, Cambodia, and Laos work longer hours for less money with no legal protection. This is where the new ethnographies of hardship need to focus.

The emergence of rapidly industrializing export-oriented economies such as Vietnam, Cambodia, Burma, and China also emphasizes the urgency for new ethnographic studies that take account of the everyday experiences of female workers. It is therefore essential, when looking at women's struggles against capitalism and their resistance to globalizing market forces, to understand the underlying material conditions in which women find themselves. It is an ethical imperative for researchers to really explore and understand women's lived realities and to let women's voices speak if we are to address and remedy the severe consequences of globalization. Ethnography can indeed be an immensely rich and constructive approach for looking at women's experiences of work and living. There are working women who have stories to tell, who are eager to tell them, and who want to be heard.

Notes

Introduction. The Condition of Women Garment Workers in Thailand

1. See Dennis Arnold, "Textile and Apparel Sourcing: The Complexity behind Low-Cost Labor in Supply Chains," *Asian Labor Update* (Hong Kong: Asia Monitor Resource Centre) 54 (2005).

2. Welcome to Sweatshop Watch. http://www.sweatshopwatch.org/. "Labour Behind the Label" is the UK motto of the CCC, which also aims to support garment workers' efforts worldwide in improving work conditions. The group focuses on raising awareness about sweatshop conditions by educating consumers, lobbying companies and governments, and encouraging international solidarity among workers. Its members include trade unions, consumer organizations, other campaign groups, and charities. http://www.labourbehindthelabel.org/.

3. "The Stark Reality of iPod's Chinese Factories," *The Mail on Sunday* (London), 18 August 2006.

4. The notion of just-in-time is one way of characterizing the flow of products through the global supply chain in what is often described as post-Fordism. It is designed to co-ordinate supply and demand and minimize stock levels at the same time. For a critical treatment of the literature on post-Fordism, see Bob Jessop, "Fordism and Post-Fordism: A Critical Reformulation," in *Pathways to Industrialization and Regional Development*, ed. Michael Storper and Allen J. Scott (London: Routledge, 1992). For another view of Jessop's treatment of these issues in the global economy, see Mark J. Smith, *Rethinking State Theory* (London: Routledge, 2000), 211–215. Labor processes in just-in-time production are also considered in Ian M. Taplin, "Recent Manufacturing Changes in the U.S. Apparel Industry: The Case of North Carolina Global Production," in *Global Production: The Apparel Industry in the Pacific Rim*, ed. Edna Bonacich et al. (Philadelphia: Temple University Press, 1994), 336–341. As Jessop and Sum explain,

> In addition to production and authority management, finished goods in the "supply pipeline" need to be exported/distributed to the global market. Distribution management, then, involves the re-articulation of factory time and global lead-time

through the activities of service-based firms in the region as well as trading and customs authorities. This trans-border private-public network is co-ordinated in the "electronic" and "social" spaces that synchronize transport schedules, export procedures of import/export licensing, custom liaison, international payments, insurance, packaging and logistic management, etc., so that goods can be delivered just-in-time and "right-in-place" for the global-regional buyers.... The subcontracting management practices that are developed and co-ordinated across the border by these various political and economic actors are a form of process innovation. (Bob Jessop and Ngai-Ling Sum, "An Entrepreneurial City in Action: Hong Kong's Emerging Strategies in and for [Inter] Urban Competition," *Urban Studies* 37, no. 12 [2000]: 2209.)

The intensification of production in business networks is also explored in Andrew Sayer, "New Developments in Manufacturing: The Just-in-Time System," *Capital and Class* 30 (1986): 43–72.

5. For a discussion of degraded production processes and brand-name companies, see Naomi Klein, *No Logo: No Space, No Choice, No Jobs* (New York: Picador, 1999).

6. During the period of British colonialism, for instance, raw materials such as cotton from India were shipped to Britain to be processed and assembled in sweatshops. Britain was then known as the "workshop of the world." The assembled goods were next shipped back to the colonies; in India, the colonial administration put a ban on indigenous cotton manufacturing to ensure it had a captive market. During decolonization and deindustrialization, from the 1950s to 1980s, transnational corporations started owning subsidiaries and using low-cost labor in the former colonies or developing countries. These companies had a more direct relation with their suppliers: raw materials were not only processed but also cut and assembled, and the finished or partially finished goods were then shipped back to the countries of origin, such as the United States. During the 1990s and to the present day, a sweatshop global economy has emerged, characterized by outsourced manufacturing: retailers and brand-name companies can outsource their entire production process to hundreds of sites around the world through contracting agents that hire workers at the lowest price possible. Hence, in the global sweatshop economy there is a contractual barrier that lets companies off the hook, so to speak: their obligation, responsibility, and liability are taken away, and manufacturers can merely sign up for codes of conduct without feeling the need to enforce them.

7. From 1999 to 2003, Thailand received between 8.5 and 10 million visitors each year (8.58 million in 1999, 9.51 million in 2000, and an average of 10 million in 2001, 2002, and 2003). According to the Bank of Thailand and the Tourism Authority of Thailand, the tourism industry during 2002–2004 contributed approximately 7.7 percent to GDP, creating, directly and indirectly, around 3.3 million jobs or 8.4 percent of the country's employment. The World Travel & Tourism Council (WTTC) projects that this employment figure will grow by 9.5 percent in 2014 and that tourism's contribution to GDP will increase from 11.7 percent in 2005 to 12.6 percent by 2014. According to the WTTC, current estimates of revenue and GDP contribution from the Thai tourism industry are higher than in other Southeast Asian countries. In 2005, 11.65 million people visited Thailand. http://www.thailandoutlook.com (1996 and 2005).

8. Thailand's major export markets are the United States, the European Union, ASEAN nations, Japan, and China. In 2004, textile and garment exports generated US$6.4 billion, according to the Thai Customs Department, representing approximately 4 percent of GDP: Focus Thailand (2005), http://www.mfa.go.th /internet/document/1861.doc.

9. For a historical account of the Hara Factory Incident of October 1975–May 1976, see Bandit Thanachaisettawut, *The Struggle of the Thai Women Labour Movement* (Bangkok: Friedrich Ebert Stiftung, 1999), 15–25.

10. According to Lavender, young female operatives employed in the Lowell mills challenged an increasingly oppressive system that exerted strict forms of control over labor

and subjected workers to deplorable conditions of work. Much discontent and resistance among the workers were due to poor work conditions, wage cuts, increasing costs in company housing, work speedups, and the imposition of "obnoxious regulations" in the factory. Less than two years after the mill opened, nearly 400 women turned out in the first recorded strike of female textile operatives in the United States. Catherine Lavender, "Lowell Mill Girls and the Rhetoric of Women's Labor Unrest" (1997). http://www.library. csi.cuny.edu/dept/history/lavender/lowstr.html.

11. Karl Marx, *The German Ideology* (New York: International Publishers, 1970), 51.

12. Michael Burawoy, *The Politics of Production: Factory Regimes under Capitalism and Socialism* (London: Verso, 1985), 39.

13. John D. French and Daniel James, "Squaring the Circle: Women's Factory Labor, Gender Ideology, and Necessity," in *The Gendered Worlds of Latin American Women Workers: From Household and Factory to the Union Hall and Ballot Box*, ed. John D. French and Daniel James (Durham, N.C.: Duke University Press, 1997), 7.

14. See Lourdes Benería and Martha Roldán, *The Crossroads of Class and Gender: Industrial Homework, Subcontracting, and the Household Dynamics in Mexico City* (Chicago: University of Chicago Press, 1987); Rita S. Gallin, "Women and the Export Industry in Taiwan: The Muting of Class Consciousness in Silicon Valley," in *Women Workers and Global Restructuring*, ed. Kathryn Ward (Ithaca: Cornell University Press, 1990); Seung-Kyung Kim, *Class Struggle or Family Struggle? The Lives of Women Factory Workers in South Korea* (Cambridge: Cambridge University Press, 1997); Louise Lamphere, *From Working Daughters to Working Mothers* (Ithaca: Cornell University Press, 1987); Eleanor Leacock and Helen I. Safa, eds., *Women's Work: Development and the Division of Labor by Gender* (New York: Bergin & Garvey Publishers, 1986); Laura Lee Downs, *Manufacturing Inequality: Gender Division in the French and British Metalworking Industries, 1914–1939* (Ithaca: Cornell University Press, 1995); Ruth Milkman, *Gender at Work: The Dynamics of Job Segregation by Sex during World War II* (Urbana: University of Illinois Press, 1987); Aihwa Ong, *Spirits of Resistance and Capitalist Discipline: Factory Women in Malaysia* (Albany: State University of New York Press, 1987); Aihwa Ong, "State versus Islam: Malay Families, Women's Bodies, and the Body Politic in Malaysia," in *Bewitching Women, Pious Men: Gender and Body Politics in Southeast Asia*, ed. Aihwa Ong and Michael Peletz (Berkeley: University of California Press, 1995); Ruth Pearson, "Industrialization and Women's Subordination: A Reappraisal," in *Patriarchy and Economic Development*, ed. Valentine M. Moghadam (Oxford: Clarendon Press, 1996); Leslie Salzinger, *Genders in Production: Making Workers in Mexico's Global Factories* (Berkeley: University of California Press, 2003); Diane Wolf, *Factory Daughters: Gender, Household Dynamics, and Rural Industrialization in Java* (Berkeley: University of California Press, 1992); Kevin A. Yelvington, *Producing Power: Ethnicity, Gender, and Class in a Caribbean Workplace* (Philadelphia: Temple University Press, 1995).

15. Ping-Chun Hsiung, *Living Rooms as Factories: Class, Gender, and the Satellite Factory System in Taiwan* (Philadelphia: Temple University Press, 1996); Devon G. Pena, *The Terror of the Machine: Technology, Work, Gender, and Ecology on the U.S.-Mexican Border* (Austin, Tex.: Center for Mexican American Studies, 1997); Susan Tiano, *Patriarchy on the Line: Labor, Gender, and Ideology in the Mexican Maquila Industry* (Philadelphia: Temple University Press, 1994).

16. Michael Burawoy, "The Extended Case Method," in *Ethnography Unbound: Power and Resistance in the Modern Metropolis,* by Michael Burawoy et al. (Berkeley: University of California Press, 1991), 272, 282.

17. French and James, "Squaring the Circle," 5.

18. Lydia Kung, *Factory Women in Taiwan* (1983; New York: Columbia University Press, 1994); Gallin, "Women and the Export Industry in Taiwan"; Hsiung, *Living Rooms as Factories*; Kim, *Class Struggle or Family Struggle?*; Wolf, *Factory Daughters*; Ong, "State versus Islam."

19. Maria Mies, *Patriarchy and Accumulation on a World Scale: Women in the International Division of Labour* (London: Zed Books, 1988), 36.

20. Edna Acosta-Belén and Christine E. Bose, "Colonialism, Structural Subordination, and Empowerment: Women in the Development Process in Latin America and the Caribbean," in *Women in the Latin American Development Process*, ed. Christine E. Bose and Edna Acosta-Belén (Philadelphia: Temple University Press, 1995), 31.

21. Zillah Eisenstein distinguishes between patriarchy and capitalism: she sees patriarchy as a system of control and capitalism as a system of economy. She describes capitalist patriarchy as a hierarchical, exploitive, oppressive system maintained through the sexual division of labor. Within a capitalist patriarchal economy, the sexual division of labor in society serves to maintain the family while it organizes a realm of work for women to perform domestic labor, resulting in the patriarchal exploitation of women's labor as it is organized by productive and reproductive arrangements. Zillah Eisenstein, *Capitalist Patriarchy and the Case for Socialist Feminism* (New York: Monthly Review Press, 1978). Similarly, Sylvia Walby defines patriarchy as a "system of social structures and practices in which men dominate, oppress and exploit women" (Sylvia Walby, *Theorizing Patriarchy* [Oxford: Basil Blackwell, 1990], 20). At the most abstract level, she conceptualizes patriarchy as a system of social relations between men and women, and "at a less abstract level patriarchy is composed of six structures" that "have causal effects upon each other...but are relatively autonomous" and "are necessary to capture the variation in gender relations" (20). Patriarchal structures within the workplace, for example, relegate women to the lowest-paying jobs. Walby points out that we need to "distinguish analytically between changes in the degree of patriarchy from changes in its forms" (23). "Changes in degree include aspects of gender relations such as the slight reduction in the wage gap between men and women" (23); changes in form occur when women move from one socioeconomic and political system to another. Walby also distinguishes between private patriarchy and public patriarchy, the former being based on the household as the main site of women's oppression, the latter on male domination in paid employment and in state structures. Patriarchal labor market structures and practices are important in determining the pattern of women's employment and unemployment. Walby does point out, however, that patriarchy is not the only concept that can account for the complexity and diversity of patterns of gender relations, which is why it needs to be examined in articulation with other systems of production such as capitalism.

22. Gallin found that male managers used gender tactics to control and divide workers and to maintain a gendered hierarchy within the workplace. Rita Gallin, "State, Gender, and the Organization of Business in Rural Taiwan," in *Patriarchy and Economic Development*, ed. Moghadam; Hsiung, *Living Rooms as Factories*; Kung, *Factory Women in Taiwan*.

23. Marilyn Frye, *The Politics of Reality: Essays in Feminist Theory* (Freedom, Calif.: Crossing Press, 1983), 59, 55.

24. Ibid. Frye explains that in order to force someone to do something, the coercer must manipulate a situation in such a way that it "presents the victim with a range of options the least unattractive of which (or the most attractive of which) in the judgment of the victim is the act one wants the victim to do" (56–57).

25. James C. Scott, *Weapons of the Weak: Everyday Forms of Peasant Resistance* (New Haven: Yale University Press, 1985), 39.

26. Tiano, *Patriarchy on the Line*, 199–200.

27. Economic Development Indicators Database. http://www.worldbank.org.

28. Tiano, *Patriarchy on the Line*, 196, 198.

29. The Central Region is made up of twenty-two provinces; the Northeastern Region of nineteen; the Northern Region, seventeen; the Southern Region, fourteen; and the Eastern Region, four.

30. The family had owned and operated twenty-two subsidiary companies.

31. According to Max Weber, ideal types should be seen as simplistic exaggerations derived from empirical reality but are not themselves literal descriptions; instead, they serve as organizing devices for making sense of the inevitably complex empirical reality we seek to explain and understand. Cited in Mark J. Smith, *Social Science in Question* (London: Sage, 1998), chap. 4.

32. My primary data were collected through semistructured informal interviews and partial participant observation. The sample groups included thirty-four nonmilitant women from F1; six militant women from F2, five of whom had been dismissed for their union activities, and one who was still employed at the factory and was head of the workers' union at the time; eighteen nonmilitant women from F3; four nonmilitant women from F4, a unionized factory and affiliate of F2; two laid-off nonmilitant women workers from the parent factory (PF) of F1 and F4; and an additional four militant women from factories located in the Omnoi-Omyai industrial zone of Samut Prakarn and Nakorn Prathom provinces, the industrial zone of Prapadaeng in the Suksawat Rathburana district, and the Bang Na Traad industrial zone of the Central Region. Nonmilitant women at unionized factories refer to those workers who were not directly involved in union activities at the factory but were members of the workers' union. The interview with one woman employee at SF1 was conducted by phone. I also interviewed three male employees and three supervisors from F1; the factory managers of F1, F3, and F4; and three labor academics and researchers. (See Table 1 on p. 33.)

The women answered an initial questionnaire dealing with general biographical information: age, provenance, marital status, family, educational background, conditions under which they were recruited, employment history, and length of employment. During in-depth interview sessions, women were asked about their work experiences, their placement within the production process, their relations within the workplace, their perceptions of their work and wages, their perceptions of men and gender equality, their social and personal lives, and their interests and activities. Women living in the dormitories at F3 were asked an additional set of questions pertaining to dormitory life. Militant women were asked about their involvement in such union activities as protests, strikes, or other forms of collective mobilization.

All interviews were conducted in Thai and were tape-recorded. I usually translated and transcribed the responses by hand in my notebook during the interview or later that day from the tape recordings. The few extra women in the sub-sample were chosen to provide supplementary material and information in addition to whatever data I had already acquired. A follow-up questionnaire and a second interview dealt with the women's daily expenses for transportation to and from work, travel time, the proximity of their homes to the factory, what time they woke up in the morning, how many hours of sleep they got a night, and what adjustments in their spending patterns were made necessary by the crisis of 1997. Most of the follow-up questions were influenced by the women's responses to my initial set of queries.

I was given access to three factories through my own personal contacts: a family member knew the owner of F1 because his daughters were her pupils at the boarding school where she taught; F3 was recommended by a friend who was a former classmate of the manager; and the manager of F4 was a personal acquaintance whose family owns and operates the majority of factories in the Rangsit industrial zone. I contacted those managers directly by phone before visiting the sites, visits that each included a tour of the production process given by the owner/manager. The militant women at F2 were referred to me by someone at the AFL-CIO regional office in Bangkok, and these women were able to introduce me to friends and fellow workers in the same situation. Through this snowball sampling method, I was able to conduct additional interviews with militant women from other factories.

Statistical and other descriptive data were drawn from annual governmental publications and documents; secondary literature, in Thai, on women in manufacturing; the *Bangkok Post* and *The Nation* newspapers' library archives. Data on militant women's activities were collected through the Thai Labour Campaign (TLC), a nonprofit, nongovernmental organization committed to promoting workers' rights in Thailand and increasing awareness of labor issues locally and globally. (The Thai Labour Campaign, started by the labor researcher and activist Junya Yimprasert in February 2000, collects information about all forms of labor violations in Thailand and publicizes ongoing abuses to a network of labor organizations nationally and internationally on its website, http://www.thailabour.org.

TLC provides extensive data on the manufacturing industry, including journalistic and investigative reports on women workers in export industries and on all ongoing demonstrations and protests at factories.) I also relied on internal factory documents obtained from former workers. Secondary sources on women in Thailand were available at research institutes such as the Thailand Information Center at Chulalongkorn University, the Gender and Development Institute, and other NGOs such as the Foundation for Women and the Committee on Asian Women.

33. Benería and Roldán, *Crossroads of Class and Gender,* 27.

34. It is estimated that about half of the transnational corporations operating in Thailand established their operations between 1963 and 1972. Kevin Hewison, *Bankers and Bureaucrats: Capital and the Role of the State in Thailand* (New Haven: Yale University Press, 1989), 58.

35. "Between 1960 and 1975, the total employed in factories with over 50 workers expanded from under 100,000 to almost 600,000," and an additional "3.3 million people were added to the total urban population, 1 million to the industrial work-force as a whole, and over half a million to the work-force in larger factories." Pasuk Phongpaichit and Chris Baker, *Thailand, Economy and Politics* (Oxford: Oxford University Press, 1995), 187.

36. The population grew from 19.6 to 56.1 million between 1950 and 1990; ibid., 187–188. Currently, the population of Thailand stands at around 64 million.

37. Medhi Krongkaew, ed., *Thailand's Industrialization and Its Consequences* (New York: St. Martin's Press, 1995), 124–125.

38. Nationwide, over 250,000 establishments are small-scale firms that employ from one to nine persons, totaling a workforce of over 864,000. Only about 112,000 nonmanufacturing and manufacturing establishments employed ten persons or more, totaling a workforce of about 7 million. The Department of Labour Protection and Welfare 1999 statistics as cited in http://www.dlpw.go.th/stat.en.html.

39. It is important to note that many small and medium factories were not legally registered and were more likely than others to violate labor regulations. Jaded Chouwilai, director of the Friends of Women Foundation, classified the NGO definition of small, medium, and large factories according to the number of workers employed: *small,* 100 workers or fewer; *medium,* between 100 and 500; and *large,* more than 500 workers. These approximate specifications make it problematic for the government to account for the total number of manufacturing establishments. Author's interview with Jaded Chouwilai on October 27, 1999, in Bangkok.

40. Nicole Bullard et al., "Taming the Tigers: The IMF and the Asian Crisis," *Focus on Trade* 23 (March 1998).

41. Phongpaichit and Baker, *Thailand, Economy and Politics,* 158.

42. Japanese investments went primarily into intermediate goods industries; the manufacturing of metal products, electrical products, machinery and transport goods, chemicals, paper, and petroleum products; and construction. Walden Bello, "The End of the Asian Miracle," *Focus on Trade* 22 (January 1998).

43. Phongpaichit and Baker, *Thailand, Economy and Politics,* 159.

44. In 1993, the net foreign capital inflow on the stock exchange was over seven times that of the previous year. Thai firms thus found it easier to raise funds on overseas markets. Bello, "End of the Asian Miracle."

45. The construction sector, which previously employed up to 1.5 million workers, was dramatically hit, affecting not only the construction workers themselves but the other industries that fed off real estate and property. Although there is no reliable estimate of the number of construction workers who were laid off, thousands were left unemployed by the end of 1997 as work on most construction projects in Bangkok came to an end. Bello, "End of the Asian Miracle."

46. Kevin Hewison, "The Political Economy of Siam, 1851–1932," *Journal of Contemporary Asia* 10, no. 3 (1980): 293–299; David Robertson, "Thailand: Asia's Bright Future," *Contemporary Review* 267, no. 1555 (1995): 57; David Robinson, "The Bowring Treaty: Imperialism and the Indigenous Perspective," *Journal of the Siam Society* 79 (1991): 2.

47. Peter F. Bell, "Development or Maldevelopment? The Contradictions of Thailand's Economic Growth," in *Uneven Development in Thailand*, ed. Michael Parnwell (Avebury, UK: Ashgate, 1996); Malcolm Falkus, "Thai Industrialization: An Overview," in *Thailand's Industrialization and Its Consequences*, ed. Krongkaew; Antonia Hussey, "Rapid Industrialization in Thailand, 1986–1991," *Geographical Review* 83, no. 1 (1993): 14–28; Jonathan Rigg, *Southeast Asia: The Human Landscape of Modernization and Development*, 2nd ed. (London: Routledge, 2003); Peter J. Rimmer, "Urbanization Problems in Thailand's Rapidly Industrializing Economy," in *Thailand's Industrialization and Its Consequences*, ed. Krongkaew; Michael T. Rock, "Transitional Democracies and the Shift to Export-led Industrialization: Lessons from Thailand," *Studies in Comparative International Development* 29, no. 1 (1994): 18; Jean-Christophe Simon, "The Thai Manufacturing Sector: New Patterns of Expansion," in *Uneven Development in Thailand*, ed. Parnwell.

48. Richard Doner and Ansil Ramsay, "Thailand in the Pacific Rim Garment Industry," in *Global Production: The Apparel Industry in the Pacific Rim*, ed. Bonacich et al., 180. The authors contend that specific state policies promoted the growth of the garment sector with the BOI making garments a promoted industry in 1967. The state further assisted with export promotion by "enacting several favorable policies including tax rebates on imported fabrics, yarns, and sewing machines; low interest rates; and reimbursement of taxes on export sales" (182).

49. Phongpaichit and Baker, *Thailand, Economy and Politics*, 144.

50. Doner and Ramsay, "Thailand in the Pacific Rim Garment Industry," 180–181.

51. Ibid., 182.

52. Phongpaichit and Baker, *Thailand, Economy and Politics*, 145–146.

53. As in South Korea, Taiwan, and Hong Kong, the development of manufacturing exports in Thailand began with the textile industry. Textile firms from Japan and garment firms from Hong Kong and Taiwan had relocated production to Thailand and other overseas sites since the 1970s. Phongpaichit and Baker, *Thailand, Economy and Politics*, 159.

54. "A 1971 bilateral agreement with the United States cleared the way for rapid export growth by placing less restrictive controls—as compared to those on East Asian NICs—on Thai garment exports. Subsequent agreements with the United States (in 1975) and the European Union (in 1976) provided Thai garment makers with assured markets, encouraging them to expand production." Doner and Ramsay, "Thailand in the Pacific Rim Garment Industry," 185–186.

55. In 1991, the estimated foreign share of the Thai garment industry was 10 percent. There was also an increase in Japanese investment in the Thai garment industry in the early to the mid-1990s. Doner and Ramsay, "Thailand in the Pacific Rim Garment Industry," 186–187; Phongpaichit and Baker, *Thailand, Economy and Politics*, 143.

56. As Doner and Ramsey indicate, between 1985 and 1989, only six other developing countries had higher annual growth rates of GNP per capita. Doner and Ramsay, "Thailand in the Pacific Rim Garment Industry," 180.

57. "Garment Sector: 'Fast Fashion' Plan Targets Small Firms," *The Nation* (Bangkok), 17 February 2005. The United States is the biggest market for Thai textile exports, followed by the European Union and Japan. In 2004, the United States took in US$1.76 billion worth of garments, or 51.81 percent of the country's total exports; the European Union, US$861 million or 25.35 percent, and Japan at US$223 million, followed by ASEAN with US$80.02 million.

58. Doner and Ramsay also point out that unionization is hampered by Thailand's flexible labor market with many urban workers returning to their villages, a situation that clearly weakens the foundation for strong unions. "Thailand in the Pacific Rim Garment Industry," 183–184.

59. Walden Bello et al., *A Siamese Tragedy: Development and Disintegration in Modern Thailand* (London: Zed Books, 1998), 75.

60. Bello reports that "By 1995, there were some 56 industrial estates throughout Thailand.... [T]hey offered tax breaks, subsidized infrastructure, exemption or reduction

in import and export taxes, and a variety of other incentives to foreign and local investors." Ibid., 80.

61. The most recent data on strikes, lockouts and grievances were recorded in 1999 but these figures do not indicate whether labor disputes occurred at one or more places, the type of manufacturing establishment, or the number of workers involved. Some cases were withdrawn, and very few cases were referred to labor court, leaving a large number of cases still pending. Bangkok and the surrounding five industrial provinces had the highest number of strikes, lockouts, and grievances filed by workers, which is not surprising, given the foreclosures of mostly unionized factories in these free-trade zones following 1997. Moreover, the numbers of strikes and lockouts were small (two and twelve respectively) relative to the number of establishments. These data are derived from the Department of Labour Protection and Welfare, 2000, as published on the Thai Labour Campaign website. http://www.thailabour.org.

62. Dan Clawson, *The Next Upsurge: Labor and the New Social Movements* (Ithaca: Cornell University Press, 2003), 153.

1. Adaptation and Accommodation: The "Nonmilitant" Women

1. Many female migrants started to arrive in Bangkok beginning in the 1960s, but the real surge of rural to urban migration took place over the next two decades.

2. I chose a larger number of women to interview at F1 and F3 because I wanted to explore the issues of accommodation, acquiescence, powerlessness, and passivity. I visited F1 on several occasions, mostly during lunch hours, to speak to the women in the canteen or in their living quarters nearby, where I became more aware of their aspirations, desires, fears, and anxieties and acquired a better understanding of their realities. These women exemplified a long-standing workforce because they had been working in textile factories for extended periods of time without disruption to production. This made for an ideal situation for looking at the various mechanisms that operated to inhibit women's possibilities for organization.

3. All the factory owners in this study were men.

4. A few old-timers started working at much younger ages: Jae Ngau was only thirteen when she was brought into F1 to do a few chores for the family; women such as Laeyd, Saiyon, and Ouan did brief stints when they were sixteen at various jobs before formally applying to work at F1.

5. Mary Beth Mills points out that women's out-migration is not limited to rural poverty but involves families from middle-income and, in a few cases, quite prosperous households. Mary Beth Mills, "Contesting the Margins of Modernity: Women, Migration, and Consumption in Thailand," *American Ethnologist* 24 (1997): 37–61.

6. Like Mills, I discovered that young women took credit for their decision to leave. Mills (ibid.) stresses that it is essential to examine the entry of young rural women into the urban labor force as a product of complex personal motivations.

7. Workers referred to overtime by initials, *oh tee*. In the inspecting department, overtime was only until 7:00 p.m., Monday through Saturday.

8. Equivalent to US$4.24 at the 1998 rate of 37 baht to US$1.00. According to Junya Yimprasert of the Thai Labour Campaign (interview in December 2002), the minimum wage rate in Thailand was stagnant for 1998 through 2000. The Thai government came under much pressure by labor advocacy groups to increase the daily minimum wage to 180 baht. Yimprasert reported that in December 2000, the Thai government agreed to raise it to 165 baht, an increase of 3 baht (8 cents) or 4.86 percent from the then 162-baht minimum. Over three years there was an actual increase of only 1 baht, or 1.62 percent. The minimum wage also fluctuates with location: e.g., 165 baht in the Bangkok metropolitan area, 143 baht and 133 baht in the outlying provinces.

As of April 2005, the daily minimum wage ranged between 137 and 175 baht. In 2006, the highest rate was 184 baht for Bangkok and the surrounding provinces and 140 baht upcountry. In May 2006, Thai workers sought to hike the minimum wage by at least 25 percent to 233 baht. "Workers Seeking Minimum Wage Hike to Bt233 per Day," *The Nation* (Bangkok), 2 May 2006.

9. It is important to note that women and men at F1 are paid the same wages per hour, contradicting the conventional wisdom that men make higher wages than women.

10. A worker must have put in the full regular hours during the week, with no absent days, in order to work overtime hours.

11. An employee is entitled to take leave to attend to his or her personal business (without pay) as necessary, in accordance with work regulations.

12. As Theresa R. Veccia found in her study of working women in São Paulo, Brazil, economic pressures were felt most by those who were the oldest. Theresa R. Veccia, "My Duty as a Woman: Gender Ideology, Work, and Working-Class Women's Lives in São Paulo, Brazil, 1900–1950," in *The Gendered Worlds of Latin American Women Workers: From Household and Factory to the Union Hall and Ballot Box*, ed. John D. French and Daniel James (Durham, N.C.: Duke University Press, 1997), 103.

13. Susan Tiano, *Patriarchy on the Line: Labor, Gender, and Ideology in the Mexican Maquila Industry* (Philadelphia: Temple University Press, 1994), 73, 92, 93.

14. According to the 1998 Labour Protection Act, a pregnant female employee is entitled to ninety days' maternity leave (including holidays during the maternity leave). According to the law, she receives her basic pay at a rate equal to a normal working day during leave up to forty-five days; the rest of the leave is unpaid. Therefore a child is usually sent away when two or three months old.

15. Rhacel S. Parreñas, *Servants of Globalization: Women, Migration, and Domestic Work* (Stanford, Calif.: Stanford University Press, 2001), 119.

16. According to the "Rights and Duties of Employers and Employees" under the Labour Protection Act of 1998, no fewer than thirteen traditional holidays per year must be granted to employees, and if a traditional holiday falls on a weekly holiday, the employee must also have the following workday off. In addition to traditional holidays, employees who have worked continually for one full year are entitled to an annual vacation of no fewer than six working days. At F1, however, employees were granted only the thirteen holidays, with no additional compensation for earned vacation days or lost holidays. In actuality, most women took only three days off a year, usually during the New Year season (December 31 to Jan. 2) and chose to work overtime hours on all official holidays.

17. When I revisited the factory in 2002, I discovered that many of the women had cell phones, which had become an affordable and integral part of life for people from all walks of life in Thailand. According to the *Bangkok Post*, Thailand's mobile phone market had grown beyond expectation, "reaching nearly 18 million users, more than 70% of them on low-margin pre-paid plans. . . . At the end of 2001, the country had 7.5 million cellular subscribers." The sudden increase was due to the removal of all phone locks by the service operators, enabling independent handset distributors to import cheaper units into the country to compete with the brand-name models. This brought down the prices of the phones significantly and made "cellular service almost universally available." The report also noted that cell phone operators were targeting untapped markets—TA Orange, for instance, was "especially aggressive" in the provinces where "cellular penetration is still low at 10% of the population, compared with more than 30% in Bangkok." Year-End Economic Review, 2002. http://www.bangkokpost.net/yearend2002/mobiles.html.

18. Parreñas, *Servants of Globalization,* 245.

19. Michael Burawoy, *Manufacturing Consent: Changes in the Labor Process under Monopoly Capitalism* (Chicago: University of Chicago Press, 1979), 24, 15.

20. At a minimum wage rate of 162 baht per day, a worker would make about 4,200 baht (US$105) per month. Subtracting 1,100 baht for rent leaves 3,100 baht, and spending 50 baht per day on food leaves the worker with only 1,600 baht for all other expenses.

21. Patricia Tsurumi, *Factory Girls: Women in the Thread Mills of Meiji Japan* (Princeton: Princeton University Press, 1990). During the Meiji era, 1868 to 1912, the numbers of Japan's first industrial workers grew rapidly but remained a small minority in a laboring population engaged mainly in agriculture. During the 1880s, 78 to 80 percent of those employed were in agricultural occupations, but by 1902, of 24.6 million in the labor force, only 67.2 percent were in agriculture. By 1912, about 863,000, in a total working population of 25.8 million, were industrial workers, more than half of them employed in textiles (3). In 1900, it was estimated that almost 80 percent of cotton spinning operatives were girls or women (5). The systematic indoctrination by management and government through lectures, lessons, published textbooks, and company songs of "sacrificing for the good of the nation" was unsuccessful because the textile workers appeared to be interested only in their families' welfare (193–196). The songs that the women chose to sing, for instance, were not nationalistic company songs but songs of surviving within harsh working conditions. Nonetheless, their labor in the factories supported the general expectation that women would work long and hard for their families.

22. Ibid., 48. Since Japan's industrialization was carried out within the framework of tradition (the Meiji restoration), it preserved rather than dissolved many traditional arrangements in the countryside. Poor tenant farmers were able to stay on the land because of the wages their daughters earned in textile mills. By helping their families pay the tax collector and the landlord, however, girls and women in the textile plants helped perpetuate the hierarchical and exploitative relationships of the pre-Meiji countryside (192–195).

23. Veccia explains that "by connecting workers to their jobs through the provision of low-rent housing, employers institutionalized a family-based labor system that in practice tended to operate more informally throughout the industry." Veccia, "My Duty as a Woman," 113.

24. Marilyn Frye, *The Politics of Reality: Essays in Feminist Theory* (Freedom, Calif.: Crossing Press, 1983), 59.

25. Harry Braverman, *Labor and Monopoly Capital: The Degradation of Work in the Twentieth Century* (New York: Monthly Review Press, 1974), 57.

26. Under the clause "Female Labour" in the Labour Protection Act of 1998, "An employer is prohibited from causing a pregnant female employee to work between 22:00 and 06:00 hours, or to work overtime, and on holidays, or perform heavy physical tasks." http://www.thailabour.org/law/thai/code.html.

27. Some of the old-timers at the factory felt that the wages they earned nearly twenty years ago were higher than what they were making now. One woman, Kuh, even stated that "The minimum wage set by the Thai government twenty years ago was mandated to cover the daily needs of at least two individuals per household" and that the daily minimum wage at present "does not meet the expenditures for even one person." However, there was no such formulation regarding the minimum wage, which, according to Phil Robertson (interview), was a constant source of complaint for the labor movement, whose members said that the minimum wage should be based on the daily needs of a family of at least two persons.

In 1972, a national wage committee was set up to make recommendations on the minimum wage to the Ministry of Interior, and under one of the clauses on labor and employment law, the minimum wage was defined as a fixed wage "which the employee should receive and be able to survive." Nikom Chandravithun and W. Gary Vause, *Thailand's Labor and Employment Law: A Practical Guide* (Bangkok: Manager Publishing, 1994), 124.

28. Christena L. Turner, *Japanese Workers in Protest: An Ethnography of Consciousness and Experience* (Berkeley: University of California Press, 1995).

29. Aihwa Ong, *Spirits of Resistance and Capitalist Discipline: Factory Women in Malaysia* (Albany: State University of New York Press, 1987), 169.

30. The factory owner, who performed a more administrative and managerial role, assumed a more distant position from the production process.

31. Nancy Scheper-Hughes, *Death without Weeping* (Berkeley: University of California Press, 1992), 126.

32. In what is defined as a family wage economy, this situation is not unlike that in the textile mills of late nineteenth-century São Paulo, Brazil, where it was common for children to work alongside their parents and for siblings to work alongside one another. Veccia, "My Duty as a Woman," 108.

33. At smaller factories, husband-and-wife teams would compete with one another to see who could produce more.

34. Tiano, *Patriarchy on the Line,* 172, 117, 176.

35. Veccia, "My Duty as a Woman," 119.

36. My very first interview in the field was with Porn, a young, pretty, fiercely independent twenty-five-year-old. Articulate, outspoken, and confident, she stood out among the women I interviewed at F1. Porn is from Ubon Rat province and comes from a nonfarming family. She had completed a sixth-grade education and said that it was her own decision to move to Bangkok. She arrived at F1 with no previous work experience but, by the time of the interview, had been working there for three years. When I returned one year later, she had left the factory.

37. Tuition at Thai public schools is free, but students are expected to pay for school-related expenses such as uniforms and textbooks.

38. Laura Lee Downs, *Manufacturing Inequality: Gender Division in the French and British Metalworking Industries, 1914–1939* (Ithaca: Cornell University Press, 1995), 270–271.

39. See Seung-Kyung Kim, *Class Struggle or Family Struggle? The Lives of Women Factory Workers in South Korea* (Cambridge: Cambridge University Press, 1997), chap. 3.

40. The percentage of women in the workforce has been estimated to be anywhere from 47 to 70 percent. Women reportedly receive only 77 percent of what men are paid in the manufacturing sector, 60 percent in the service sector, and 84 percent in the farming sector. Kulavir P. Pipat, "Thai Women Continue the International Women's Day Struggle," *Forum News* 18, no. 1 (January—April 2005). Women's Studies Center, Chiang Mai University, Thailand. http://www.apwld.org/vol181–04.htm.

41. Busakorn Suriyasarn, "Socio-economic Change and the Changing Roles and Status of Thai Women" (1993). http://www.busakorn.addr.com/women/women-socio-transfor mation.htm.

42. In Thailand, daughters, especially in rural communities, are expected to care for their elderly parents and other family members. For Mills, the "good daughter" is the young female migrant who has a deep sense of responsibility for her rural family. Mary Beth Mills, *Thai Women in the Global Labor Force: Consuming Desires, Contested Selves* (New Brunswick, N.J.: Rutgers University Press, 1999), 92.

43. Mills, "Contesting the Margins of Modernity, 43, 55.

44. "Older women" are thirty-six years of age or more; fourteen women, or 41 percent of my sample, fell into this category.

45. Tiano, *Patriarchy on the Line,* 197.

46. Ong, *Spirits of Resistance,* 165–166.

2. Resistance and Worker Rebellion: The "Militant" Women

1. In April 1994, Sripai took a leave of absence, as permitted under Thai labor law, so that she could help organize workers at another factory. She was fired from F2 for missing thirty-three days of work. She took her case to court, but the court ruled against her on the basis that her leave of absence was taken on behalf of workers at another factory, one of F2's subcontract factories.

2. Women's ages are based on the time at which the first phase of interviews was conducted in 1999.

3. "Sweatshops" may be defined here as small-scale firms that are not legally registered and that may employ from one to ten workers.

4. I never had an opportunity to sit down with Taan and talk to her at length (as I did with the other women) about her experiences of coming to work at F2.

5. "Introducing the IYCW." http://jociycw.net. Today, YCW groups organize workers of all nationalities and religions throughout the world. Their main activities involve improving workplace and living conditions and campaigning against unemployment, unfair dismissals, and racial discrimination. The organization maintains operational relations with UNESCO and has members in fifty-nine countries, seventeen in the Asia Pacific region.

6. YCW has been a helpful instrument in the organization of militants and young workers and maintains close ties with local churches, trade unions, and other human rights organizations. In the Paknam chapter, 300 young factory workers organized successfully— through rallies, advocacy, public campaigning, and protest—to demand bonus pay and higher wages (ibid.).

7. As of January 2000, there were only about 200 women remaining at F2 owing to continual layoffs since 1995 and the company's expansion of its production to three subsidiary factories located in other provinces.

8. The minimum wage rate in 1999–2000 was 162 baht per day (US$3.86 at 42 baht to US$1.00). A worker received the same minimum wage regardless of how long she had been employed.

9. *Kwai*, "water buffalo," is a derogatory term meant to imply a "slow and stupid worker." It is commonly used by factory managers and supervisors to demean and humiliate workers.

10. The factory added seven more toilets after the establishment of the labor union in 1990.

11. After the labor union was established, Pik successfully lobbied for improved transportation for the workers by writing up a contract that was signed by the factory owner. But the factory subsequently refused to abide by the stipulations in the contract.

12. According to the women in the factories I visited, the engine oil used to run sewing machines is prescribed as a common remedy for minor cuts and scrapes during work.

13. Bum was also the chair of the workers' union at her factory.

14. At the small clothing factory where Prayao was employed, there was an informal alliance between old-timers and the employer. Prayao was one of the factory's first and "finest" employees, and thus she was able to speak out on behalf of the other workers and demand benefits in exchange for helping the factory recruit more workers. Because of her efforts, the factory expanded its business, and in return the owners acceded to some of her demands. In this particular factory, the reciprocal relation between management and a handful of "trusted" workers acted in lieu of a labor union.

15. Michael Burawoy, *The Politics of Production: Factory Regimes under Capitalism and Socialism* (London: Verso, 1985), 172.

16. The mill girls in Lowell banded together and went on strike, forcing the mills to be shut down in what became the first recorded strike of female textile operatives. And even though their first attempt at rebelling against low wages was not successful, their action set a precedent for many successful strikes that followed. See Harriet H. Robinson, "Early Factory Labor in New England," in Massachusetts Bureau of Statistics of Labor, *Fourteenth Annual Report* (Boston: Wright & Potter, 1883), 38082, 38788, 39192.

17. In fact, during the time of their involvement in the establishment of the first workers' union at F2, Sripai, Saneh, Pik, Soey, Nay, and Taan were all single and had no plans to marry. Other militant women mentioned in this chapter, such as Wilaiwan and Bum, were also single.

Because organizing activities consumed all their time, the women often joked about not being able to have a normal social life: meeting men, going on dates, and so on. While I was having lunch with the women at the workers' center one afternoon, someone said, "Did you hear about the woman who was sexually assaulted in a *soi* [street] not far from here?"

Two women answered in unison, "God, that's terrible." And a moment later added slyly, "So what's the name of this street again?" The women in the room all burst out laughing. The joke spoke to the complete absence of a sex life for many of the women in the factory and what was missing from their personal lives. Self-deprecating humor was a shared aspect of their camaraderie.

18. There were ten members in the union committee (*pratharn raeng ngarn*) with one person holding two positions: chair of the workers' committee (*pratharn look jarng*) and chair of the union committee, a position that Nay had held in 1994.

19. Michael Burawoy, *Manufacturing Consent: Changes in the Labor Process under Monopoly Capitalism* (Chicago: University of Chicago Press, 1979), 156.

20. John D. French and Daniel James, "Oral History, Identity Formation, and Working-Class Mobilization," in *The Gendered Worlds of Latin American Women Workers: From Household and Factory to the Union Hall and Ballot Box*, ed. French and James (Durham, N.C.: Duke University Press, 1997), 305.

21. The number of signatures had to add up to at least half the total number of employees, at that time about 700 women.

22. In January 2001, Thom married a man from her village and left the factory to return to her home province in Loi-et.

23. In the greater Bangkok area, there were seven *klum yaan* (workers' zone groups) in 1996. Like the worker-run labor union at F2, these are freestanding organizations that are independent of the national labor congresses and industrial trade union federations. See Stefan Chrobot, *Trade Unions in Transition: Present Situation and Structure of the Thai Labour Movement* (Bangkok: Friedrich-Ebert-Stiftung, 1996), 18–19.

There are ten labor federations in Thailand, organized by industry: Federation of Bank and Financial Workers' Unions of Thailand, Federation of Thailand Siam Motors Automobile Industry Workers' Union, Paper and Printing Federation of Thailand, Petroleum and Chemical Workers' Federation of Thailand, Petroleum of Thailand Federation, Textile, Garment and Leather Workers' Federation of Thailand, Thai Automobile Workers' Federation, Thailand Electrical Appliance Workers' Federation, Thailand Metal Workers' Federation, and the Transport Workers' Federation of Thailand. *Thai Labour Federations*. http://www.thailabour.org/orgs/federation/index.html.

24. Thai labor law stipulates only that "an employer may require an employee to work overtime as necessary," but there is no clause either explicitly limiting the number of overtime hours or prohibiting an employer from banning an employee from OT work. "Rights and Duties of Employers and Employees," Labour Protection Act of 1998. http://www.thailabour.org/law/thai/code.html.

25. Freestanding or independent workers' unions at factories had to rely on their own sources of funding. At F2, workers were required to pay 20 baht (equivalent to US$0.80 in the early 1990s) to join the union and 20 baht every month in membership dues, which were later increased to 40 baht per month. According to Sripai, "Even though the dues were very low, many workers just weren't able to contribute any money, given their low wages," and during her tenure as union chair and representative, the union never received more than 2,000 baht (US$80) at the end of any given month. Because this left the union without enough funds to carry out its activities (including transportation, photocopying, and communication expenses) throughout the period of their struggle, F2 women had to rely for financial support on a number of well-established nongovernmental organizations and labor advocacy groups in Thailand, such as the Thai Labour Campaign, American Center for International Labour Solidarity, Arom Pongpangan Foundation, Friedrich-Ebert-Stiftung, Friends of Women Foundation, Thawatchai-nan Foundation, Women Workers' Unity Group, and the Young Christian Workers. Many of these groups, however, were already operating on limited budgets and unable to extend financial assistance. (All of these groups are actively involved in labor organizing, worker support, education, and training. Thai Labour Campaign is a Thai-run, nonprofit NGO committed to promoting workers' rights in Thailand and increasing awareness of labor

issues globally. Friedrich-Ebert-Stiftung is a private, not-for-profit research and educational center committed to improving the situation of women in Thailand. The Women Workers' Unity Group is an intersectoral association formed by leading women unionists and committed to strengthening the role of women in labor unions; an independent network, it has campaigned for maternity leave and has raised the issue of the lack of day-care nurseries at factories.)

26. John D. French and Mary Lynn Pedersen Cluff, "Women and Working-Class Mobilization in Postwar São Paulo, 1945–1948," in *The Gendered Worlds of Latin American Women Workers,* ed. French and James, 194.

27. In examining cases of women's activism in Brazil, Chile, El Salvador, and Mexico, Lynn Stephen writes about the thoughts, ideas, and experiences of women who have chosen to participate in collective action: "The lens through which Morena and other women...view their past and present political experience reveals the whole person they have become through the process of political activism....As whole people, Morena and others integrate their own lived experience with everything they speak and think about. As political activists, the women highlighted here vary tremendously in what they bring to their movements, how they participate in them, and how they interpret what those movements mean." See Lynn Stephen, *Women and Social Movements in Latin America: Power from Below* (Austin: University of Texas Press, 1997), 20.

28. Lydia Kung, *Factory Women in Taiwan* (Cambridge: Cambridge University Press, 1983), 171.

29. Their new contacts included the Center for Labour Information Service and Training, Church of the Christ Social Development Department, Labour and Welfare Development Department, Labour Coordination Center, Labour Development Center Faculty of Economics, Society for Labour Law, and Thai Labour Museum.

30. In 1996, about 180 labor unions belonged to various workers' zone groups throughout the urban industrial zone. Some of them had memberships with the national trade union federations, but for the most part, these local workers' zone groups held only a lobbying position. They did, however, work closely with the more "radical," grassroots-oriented NGOs, which provided mainly moral, political, and educational (rather than monetary) support. The F2 workers' union allied itself with the strongest and most influential workers' zone groups during the turbulent period in F2's history.

31. Susan Tiano, *Patriarchy on the Line: Labor, Gender, and Ideology in the Mexican Maquila Industry* (Philadelphia: Temple University Press, 1994), 198.

32. Burawoy, *The Politics of Production,* 171.

33. Tiano, *Patriarchy on the Line,* 198.

3. Workers in the Post–Crisis Period

1. According to a 2001 report, official unemployment was "at a low of 1.5% in the last boom years, 1996 and 1997, and then peaked at 4.4% in 1998. Post-crisis, unemployment rates have slowly declined to 4.2% in 1999, 3.6% in 2000, 3.3% in 2001 and a projected 3.2% in 2002." *Thailand: Economy.* http://www.nationsencyclopedia.com/Asia-and-Oceania/Thailand-ECONOMY.html.

2. The piece-rate system was not a new development—it had been in place in apparel factories such as Hara in the 1970s—but a return to piecework production in large manufacturing establishments such as F2 and its subsidiary companies. According to Sripai, piecework had informally existed in a marginal way alongside assembly line production at F2 as an option for women who wanted to take on heavier workloads, but after the crisis the factory became increasingly reliant on piece-rate production, downsizing its workforce and gradually eliminating the assembly line. It is no longer piecework in the context of the local or national supply chain but piecework in the context of the global supply chain.

3. "Japanese firms moved the more labor-intensive phases of their production processes to cheap labor sites mainly in Southeast Asia. ... In the case of Thailand the Japanese investment that flowed into the country in 1987 exceeded the cumulative Japanese investment for the preceding 20 years." Walden Bello, "Siamese Twins: The Currency Crisis in Thailand and the Philippines," *Focus on Trade* 17 (August 1997).

4. In Thailand, property-related loans accounted for 50 percent of all investment, and property development contributed 30 to 50 percent of annual growth of the GDP. Ibid.

5. Walden Bello et al., *A Siamese Tragedy: Development and Disintegration in Modern Thailand* (London: Zed Books, 1998), 20–36.

6. These industries included textiles and apparel, footwear, toys, food processing, and gems and jewelry, as well as service industries and banking and financial sectors.

7. Statistics quoted in Thitiprasert, "Thai Women's Rights Situation in 1998," 4.

8. In a survey of unemployed people in the province of Nan, Thitiprasert indicates that about 80 percent of those interviewed had returned to their provinces because of the economic crisis. Ibid.

9. Jaded Chouwilai, "Braving the Slump," *FOW Newsletter* 9 (1998): 19.

10. According to Junya Yimprasert and Peter Hveem, the Thai government has reclassified its export processing zones (EPZs) as Special Economic Zones (SEZs), which no longer cover only exports but encompass other sectors of the economy including tourism, agribusiness, services, and commerce. Junya Yimprasert and Peter Hveem, "The Race to the Bottom: Exploitation of Workers in the Global Garment Industry," *Occasional Paper Series, Norwegian Church Aid* (2005): 24–25.

11. Migrant workers are also forced to live in overcrowded accommodations that are unsafe and unhygienic. See *Amnesty 2005 Report*, "Thailand: The Plight of Burmese Migrant Workers," Amnesty International ASA 39/001/2005 (June 7, 2005). http://web.amnesty.org/library/Index/ENGASA390012005

12. David Harvey, *The Condition of Postmodernity: An Inquiry into the Origins of Cultural Change* (Cambridge: Mass.: Blackwell, 1989), 155–156.

13. Beverly Silver, *Forces of Labor: Workers' Movements and Globalization since 1870* (Cambridge: Cambridge University Press, 2004), 70–71.

14. Nukul Kokhit, "Labor in the Informal Sector in Thailand," *Asian Women Workers Newsletter* 17, no. 4 (1998): 8.

15. In 1995, F2's workforce was down to 500; by the end of 1998, there were only 270 workers and, as of January 2001, only 150. The factory not only decided to reduce the number of workers but started cutting down overtime and eliminated some departments.

16. Pik and Nay were key informants to the gathering of information on F2's two subcontract factories. Their primary contact was a young woman employed at SF1 who was aware also of conditions at SF2. A phone conversation was set up with the woman on her only day off, Sunday. They asked her questions regarding wages, overseas clients, volume of work, and the number of orders coming in. The actual number of workers at both factories was uncertain, since conflicting estimates ranged from 300–400 to 400–600 workers for the two factories respectively.

17. This interview was conducted in November 1999. The worker asked that her identity be kept confidential for fear of dismissal or other penalties for revealing conditions at the factory.

18. The extraction of absolute surplus value denotes a situation in which labor comes at absolutely no cost to the owner of production, so that, by definition, the owner of the means of production is absolutely "winning." The rate of surplus value can be raised only by prolonging the working day in absolute terms, but this prolongation is effected by the workers themselves out of economic necessity—that is, the need to survive—via the setup of such a system of production. See Karl Marx, *Capital* (London: Penguin Books, 1976), 1:646.

19. For discussion about the emergence of a "new slavery," see Kevin Bales, *Disposable People: New Slavery in the Global Economy* (Berkeley: University of California Press, 2000).

20. Excerpted from a report by Junya Yimprasert and Suthasini Kaewleklai, "Par Garment—Endless Struggle," May 17, 2000. https://www.cleanclothes.org/companies/pargar00-05-17.htm. The report noted that besides the dangerous work environment, there were labor violations in the written and signed agreements between the factory and the workers' union.

21. David Harvey, *The Condition of Postmodernity*, 150, quoting from the Institute of Personnel Management, "Flexible Patterns of Work" (London, 1986).

22. After the items were shipped overseas, any leftovers were sold locally by the factory or warehoused before being sent to local department stores.

23. John French and Mary Lynn Pedersen Cluff, "Women and Working-Class Mobilization in Postwar São Paulo, 1945–1948," in *The Gendered Worlds of Latin American Women Workers: From Household and Factory to the Union Hall and Ballot Box*, ed. John D. French and Daniel James (Durham, N.C.: Duke University Press, 1997), 188.

24. Kokhit, "Labor in the Informal Sector in Thailand," 8; and Thitiprasert, "Thai Women's Rights Situation in 1998."

25. William I. Robinson, *A Theory of Global Capitalism: Production, Class, and State in a Transnational World* (Baltimore: Johns Hopkins University Press, 2004), 87.

26. Pasuk Phongpaichit and Chris Baker, *Thailand, Economy and Politics* (Oxford: Oxford University Press, 1995), 149, 159, 409.

27. Bello et al., *A Siamese Tragedy*, 48, 87.

28. Ibid., 91.

29. Phongpaichit and Baker, *Thailand, Economy and Politics*, 409.

30. Junya Yimprasert and Christopher Candland, "Can Corporate Codes of Conduct Promote Labor Standards? Evidence from the Thai Footwear and Apparel Industries," in Hong Kong Christian Industrial Committee, *The Asia Monitor Resource Center* (December 2000). http://www.thailabour.org/docs/CodesReport/index.html.

31. Junya Yimprasert and Christopher Candland, "The Violation of the Codes of Conduct in the Apparel Manufacturing Industry That Produce Nike and Adidas Products" (2000). http://www.thailabour.org/docs/CodesReport/Codes.html.

32. Yimprasert and Candland, "Can Corporate Codes of Conduct Promote Labor Standards?"

33. Thitiprasert, "Thai Women's Rights Situation in 1998," 5.

34. Excerpted from Yimprasert and Kaewleklai, "Par Garment—Endless Struggle." http://www.cleanclothes.org/companies/pargar00–05–17.htm.

35. Silver, *Forces of Labor*, 183. Silver calls attention to acts of resistance that involve everyday, nondirect forms of resistance such as "undeclared slowdowns" (as at F1) and "desertion and absenteeism" (as at F2), 181–203. Refer to Appendix A in Silver for concepts and definitions of labor unrest.

36. Among the workers surveyed in thirty-five Juarez-area *maquiladoras* on the issue of output restriction, 62 percent had resisted work speedup. Devon G. Peña, *The Terror of the Machine: Technology, Work, Gender, and Ecology on the U.S.-Mexican Border* (Austin, Tex.: Center for Mexican American Studies, 1997), 113–114.

37. Leslie Sklair, *Assembling for Development: The Maquila Industry in Mexico and the United States* (San Diego: Center for U.S.-Mexican Studies, 1993), 215.

38. Michael Burawoy, *The Politics of Production: Factory Regimes under Capitalism and Socialism* (London: Verso, 1985), 172.

39. Yimprasert and Hveem, "The Race to the Bottom," 18. In July 2005, the Ministry of Labour decided to increase the minimum wage rates, for Bangkok and other industry-based provinces across the country, ranging from 2 to 8 baht per day, effective August 1—a raise that labor activists believed would not help workers deal with soaring inflation. Thousands of workers and local labor groups were demanding that the government increase the daily minimum wage to 233 baht nationwide. The Central Wage Committee had increased the minimum wage in the some provinces as follows: "the upper southern province of Prachuap Khiri Khan by Bt8 a day—the highest—followed by Bt6 a day in Bangkok and

15 other provinces, including Nonthaburi, Samut Prakan, Samut Sakhon, Chacherngsao, Saraburi, Nakhon Pathom, Pathum Thani, Ayutthaya, Nakhon Ratchasima, Kanchanaburi, Chonburi, Rayong, Trat, Lopburi, and Ranong. The committee also approved a pay rise of Bt4 a day for the country's northern provinces of Chiang Mai and Lamphun, and Bt2 a day—the lowest—for the northeastern province of Ummajjaroen." "Labour Ministry Concludes New Minimum Wage Rates," *MCOT News*, July 18, 2005.

40. Sklair, *Assembling for Development*, 214.

41. See Michael Yates, "Poverty and Inequality in the Global Economy," *Monthly Review* 55, no. 9 (2004): 37–48.

42. Arlie Russell Hochschild, *The Time Bind: When Work Becomes Home and Home Becomes Work* (New York: Henry Holt, 1997), 41, 209.

43. Yimprasert and Candland, "Can Corporate Codes of Conduct Promote Labor Standards?"

44. Junya Yimprasert, "The Case of the Par Garment Manufacture" (1999). http://www.thailabour.org/docs/ParGarmentStudy.html.

45. On September 13, 1998, management announced that they were going to stop operating for four days, from September 26 through 29, and every Saturday through Tuesday in October and November, totaling thirty-six days of work stoppage.

46. Harvey, *The Condition of Postmodernity*, 192.

47. Thitiprasert, "Thai Women's Rights Situation in 1998," 6.

48. These informal occupations are also referred to as *nonsystematic forms of labor*. But because there were few rural employment opportunities, as Thitiprasert notes, "about twenty percent of laid-off women workers who return[ed] to their rural homes have had to return to the city" (ibid., 5–6).

49. Ibid., 19.

50. In most developing countries whose economies have come under structural adjustment programs of the IMF, health and education are the first sectors to feel the pinch as these nations work on repaying their debt. Ordinary people suffer as a result of cutbacks in basic social welfare expenditure for health-care services and access to education, and in the lack of employment and reduced ability to become self-sufficient. When schools are forced to charge fees, fewer people are able to send their children, and education is mainly available only to those who can afford it. In sub-Saharan Africa, for instance, the percentage of six- to eleven-year-olds enrolled in school fell from nearly 60 percent in 1980 to less than 50 percent in 1990. The decline in primary and secondary school enrollment, especially for girls, was a direct result of the mandatory school fees introduced as part of structural adjustment policies. Thus, more than 130 million school-age children, 73 million of them girls, are growing up in the developing world without access to basic education. See "A Silent War: The Devastating Impact of Debt on the Poor" (1998). http://www.globalissues.com/TradeRelated/Debt/ExternalArticles/silent.asp.

According to Andrew S. Downes, "Macroeconomic policies have adversely affected the education sector via shortage of staff and supplies, the de-motivation of teachers due to the decline in their standard of living and higher teaching loads, reduced teacher training, greater absenteeism, the deterioration of physical plants, reduced availability of materials and equipment and higher teacher pupil ratios." A. Downes, "The Impact of Structural Adjustment Policies on the Educational Systems of the Caribbean" (2002). http://www.iacd.oas.org/La%20Educa%20116/downes.htm. See also Anup Shah, "Structural Adjustment: A Major Cause of Poverty" (2005). http://www.globalissues.org/TradeRelated/SAP.asp.

51. These included 2,306 preschoolers, 15,907 primary pupils, 8,803 secondary pupils, and 1,616 college students. Chouwilai, "Braving the Slump," 20–21.

52. Ibid.

53. Ibid.

54. "Under capitalism, surplus labor takes the form of *surplus value*, which is realized as profit in the market." Michael Burawoy, *Manufacturing Consent: Changes in the Labor Process under Monopoly Capitalism* (Chicago: University of Chicago Press, 1979), 23.

55. Marx, *Capital*, 1:646.

56. Stephanie Black, *Life and Debt* (New York: New Yorker Films, 2001), chap. 12.

57. Lynn Stephen, *Women and Social Movements in Latin America: Power from Below* (Austin: University of Texas Press, 1997), 24.

58. Susan Tiano, *Patriarchy on the Line: Labor, Gender, and Ideology in the Mexican Maquila Industry* (Philadelphia: Temple University Press, 1994), 199–200.

Conclusion. Looking Back, Moving Forward

1. See *We Shop, Who Pays? Western Companies Using Slaves for Manufacturing Overseas*, a documentary about Western companies producing clothes and shoes in developing countries such as India and Bangladesh (Lotta Ekelund/LottaFilm, 2006). http://video.google.com/videosearch?hl=en&q=western%20companies&sa=N&tab=wv.

2. Philip Robertson and Somsak Plaiyoowong, "The Struggle of the Gina Workers in Thailand: Inside a Successful International Labour Solidarity Campaign," *Southeast Asia Research Centre Working Paper Series* No. 75 (Hong Kong, November 2004), 1.

3. Penchan Charoensuthipan, "Lingerie Firm Workers Plan to Defy Ban," *Bangkok Post*, 7 October 2006. The workers demanded an estimated 97 million baht (US$2.6 million) in severance payment. "Some 1,000 Workers to Protest at US Embassy," *The Nation* (Bangkok), 7 October 2006. The Gina factory closed on October 20, 2006. In November, the Clover Group reached a settlement with the workers and agreed to pay "all outstanding bonuses and legally required severance pay and approximately three-and-a-half months' additional salary above the legal minimum severance pay for each worker." "Clover Group Reaches Settlement with Gina Form Bra Factory Workers" (29 November, 2006). http://www.cleanclothes.org/urgent/06-11-17.htm.

4. See for a discussion of TANs, Margaret E. Keck and Kathryn Sikkink, *Activists beyond Borders: Advocacy Networks in International Politics* (Ithaca: Cornell University Press, 1998).

5. Robertson and Plaiyoowong, "The Struggle of the Gina Workers in Thailand," 26.

6. Piya Pangsapa and Mark J. Smith, "The Political Economy of Borderlands, Migration, and Environmental Sustainability: The Responsible Conduct of Developing-Country Firms in Southeast Asia" (under review).

7. Robertson and Plaiyoowong, "The Struggle of the Gina Workers in Thailand," 4–6.

8. "Thai Garment Industry Faces Labor and Raw Material Shortages," *MCOT News*, 23 July 2005.

9. Mark J. Smith and Piya Pangsapa, "New Controversies in Phenomenology: Between Ethnography and Discourse," in *Sage Handbook of Social Science Methodology*, ed. William Outhwaite and Stephen Turner (London: Sage, 2007).

10. See Anthony Giddens, *The Constitution of Society* (Cambridge: Polity Press, 1986).

11. Seung-Kyung Kim, *Class Struggle or Family Struggle? The Lives of Women Factory Workers in South Korea* (Cambridge: Cambridge University Press, 1997). See also studies in *Women's Working Lives in East Asia*, ed. Mary C. Brinton (Stanford, Calif.: Stanford University Press, 2001).

12. Helen I. Safa, "Runaway Shops and Female Employment: The Search for Cheap Labor," in *Women's Work: Development and the Division of Labor by Gender*, ed. Eleanor B. Leacock and Helen I. Safa (New York: Bergin & Garvey, 1986); Susan Tiano, *Patriarchy on the Line: Labor, Gender, and Ideology in the Mexican Maquila Industry* (Philadelphia: Temple University Press, 1994).

13. Susan Tiano, *Patriarchy on the Line: Labor, Gender, and Ideology in the Mexican Maquila Industry* (Philadelphia: Temple University Press, 1994), 192.

14. Michael Burawoy, *Manufacturing Consent: Changes in the Labor Process under Monopoly Capitalism* (Chicago: University of Chicago Press, 1979), 14.

15. James Petras and Morris Morley, *U.S. Hegemony under Siege: Class Politics and Development in Latin America* (London: Verso, 1990), 166.

16. Neil J. Smelser, "On Theory, Case Study, and Comparative Research," *Comparative and Historical Sociology* 13, no. 1 (Fall 2000): 3.

17. Michael Burawoy et al., *Ethnography Unbound: Power and Resistance in the Modern Metropolis* (Berkeley: University of California Press, 1991), 271.

Glossary

All words and phrases are based on my own phonetic spelling of Thai in the vernacular capturing the way that the women understood the meanings and nuances of these words and phrases. Thai is a complex tonal language and there is no universal standard for transliterating Thai into English. As an ethnographic research project, this study focuses on how respondents construct meanings in their lived experiences—thus this book should offer a space for the women's own voices. Consequently, I chose to spell the words and phrases in a way that best captures the pronunciation of standard spoken Thai in the context of the lives of the women at the heart of this study.

ajarn	professor
batr pra cha chon	citizenship identification cards
chiwit jing jing	the "nitty gritty" of life
chorb	like
chood meeh	teddy bear outfit
chuey	old-fashioned
condo	small flat or apartment
choom chon	urban slum community
dek baan nok	country girl
dek loon mai	younger generation
dek pump	gas station attendant
dek thaloh kan	kids fighting with each other

dhet	bold, daring, fearless
doo rae tua eng	taking care of oneself
farang	Western foreigner
hua khaeng	hard-headed
hua na	supervisor
im tua	satisfied
itch chaah	jealous
jai dee	kind, generous
jai rai	mean, cruel
jitsamnukh	consciousness
jungwat	province
kae kurn pai	too old
kamakorn	laborer
kana kamakarn	committee or group
kau nah	advanced/progressive
khao dum	black and white
khid maak	to think too much
khon krungthep	urbanite/Bangkokian
khon ngarn	worker
khon ngarn pi seth	special worker
khunna parb chiwit	quality of living
klum puan	social clique of friends
klum yaan	district labor group/workers' zone group
kra dook suaham	bone frailty
krating daeng	Red Bull
kra toon jitsamnukh	the act of raising consciousness
kurd phen khon chon	to be born poor
kwai	buffalo
kwarm kuey chin	out of habit or routine
kwarm ob oohn	warmth/feeling of comfort and security
kwarm rab pid chorb	responsibility
maatra jet sib hah	Article 75
mae	mother
mai chorb	dislike
mai duad rhon	no worries
mai mee kang wohn	to have no worries
mai mee nam ya	no substance
mai puad hua	without headache
mai sohn jai	we don't care
maw saam	the equivalent of the 9th grade

mee ngarn kor dee laew	having a job is good enough
mee rabeyb	to be a proper person/orderly
mop	demonstration
nai jarng	factory boss/employer
ngarn leng	rush orders
ngarn rahb mao	piece-rate job
njuad	production line
pah	aunt, elderly woman
pa-ra	a burden
paw jai	satisfied
paw yoo dai	livable
pee pee nong nong	siblings
pew kao neyn	fair, smooth skin
pew kao phong	whiter, fairer complexion
pew klaam pew dum	darker skin
phen tua rau eng	to be myself
plern plern	gradually
poo ying than samay	modern woman
por hok	the equivalent of the 6th grade
pratharn look jarng	worker/employee representative
pratharn raeng ngarn	union representative
puan sanid	closest friends
rabob rahb mao	piecework system
reyb roi	proper
rohng	a place/shelter
rohng ngarn	factory
rohng reyn ratr	city public school
rohng reyn wat	temple school
rohng sohb	coffin
roo dee	to know too much
saat tru	enemy
sabai-sabai	easygoing
sahaparb	union
sahaparb raeng ngarn	labor union
sahmakee	unity
samosohn	food coop
sao rohng ngarn	factory girl
sawatikarn	worker benefits
seya lek	younger or junior factory boss/employer/owner
seya yai	older or senior factory boss/employer/owner

sithi	rights
soi	street
suam	toilets
tahng ratr	shortcut
tham jai	to prepare yourself
tham hai pew kao	to whiten the skin
tham ngarn pua luke	to work for one's children
tha na	class
thansamay	modern
thon mai dai	"can't stand"/unbearable
tid khun yai	attached to grandmother
toong ngarn wai	to delay the workload
tua tan njuad	production line representative
tu raed	ridiculous
tukh taew	townhouse building
tukh taew saarm chun	three-story building
tukh taew see chun	four-story building
yoo dai pai wan wan	getting by day to day
yudh amnard	to take over

Index

Piya Pangsapa is Assistant Professor in the Department of Global Gender Studies at the University at Buffalo, State University of New York. Her current work considers the impact of corporate responsibility on the global supply chain, the changing nature of factory production, and the status and citizenship rights of migrant workers.